GENERSHIP 1.0

BEYOND LEADERSHIP TOWARD LIBERATING THE CREATIVE SOUL

DAVID CASTRO

ARCH STREET PRESS

BRYN MAWR

ISBN: 978-1-938798-01-6

for JULIA

LEADERSHIP

The office or position of a leader;
the capacity to lead; the act of leading.

CREATIVITY

The conscious effort on the part of an individual
or group to bring into being any circumstance,
condition, object, relationship or activity.

GENERSHIP

The capacity to create with others;
the community practice of creating.

CONTENTS

ACKNOWLEDGMENTS

Genership 1.0 grows out of an entire community of practice. I thank our whole team at I-LEAD for helping to generate the ideas included in *Genership* over the many years we have worked alongside one another. Angel Figueroa, Denise Kirkland and Phillip Thomas deserve particular thanks for their generous and generative dialogue at many points in the process. I also want to thank Cheryl Lang, Cynda Clyde, Chris ("Krysss") Nash and Barbara Sykes. From our board of directors, I give special thanks also to Robert Natalini and Lynne Abraham, our cofounder and chair, for inspiration, feedback and important suggestions about the content.

I thank my gifted partner in this creative effort, Robert Rimm, for serving as a simply fantastic coach, editor, mentor and friend during the writing process. Robert also wrote a number of the call-outs instrumental in explaining genership, which are identified in the text. *Genership* would not be what it is today without his patient help and invaluable contributions.

I am also deeply thankful for my experiences in the Kellogg, Eisenhower and Ashoka Fellowships. My exposure to so many dedicated and inspiring individuals through these networks has greatly enriched this work. Much of what I write about here is modeled in these organizations, especially within Ashoka's worldwide network of social entrepreneurs.

Heartfelt gratitude also goes out to my children and my parents, Joan and Carlos, who provided emotional support and encouragement throughout the project. You are the reason I get up in the morning.

Most important of all, I thank the inspiration, the love and the lion of my life, my wife Julia. What we create should always be an act of love; I dedicate this act of love to you.

PREFACE

So God created mankind in his own image,
in the image of God he created them;
male and female he created them.
—Genesis 1:27

Living the Questions

Be patient toward all that is unsolved in your heart and
try to love the questions themselves like locked rooms
and like books that are written in a very foreign tongue.
Do not now seek the answers, which cannot be given you
because you would not be able to live them. And the
point is, to live everything. Live the questions now.
Perhaps you will find them gradually, without noticing it,
and live along some distant day into the answer.
—Rainer Maria Rilke, *Letters to a Young Poet*

What makes a journey of self-discovery so compelling? We have no choice but to be ourselves, yet our true nature remains mysterious, as if the practice of self-reflection necessarily entailed dark matter and blind spots. Self-knowledge seems always to demand hard work and difficult searching. We prepare for daring adventures and painful trials. Like mythic wanderers, we imagine that only after such pursuits can we begin to discover our true selves: our origin, talents, curses, fate and

1

raison d'être. Should we survive, we hope eventually to come home changed, imbued with a new capacity to see what before was invisible. Only then can we know what to believe and do.

As the poet Wallace Stevens wrote, "Perhaps the truth depends on a walk around the lake." The journey of self-discovery involves the possibility of transcendence. The effort to see ourselves changes us. Thomas Mann reminded us that "[n]o one remains quite what he was when he recognizes himself." We are the sculptor; we are the stone. The strangely transformational search for true human nature belongs not only to myth-makers, poets and philosophers. We experience the quest for our identity as social beings. Through families, organizations, communities and nations, humanity writ large shares the pilgrimage toward the self. Religion, philosophy, art, science and history undertake the same fundamental inquiry: Who are we?

Western civilization has deemed *reason* to be the most central human capacity, the most fundamental aspect of human nature. While competing religious and philosophical traditions have debated the nature of truth, they have generally agreed that humanity's most important purpose is to use the faculty of reason to perceive it. This is why we tend to see knowledge of the world, society and the self as fundamentally reflective and mimetic. We are the mirror held up to the universe we inhabit. We are cast in the role of detectives or researchers piecing together information so that it forms a complete picture of reality. Success requires faithful observation and the understanding that follows it, even if this inquiry entails the difficult task of coming to grips with how our humanity shapes reason's lens. This is our approach to both the natural universe and God. Reason provides the primary means. In the pursuit of wisdom, faith in reason is shared alike by idealists, skeptics, empiricists, pragmatists and even postmodern thinkers intent on employing reason to question objectivity itself. They may disagree about the nature of reality, the mind and society, but they agree that reason is the primary human faculty through which to understand ourselves, the universe and what to do.

But what if all this while, humanity has been missing something central to our identity? The chapters that follow take inspiration from this simple but profound question. Suppose there has been a different

2

critical energy evolving within human beings—something that our most fundamental beliefs and narratives suggest, but do not yet fully express. This missing part of the story is like a thematic statement early in a symphony, a leitmotif, a few notes at the start of the first movement that we can only fathom later, when we hear them developed in a complete orchestral guise.

Creativity

What if our most critical human goal, the most fundamental human activity, is not to *know* or to *understand*, but rather to *create,* to *generate?* What would it mean if at the heart of human nature we discovered not reason, not rationality, not the capacity to grasp the world in the mind, but rather the capacity to imagine and invent that world?

How does creativity, as distinct from reason, emerge within human experience? Human beings feel tossed from oblivion into life, compelled day by day to question its meaning, slowly becoming self-aware as we emerge from infancy into childhood. Entering maturity we work toward understanding our community, our environment and ourselves. Eventually we strive for some measure of control over our minds, bodies, relationships and surroundings. All the while, we rely primarily on reason as our capacity to comprehend reality swirling around us.

But a critical transition occurs as we begin to make fully conscious decisions. We cross a bridge from reflection to intentional action. At that moment, we become something far more than rational beings interested in knowing the world; we become *creators.*

Our personal evolution from unconsciousness to reflection and then to intentional action gives rise to an ongoing stream of decisions that define the rest of our days. What to observe, what to eat, where to go, what to do. What to attempt, what to flee, how to respond. Who to avoid, who to combat, who to befriend, who to love. We can describe these and similar choices in a single question: *What should we create between birth and death?* Through our intentional actions we author our particular stories at each moment of our waking lives.

As adults we often strengthen our command—our capacity for careful deliberation and intentional action—and recognize that our creative choices present a broad (by some measures, infinite) spectrum of possibilities. Of course, we cannot do everything and anything we want; yet even within the severe limitations that our skills and circumstances impose, our span of influence offers countless potential courses of action. Like a game of chess, life presents powerful rules and boundaries. Our bishops must live and die on their colors and may only move diagonally. Our rooks can only move vertically and horizontally. Our knights must turn sharp corners. And yet, despite the maze of strict rules that make so many moves completely impossible, and notwithstanding the lack of any element of chance in the game beyond who moves first, *more theoretically possible chess games exist than particles of matter in the universe.*[i] There is much in chess that we cannot do, but there is also no meaningful limit to the possibilities. So also with life's choices, constrained and at the same time limitless.

As essentially social beings, the activities of expanding, refining and acting upon our vast personal spectrum of possibilities take center stage in the theater of our community discourse. We are inescapably the product of our network of relationships. In the spotlight of *interpersonal* consciousness, our dramatic internal and external dialogue concerns the most profound matters (What should I believe? What should I learn? Whom should I love? What work should I perform?) and also the most trivial (What color socks should I wear? What kind of tea should I drink and serve?). Through these choices we construct who we are, as much by whether we are Christians, Jews, Muslims, Buddhists, agnostics or atheists as by whether we drink Earl Grey or wear argyle. In our effort to master this stream of personal decisions defining our identity (choices that our social network both informs and evaluates), we seek overarching truths about human nature, existence and experience, hoping to employ reason in support of creativity, searching for rules or at least guidelines in managing our freedom.

It is strange that in coming face to face with our unique potential (limited yet unbounded), we do not find ultimate guidance in the domain of science and its fortress of rationality, but rather must look toward history, religion and philosophy, even if only implicitly; these take up life's ultimate purpose and meaning in ways that pure science cannot reach. Why is science of limited service? To be valid, truly scientific knowledge must restrict itself to conjectures that can be falsified through controlled observations. We must carefully design our experiments to isolate the factors we want to observe and measure, for without such discipline, we cannot replicate or trust our observations. Moreover, even when our theories successfully explain ongoing experimental evidence, they cannot be credited as ultimate truth. Scientific theories cannot achieve more than consistency with what we observe in controlled experiments. This serves as the ground for predictions, but invariably, as our experiments expand and evolve, even our best theories encounter limits. Science has discarded as many theories once deemed promising as it currently retains. Properly understood, science can surely shed some light upon the present moment; it can describe patterns of experience that demonstrate consistency in controlled environments and thus can be perceived. What is, simply *is*; we have no choice about it. But science cannot enter the domain of making choices. It can never tell us what *should be*, cannot specify what to do when many future outcomes are possible. Hume's guillotine separating "is" from "ought" remains razor sharp. Science at best can tell us how to accomplish efficiently the objectives we select from a bottomless pool of possibilities. It cannot select our objectives nor tell us what conjectures we should investigate. Science cannot determine our ultimate ends. It cannot tell us what we should do with the patterns in nature that our experiments may reveal. Scientific knowledge falls silent wherever predictable patterns cease and only possibilities emerge. And where science encounters our free will, it shuts down entirely. At this crevasse, only creativity can find purchase and beat a path toward tomorrow. Creativity must take over the reins of experience at that point. Knowledge retreats and creative choice ascends.

We cannot choose the speed of light, the law of gravity or the elemental composition of water, but we can choose whether to study physics, law or medicine. We cannot change the natural laws governing how light travels from a book or a computer screen to our eyes, but we can choose what to read and what to watch. We cannot decide whether to have instincts, but we can choose how we eat, how we love, how we play and even how we face death itself. We come to learn that if *true* answers exist for these distinctive decisions—those through which we weave the fabric of our creative freedom—these answers are not right or correct in the same sense that predictions about well-defined experiments can be. They are accurate in a different sense, in the way that justice can be right and true even when humans fail to achieve it, or as a work of art can illuminate an ideal of beauty while falling short of it. Certain moral truths of human nature persist in the wake of contradictory experience, like the truth that all men are created equal. Creative freedom draws upon this special kind of truth, one not dependent on experience or experiment. What we choose to create with our free will can be true in this way even when the material world resists or even defies its existence. When Rousseau famously observed that "man is born free, and everywhere he is in chains," he did not take the observation of pervasive bondage as evidence refuting the ideal of freedom.

What if our creative power—the power to *create* the truth rather than merely to observe it—is the most important feature of human nature, more important than reason itself?

Creativity, Reason and Faith

Approximately 15% of the world's population self-identifies as nonreligious. Within this minority, a much smaller group—by some reckonings less than 3%—identifies as atheist. The remaining nonreligious individuals are agnostics along with theists who nevertheless do not adhere to any particular religion. As a group, nonreligious individuals tend to credit rationality and science over faith as tools for comprehending the fundamental elements of human nature. For this nonreligious audience, creativity offers a kind of limit or threshold allowing humanity to transcend the boundaries of purely rational, scientific discourse limited by mechanistic, deterministic thinking.

Philosophical & Faith Foundations of Genership

First Commandment

Golden Rule

Genesis

For the approximately 85% of readers who understand human affairs and human nature as being circumscribed by the divine, the perception of creativity rather than rationality as the most fundamental element of human nature admittedly does not emerge from traditional religious doctrine. But it need not be so. It is possible to see human creativity as the most fundamental element of human nature and nevertheless remain consistent with the most deeply held religious precepts across the Abrahamic religious traditions. Equally important, to understand how faith can support a primary emphasis on human creativity provides an illuminating backdrop against which to understand the central critique of traditional leadership concepts introduced and advanced within genership: the Messiah Fallacy.

The focus in Western philosophy and theology on the primacy of reason offers a partial explanation for humanity's willingness to subordinate human creativity. The search for truths beyond human nature—absolute truths perceived by reason—often inspires us to seek the limits of human freedom rather than its example. The reverence and awe we may feel for the divine, or for natural powers resplendent in the observable universe, may also make us feel small and insignificant. The sun and the stars appear beyond our capacity to change. Our feelings of wonder may spur us to seek meaning only in relation to God's law, or to natural laws that can appear to be eternal. In the face of such truths we confront our creative limitations, our utter finitude. This duality—the manner in which our sharp perception of finitude dampens the appreciation of our creative power—is captured in Hamlet's famous lines:

> What a piece of work is a man, how noble in reason,
> how infinite in faculties, in form and moving how express and
> admirable, in action how like an angel, in apprehension how like a
> god! The beauty of the world, the paragon of animals—and yet,
> to me, what is this quintessence of dust?
>
> —*Hamlet*, Act II

Hamlet's reference to dust recalls its mention in Genesis: "[F]or dust you are and to dust you will return" (Genesis 3:19). The thought of humanity as mere dust does not fill us with a sense of our creative potential.

But man is so much more than mere dust. The core tenants of the Abrahamic religions can also be read to encode seminal ideas about human creativity and equality. The philosophical and religious frameworks that define human freedom operate initially by excluding options, telling us what our choices should avoid. Think of the injunctions within the Ten Commandments. Do not lie. Do not hurt others. Do not take what belongs to others. Such maxims teach us what not to do, what not to create. In most of the Commandments, we encounter negative visions, what is wrong, what should be denied existence, without clearly embracing a definitive picture of what should be nurtured into being. Where does humanity turn within faith traditions to find an affirmative vision of human nature?

Monotheism carries a special meaning regarding creativity and personal freedom. The idea that there is only one God means that our creative choices—our assessments about how to use our freedom (all those choices not determined by inalterable laws of nature)—can be informed by a personal relationship with a single Supreme Being. The message is that we can have a personal relationship with God as a creator, as a living intelligence, as a personality who inspires and informs us as we choose what to create for ourselves, in our relationships and through our interaction with the world.

This special relationship that we may have with a single God also articulates a singular truth about the necessary nature of our relationship with other human beings: We are all equals. In this way, monotheism speaks about human as well as divine nature. It states unambiguously that humans are not gods, that no man is or could be a god. So we must take care not to confuse the two. If we are not to worship idols, then we must not worship our own ideas, and it follows just as certainly that we must avoid revering other men or their ideas. We must not make any man into an idol, nor bow down and worship any man. Encoded within monotheism we find a thought that contains the germinating seed of our commitment to human equality.

In modern Western culture, most people perceive the concept of equality as an inherently *secular* value. The political thinkers whose work gave birth to modern constitutional democracies that embrace equality (e.g., Rousseau, Locke, Jefferson) did not ground their thinking in faith, but rather in natural law. And while natural law often references a creator, it speaks of that creator as part of nature itself. The famous source of power identified within the Declaration of Independence is described as "the Laws of Nature and Nature's God." This makes sense, especially given the historical reality well known to the framers: Organized religion tended to buttress the authoritarian state and similarly opposed the concept of human equality.

Nevertheless, in confirming the non-divinity of all men, the concept of monotheism contains a critical idea pointing toward human equality before God. This corollary of the First Commandment, that no man is a god, speaks volumes about leadership and creativity. It says that no man should come to any other man with creative ideas and pretend to have the qualities of God, to be all-knowing, infallible or always entitled to deference. Another element of this insight is that in creative matters the relationship between God and each human must always supersede the relationship among humans. If we relate to God through our own individual consciousness, through our own personal relationship with him, then it must follow that in matters of personal conscience the dictates of our individual spiritual reflection will always have at least equal importance with those that arise in dialogue with other men.

This striking idea—that each individual must bear personal responsibility and accountability for his own creative choices through his relationship with God—is also the specific concept that animates the golden rule. Consider these articulations across the ages:

"The stranger who resides with you shall be to you as one of your citizens; you shall love him as yourself, for you were strangers in the land of Egypt: I the LORD am your God."

—Leviticus 19:34 (c. 1400 BCE)

"Do not to your neighbor what you would take ill from him."

—Pittacus (c. 640-568 BCE)

"Never impose on others what you would not *choose* for yourself."

—Confucius (c. 500 BCE)

"Hurt not others in ways that you yourself would find hurtful."

—Udana-Varga (c. 500 BCE)

"Thou shalt love thy neighbor as thyself."

—Matthew: 22:39 (c. AD 55)

On the golden rule's compass of moral choices, true north lies within the individual consciousness as shaped in dialogue with the divine:

"Nothing in all creation is hidden from God's sight. Everything is uncovered and laid bare before the eyes of him to whom we must give account."

—Hebrews 4:13 (c. AD 64)

As a guide to positive behavior (what to do as distinct from what to avoid), the golden rule does not say, "Do as God says you should do" or "Follow those who have power in your community" or "Do as those who are wise advise you to do." It does not suggest that any one individual should impose his will upon another. Instead, this rule requires each individual to answer profound questions, calling forth personal creativity:

"What do *I* desire?"

"How do *I* wish to be treated?"

"How should *I* love myself?"

Within the Judeo-Christian tradition, even prophets, generally understood as God's messengers, clearly had faults and were fallible. Since the prophets were not more than men—and since an element of personal reflection always comes into play when assessing the thoughts of men, as it must—then each individual through his personal relationship with God must remain the final judge in answering moral questions and making moral choices. The foundation of ethics and morality in human culture thus requires creativity and individual choice.

Genesis itself, the creation story shared not only through Judaism and Christianity but also Islam, can be reread to posit creative freedom as human nature's most essential feature. This may seem a provocative claim, but consider: Rather than present the universe as a timeless entity preexisting and giving rise to divine and human personality (as in creation stories from other cultures), the Genesis account tells of a self-existent creator who brings forth heaven and earth from the void. After God creates light, night and day, land and sea, and all the flora and fauna of the earth, he creates humans in his image and likeness. At this point in the narrative, the only attribute revealed about God is his status as a creator. To be "in his own image" thus means to be a creator.

Most importantly, Genesis' central drama involves humanity's creative moral choice. In what sense can we see the choice at the heart of Genesis as *creative*? The story recounts God's creation of the universe, all life within it and humanity itself. Adam and Eve, in the likeness of God, also enjoy creative freedom. In setting forth his rule not to eat from the "tree of the knowledge of good and evil," God acknowledges that man has the creative power to diverge from his instructions, the capacity to take the world off in a direction that completely differs from God's will. Surely we must imagine that an all-powerful God has the power to make disobedience itself impossible. But it turns out that

God's creatures are not bound to his law by force. Indeed, if disobedience were logically or physically impossible, there would be no need to articulate a rule in the first place. A rule of conduct necessarily implies the potential for departure. In this sense, Genesis offers us the most compelling possible evidence to demonstrate the reality of human creative freedom: the primordial act of disobedience itself. God points the way in a dialogue with man, but man (in the image of God) has the divine power to choose. Genesis thus conveys the idea that it is man who takes responsibility for human destiny. In this sense, moral choice—the fall itself—can be seen as the primal creative act. Indeed, this choice brings forth human civilization and history as we know it.

Within Christian doctrine specifically, God offers salvation, but man must choose it. Without the reality of creative free will, this choice would be drained of meaning. The very idea of choice requires freedom, an idea later echoed in the golden rule's fundamental moral precept: Do unto others as you would have done unto you. The concept that we must do to others as we would have them do to us lacks all meaning without introspection and insight about *what* exactly we would have them do to us. We must freely choose. Similarly, the concept that we must love our neighbors as ourselves requires us to say specifically how we should love ourselves. Throughout history, humans have *invented* answers to give meaning to God's moral code when choosing what and how to create.

Think of the free market with its famous ethic of selfishness. Men bargain selfishly with one another knowing and expecting that others will be similarly selfish to them. They practice the selfishness they would expect from others. Of course, they do so believing that the overarching system of selfishness will produce efficiency that serves the needs of all. In this sense, man invented the market consistent with the golden rule. The market arises from human choice. It does not exist within all spheres of human existence. Inside organizations, families and philanthropies, men and women choose an ethic of selflessness, giving rise to another kind of reality. Such answers about how humans should live, what to create in society and how to influence the world arise through personal freedom. They are not specified in God's law, but they can be guided in their development through prayerful dialogue between the Almighty and free spirits he has brought forth. God himself does not choose to lead. His most fundamental precepts present us with open-ended questions: How would we ourselves wish to live and be loved? He gives man freedom to create.

So at the center of our human nature we find not a singular answer but rather an unanswered question. As human beings we are ultimately called not to *know* the world but rather to *create* it. We are called not to *understand* the world but rather to *invent* it. We are not traveling to an existent promised land already fully formed in the mind of God, but rather inspired to *create* that land. To do this work giving meaning to our lives—not *answering* but rather *living out* the questions at the core of humanity—requires a set of abilities and practices as yet emerging within humanity, only just becoming consciously visible, coherent and distinct. The pages that follow strive to describe—to call forth this emergent way of being in the world—the practice called *genership:* our divine capacity to create with others. Genership differs from practices that have come before it, including *leadership.* At journey's end, we will have gained an incisive understanding of this new capacity, like adventurers calling forth a new world, hewing it from a yet undiscovered continent of imagination.

PROLOGUE
BEYOND LEADERSHIP

I've spent more than 20 years engaged in a concerted effort to practice, analyze and teach effective leadership. In 1995, my passion for leadership work led me to found a nonprofit organization, the Institute for Leadership Education, Advancement and Development (I-LEAD). Its mission is to liberate human potential in America's most challenged communities through leadership development.

Through my work over the last two decades with leadership thinkers, scholars, practitioners and learners, I came to notice that leadership practices in our communities have been evolving. This is not surprising. Many entities in our experience evolve: living beings, communities, natural systems, the earth and the universe itself are not what they used to be. They are continually changing into something different. Leadership is part of evolution; it too is changing and has the potential to improve.

In reflecting on how leadership practices are evolving, I have noticed specific positive trends. Some problematic approaches are slowly giving way to new practices that I and many others perceive to be better for the individuals and communities who participate in them. Reflecting on these positive trends—what is coming and what is receding—has inspired me not only to attempt to describe what I see but also to encourage and develop it. Readers can think of this work both as chronicling evolution in leadership practices and a stimulant to the evolutionary process itself.

The effort to describe the evolution that I am both witnessing and fomenting, has called forth a new logos, *genership*. I hope that one day soon people across the world will be talking about genership rather than simply leadership skills. What is genership? While leadership involves the ability to point the way, to lead others toward a destination, vision or common goal, genership entails a quite different dynamic that displays the abilities required to create with others, together with the capacity to engage and stimulate creativity within a community. Genership relates closely to the word generate, with the same connotation of energy, life, origin, birth and growth. It intentionally departs from traditional connotations of leadership that involve power, prestige and ego.

While genership presents a critical evolution in leadership practices, it also expresses something fundamental carried in the roots and seeds of human nature. For those of us who have a faith-based orientation to life and work, we can see genership as being connected to our God-given free will. It captures the idea that when God made humanity in his image, he gave us a fraction of his creative powers, so that, as Thoreau wrote, "The world is but a canvas for our imaginations." Those who may be agnostic or even atheist can understand genership in existential terms, as humanity's connection to the powerful concept of emergence, the insight that higher-order systems are capable of transcending deterministic, reductive theories. Human beings and their communities are more than the sum of their parts. Whole systems have qualities not found in the parts. The rules that govern the parts frequently can neither predict nor adequately describe the behavior of the whole. The future is not preordained with reference to as yet undiscovered or unfathomed theories; it is ours to make freely.

Why do we need genership? What is wrong with leadership? First, leadership is an extremely broad concept that in current usage sweeps together so many diverse characteristics and dynamics of group process that it almost becomes like a Rorschach image, with participants able to project whatever they please onto it. By contrast, genership specifically references group processes related to production and creativity.

Beyond their ambiguity and overbreadth, traditional leadership practices often entail dysfunctional ideas that inhibit group processes while undermining team creativity and success. After much reflection over many years, I have identified three such specific areas—fallacies—associated with traditional thinking about leadership.

The Messiah Fallacy refers to the idea that a group's success depends upon the success of one extraordinary individual who serves as a messianic leader. In my experience, groups suffering under this fallacy often waste precious time and resources focusing on this messianic leader, obsessing about whether the person who wears the messianic robes is the true messiah, and about his or her actual progress in serving the organization's needs. This obsession ultimately creates both paralysis and helplessness.

The Hero Fallacy describes a situation that often takes hold when there is no visible messianic leader or where that leader fails. Groups suffering under this fallacy hope that a messiah will emerge from a contest among warring heroes. Groups believe that the process of combat among the heroes somehow imbues the successful contestant with messianic qualities. Again, groups suffering under the weight of this fallacy tend to ignore the abilities of their members to engage in productive work while they wait for a messiah to emerge from the hero wars.

The Fallacy of Leadership Nostalgia involves a group's efforts to enshrine the ways and wisdom of leaders who have departed or died. When laboring under this fallacy, groups often wrongfully attribute the creative work of many community members to the efforts of a singular genius. They then attempt to create parables and codes of conduct that supposedly describe and analyze this person, behaving as if the group's present members can achieve messianic leadership if they dutifully follow those recipes. This fallacy causes groups to look backward, attempting to recreate a faux past instead of collectively and equally grappling with the creative opportunities of the current moment.

The Fallacies form a recurring dysfunctional cycle:

Cycle of Fallacies

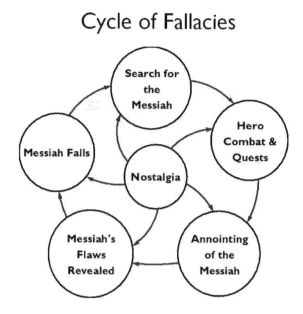

This ultimately pointless loop causes groups to divert critical energies from teamwork to leadership processes bound up with the Fallacies under the mistaken belief that the selection of a true messianic leader is necessary for the group's ultimate success. This focus causes groups to move more slowly and miss opportunities to make meaningful progress.

In contrast genership takes certain core practices of leadership and evolves them into more functional practices that enable teams to unite their creative energies effectively:

New genership practice	Former leadership practice
Listening	the messianic leader's projection
CoThinking	the messianic leader's directed thinking
CoVisioning	the visions of a singular messianic leader

Development of effective team creativity	strategic management through the messianic leader acting alone or with a small subgroup
Development of an open, level genership culture	autocratic, hierarchical culture developed through a messianic leader

Teams working within a leadership culture tend to rely on one person or a small subgroup to engage in visioning, assessment and strategic thinking while generating energy and commitment, whereas teams practicing genership encourage all members to share equally and efficiently in the work of visioning, assessing reality, surfacing creative impediments (both external and internal), and developing the emotional and motivational resources to sustain highly innovative and productive efforts. My life's work continues to explore these elements of group creative processes.

Genership describes a new ideal of human interaction, one that embraces the emergent evolution away from traditional leadership toward more creative, liberating, beneficial and productive ways of working together. It also offers individuals—and the communities they inhabit and sustain—a way of living and working together that releases aspiration essential but latent within human nature: our capacity to become more than we are at this moment, to transcend history and circumstance, and ultimately to express our connection to a power deeply rooted in faith.

CHAPTER ONE
LEADERSHIP: *EVOLVING INTO GENERSHIP*

In the Stream of Human Change and Progress

Think back to the earliest moment you can remember in your life. Where were you? What were you doing at that moment? Can you remember it clearly?

Now take your current age and divide it into parts. Think of yourself at a quarter of your current age, at half, at three quarters. Where were you at each of those moments? What were you thinking, feeling and doing at each point?

What do you notice about yourself as you think about your life from all of these perspectives? One feature of your existence will surely become starkly visible: You have changed considerably and are continuing to change. As we age, the changes in us become more profound. Sometimes they become so pervasive that we can no longer recognize ourselves as the people we once were. If you've attained middle age, a powerful illustration is to look through the stack of your expired driver's licenses.

What is true of our individual lives is also true of human society as a whole. Modern society has a collective memory extending back over thousands of years. This is not simply a recollection of the past; we have developed a historical consciousness of human progress. It is worth reflecting on the idea that the past is not *necessarily* more primitive. It is quite possible that we could look into the past and see times that were the same or that *exceeded* the present in complexity and development. But when we look toward the past, we see something different: *progress*. The concept is simple: Human organizations and quality of life are slowly improving over time, so much so that our ancestors would barely recognize life today. Over the past few centuries, with the advent of significant technological developments, the idea of human progress has acquired exponential force.

There is also widespread consensus that our modern political and economic systems, while deeply flawed, represent vast improvements over prior systems in human history. Few in the West would wish to trade democracy for monarchy or capitalism for feudalism. If you were offered the chance to trade places with someone of great wealth who lived 50, 100 or 500 years ago, would you accept? Probably not, in view of the benefits of modernity that you would have to sacrifice. In a sense, the common citizen today—with access to modern conveniences, devices and human know-how—has powers that rival and generally exceed those enjoyed by ancient royalty. This is the meaning of progress in human society as a whole; in tangible ways—access to food, shelter, entertainment, healthcare and security—the commoner of the present lives as the emperor of the past.

Leadership Evolving

In modern society we understand leadership practice as an ideal within organizational life. Consider the quote below from a mainstream business seminar on the importance of leadership:

> Nothing happens without leadership. Nothing changes without leadership. Nothing develops without leadership. Nothing improves without leadership. Nothing is corrected without leadership. Everyone, everywhere, every time is always being led. Whatever conditions, circumstances or predicament in which a person, family, community, organization or nation may find itself, someone led it there.

In such an environment, it may be difficult to imagine that leadership as an ideal may be evolving into something else, transforming into something better and stronger. Imagine walking into the International Academy of Management and suggesting that management is an idea whose time has passed.

But as with human society itself, leadership as a practice does have the potential to evolve into something better. This may seem to be a provocative, even outrageous assertion considering the high value placed on leadership processes in Western culture today. But seen through the lens of history, not so. Remember, there was a time in which men did not imagine living without kings. There was a time in which there was really no such thing as private property as we think of today. There were cultures in which most individuals, and particularly women and racial minorities, had no participatory rights in the political process.

Our sense of historical progress, wrapped within our understanding of the course of evolution, reminds us that in the future humans will not live as they do today. The truth of evolution—progress—at this moment in human history is undeniable. We must consider the implications of this truth. The unfolding of the universe, the truth of progress, calls upon us not to view existing forms of behavior with great reverence. We must banish our sense of nostalgia. It is very likely that at some point in the future, the conduct of our affairs today will seem primitive and even vestigial in nature. The world we think of today as modern will likely be seen as a way station on the journey to something more complex, powerful and valuable. Human evolution has discarded tails and the need to grow fur for warmth. Surely, many aspects of human life that seem almost sacred to us today will in the future seem like furry tails: things needed before, but now—if we still had them—superfluous, ridiculous and annoying.

Is it possible to imagine a world in which the traditional idea of leadership itself were to become a concept that is no longer useful, like monarchy and feudalism? What would it mean to transcend the concept of leadership in human affairs?

Leadership as a central method and strategy for human progress is evolving. As human societies transcend leadership, a better and more promising strategy for work in human communities emerges, slowly becoming visible and staking claim as a new strategy in human affairs. *Genership* represents the capacity to collaborate with others in a liberating creative process. This work describes, understands and accelerates this trend.

The Nature of This Work

This work emerges from the experience of a team of leaders, consultants, researchers and thinkers at the Institute for Leadership Education, Advancement and Development (also known as I-LEAD) over the past decade. The work has also been informed by energetic dialogue and learning during this time frame among the Kellogg Fellows Leadership Alliance, the Eisenhower Exchange Fellows and the Ashoka Fellows, groups representing more than 5,000 gifted leaders in the United States and around the world.

Over many years helping groups and individuals increase their leadership abilities, one of our most difficult challenges has been the growing awareness that there are more counter-examples than examples. One can easily point out what *not* to do, but finding cases of people modeling exemplary practices is difficult. Coming to grips with this reality forces one to think carefully about the nature of the project, yielding some key framing ideas.

The first is that we are not necessarily describing the work of existing leaders, but rather advocating new models of leadership and different approaches to working with groups. In many cases, the practices genership advocates are honored in the breach. Too often, the work of actual leaders does not exhibit the best practices that lead to success. What we can see in the field often showcases organizational failure or stagnancy resulting from deficient leadership. We can talk about what goes wrong in organizations without being able to point to large numbers of people getting it right. The examples and cases involving role models are isolated and emergent; there is at best a hopeful trend showing that more successful organizations model genership behaviors.

At the deeper level, genership does not merely advocate practices that work, but calls for change. Our work is normative, not descriptive. We seek to promote a new kind of relationship between people in organizations grounded in a celebration of human dignity and creativity—in other words, genership promotes the practice of moral philosophy of organizational work. We say to our learners, this is how you *should* work, not only because it succeeds, but also because it represents the right thing to do, while both productive and *good*.

Genership explicitly rejects one extant mental model; specifically, it is not science. In the realm of creativity and innovation, the application of science has limits. Think of Bill Gates and Steve Jobs, working on their innovations, trying to prove scientifically that they would have a large market, leading Microsoft and Apple to become among the most powerful organizations in human history. When the companies began work on their products, there was no worldwide market for personal computers. Now, one might make the mistake of thinking that Gates and Jobs predicted such a future, that they saw the market emerging with or without them. But the reality is different. They established the market by contributing to the invention of the device. They did not predict the world. They changed the world through their work. There was no empirical evidence to suggest that personal computers would be ubiquitous at the moment when Gates and Jobs (along with many others, of course) were inventing the industry. Given the analogy to the mainframe business, an effort to scientifically prove the market for computers would have assuredly failed. Hence the famous 1943 quote from the otherwise astute chairman of International Business Machines, Thomas Watson: "I think there is a world market for maybe five computers." Or what Ken Olsen, President of Digital Equipment Corporation said in 1977, "There is no reason anyone would want a computer in their home." DEC did not survive the 1990s.

On a moral—as opposed to a technological level—imagine if Jefferson had been asked to prove experimentally that democracies provided the most successful process for developing human societies. Or imagine if he had been asked to conduct a study proving that all men are created equal and endowed with inalienable rights. No such studies would have been possible; even if so, they would have evidenced the opposite of Jefferson's assertions.

Human advancement cannot be justified through studying existing leaders and practices. Instead, genership articulates new approaches to leadership, changing how it is conducted in the world, and letting others study the changes we cause after the fact. We offer the work presented here in that spirit, with clear knowledge of its transformative potential.

Genership involves normative rather than descriptive work. This is a critical distinction. Descriptive work finds its justification in the concept that human practices follow scientific laws and principles. The theory is that if we observe the laws carefully, we can describe them and employ them in our work, just as one who understands the principles of electro-magnetism can use them to build an electric motor. But normative work is different. It finds its justification in the human capacity to change itself and the world, to bring entirely new practices, products and outcomes into being. These cannot really even be finally judged in terms of merit until they exist. Normative work is what led us to envision the electric motor itself.

The ultimate purposes of human life are beyond the boundary of scientific knowledge because of the limits of the scientific method, bounded by the concept of the experiment and the falsifiable hypothesis. Science can only know what is proven in valid experiments. Even the hypothesis that survives experiment is not necessarily true forever. It merely remains consistent with observation. And there may be many such theories that show consistence, coming from different and divergent systems of knowledge.

Scientific methods can help us describe. They can tell us about patterns that are already extant in the world. We can make predictions and then run experiments to see whether those predictions are observed in reality. But scientific knowledge cannot tell us which patterns are important to understand. Most importantly, it cannot tell us what patterns to set in motion using our own creative energies. Human potential in the world is itself a force of nature. The spectrum of possible outcomes within human communities is unlimited. What guides us toward certain outcomes and away from others is not a descriptive scientific inquiry, but rather our normative visions and values. As cognitive scientist and philosopher Jerry Fodor has stated, "Science is about facts, not norms; it might tell us how we are, but it couldn't tell us what is wrong with how we are."

The questions about what human communities want, how they should live and what they should try to create are matters for another domain of human understanding. They cannot be resolved through study and experiments. We cannot use science to understand patterns of experience that do not yet exist, that are emergent. We know from observation that there are an enormous number of changes in the world introducing new patterns that have never before existed. We could not, for example, have used science to investigate human interaction with computers in 1900. In the words of American physicist and Nobel laureate Phillip Warren Anderson:

> The ability to reduce everything to simple fundamental laws does not imply the ability to start from those laws and reconstruct the universe. The constructionist hypothesis breaks down when confronted with the twin difficulties of scale and complexity. At each level of complexity entirely new properties appear. Psychology is not applied biology, nor is biology applied chemistry. We can now see that the whole becomes not merely more, but very different from the sum of its parts. [ii]

In just this way, genership is more than an observation of emergent patterns of human behavior. It is a stimulus to the emergence of those patterns as a whole, part of the change in the world, not an after-the-fact report about it. What follows describes the new pattern emerging from the complexity of the whole, not an echo of abstract rules receding in history.

Three Fallacies That Underlie Leadership

A fallacy is more than a mistake or lie, more than an untruth. The world is, after all, riddled with non-material mistakes and errors, imprecisions that don't matter much. When asked his age, a person generally answers with a rounded-off year. Technically, that's wrong. He is not exactly the age replied. But people rarely care about such details. Of course, there are circumstances in which precision is important. If one takes a potent medicine, it is necessary to get the dose exactly right. But a fallacy suggests a different order of magnitude, something *important* that was believed to be true at some point, and later discovered to be false. The word "fallacy" also conveys the idea that the discredited belief may have been central to other beliefs or actions, like a support beam inside a house. It's not a picture that's hanging askew on the wall or a window that needs to be replaced or painted. Rather, it's a floor about to give way. It's a roof about to fall in. A wall about to come down. A fallacy is an error that really matters.

An important logical and legal fallacy is called post hoc, from the Latin "post hoc, ergo propter hoc," meaning *after the fact, therefore because of the fact*. This is the fallacy that because one event occurs shortly after another, we can induce that the earlier event caused the later one. This fallacy drives an enormous amount of bogus analysis in the world; for example, when stock-market moves are attributed to particular pre-occurring events within a vast field of them. Presidential elections often receive credit or blame for movements in stock averages, but we know that elections are only one of more than thousands of variables influencing the markets. The mind is predisposed to seek connections; it searches constantly for reliable patterns and sequences. The reason for this is our desire to predict and control the future. If one knows that a pattern is real, then if the first part of the pattern presents, then the second part will follow. This knowledge allows for action. If a smoke alarm goes off when there's something burning, then one can stop the burning before it gets out of control. If a car sensor beeps before the vehicle runs out of gas, then the tank can be filled, breaking the sequence one wants to avoid.

Unfortunately, the mind generates a large number of false positives, seeing connections between events that, with subsequent effort, it can determine coexist only because of serendipity or random coincidence. The colloquial expression for this is "crying wolf," from Aesop's fables. If a boy continually cries wolf when no wolf is there, then those around him soon discredit his claim. They will ignore him, just as one would ignore a faulty gas sensor that beeps when the tank is full.

For this reason, understanding the false connections in life is extremely valuable. As experience teaches us all too well, the world is not as it appears and often not as described in commonplace narratives or theories. Our sense of the world is informed by experiences and stories that predispose us to seek out certain kinds of connections between events and ignore others.

A natural scientist lives in a hut with a witch doctor and a monk from the middle ages. In trying to understand the world around them, the different experiences and knowledge informing their observations will cause them to seek and then to see very different kinds of connections between events. If the hut were struck by lightning, the monk would likely attribute this to an intentional act of God; the witch doctor, to some element of the natural spirit world; the scientist, to the random behavior of electric fields in midair.

Many human beings and communities are influenced by competing narratives, causing them to search for widely divergent sets of connections in understanding the world. An individual who understands Christianity, psychology, political science, philosophy and economics might comprehend events in many diverse ways and at different levels. A downturn in the economy, for example, might be explained as the wages of sin, a sense of ennui or fear taking hold of the public, class conflict, global market competition or faulty accounting mechanisms. Often people will hold in their minds simultaneously contradictory ways of understanding the world. If a person experiences financial success, he might say that he is benefiting from God's grace, hard work or modern technology. Think of the football player who evades and breaks tackles down the field, and then crossing into the end zone, points to the heavens. "God did that," is what he means. Meanwhile, the announcers are praising not God, but the player's athleticism and his teammates' work.

Truth and Pragmatism

"What works is true and represents a reality,

for the individual for whom it works."
　　　　—William James, *The Meaning of Truth* (1909)

Years ago, when I was in law school, I had a professor of torts who delighted in showing the class that if you thought long and hard about anything, you could reduce it to nonsense. The pattern of his lectures was always the same. He would begin by asking questions. Then no matter how students answered, he would offer a series of penetrating challenges to their reasoning. At the end of the lectures, all of the theories and arguments presented by the students were decimated and their proponents shown to be silly and shallow. My professor always summed up by laying out all of the arguments for and against whatever the question was, often on multiple sides. He would then insist on leaving the matter in a state of equipoise, if unsettled. Nothing was ever shown to be right. In frustration, I approached him toward the end of the semester.

"Is there always a good counter-argument?" I asked. "Can everything be shown to be wrong and is nothing ever clearly right?"

His eyes were full of amusement. "Well," he said, "that depends."

"Depends on what?" I asked.

"On how long you want to think about it."

"But isn't there anything such as *truth*?" I asked.

"That depends too," he replied again.

"On what?"

"On what you mean by *truth*."

"The truth is *what is*." I had it all figured out.

"But what if you can never know *what is*?" He smiled at me knowingly.

"Then can I ever know anything?" I was searching.

"Well, if you know how something isn't true, the sense in which your idea about something is coming up short, does that count as knowing *something*?"

"I guess so."

"So then knowing *what isn't* gets you closer to *what is*?"

"But when do we get *there...* to *what is*?" I paid a lot of money to go this law school. I didn't just want to get closer. I wanted to arrive.

He shrugged his shoulders. "That's for you to figure out."

My efforts over the years have yielded many important insights. One of the most critical was basically that seeking the truth is sometimes like chasing a rabbit through the underbrush. As you approach, it darts away from you. At any given moment, you're not sure exactly where it is. But you do gain certainty about where it isn't. That knowledge is useful; it matters. To know what is not right, what doesn't work, can be an important part of making progress, of moving toward the truth. Some of the greatest discoveries are through trial and error, and the identification of error is critical to progress.

In the pragmatic approach, the truth is not a universal, eternal or ultimate set of ideas proven to be correct, but rather a tool for working with reality that either helps you accomplish your goals or doesn't. Whether it works depends of course on what you're trying to accomplish. Since the goals of human action evolve and extend into the future, our ways of thinking about the world can never be discovered to be correct once and for all time. A pragmatist works with an idea as long as it proves to be useful, while it helps achieve his ends. For this reason, a pragmatist gains certainty about what does not work, but holds lightly to the ideas that have not yet failed him, ready to discard them if they do.

The fallacies presented here are ideas whose time has passed in the sense that they are no longer useful, if ever they were.

Three Fallacies

The Messiah Fallacy

The Hero Fallacy

The Fallacy of
Leadership Nostalgia

More than a decade of working with organizations and individuals thinking about leadership has surfaced three fallacies closely related to the fallacy of post hoc. They describe deeply engrained patterns of behavior among leaders and followers in which success is attributed to forces that may coincide with success but do not cause it.

1. *The Messiah Fallacy.* This is the fallacy that a group's success depends upon the success or failure of a singular extraordinary individual, a messiah. Under this spell, the concept of leadership itself arises in part from a disabling pattern of thinking and behavior in which members of a group fall into a state of crisis and then seek a messiah figure whom they believe will rescue and lead them—in the manner of sheep—to a better future. This pattern of thinking finds its roots both in experiences of childhood and in religious narratives deeply embedded in Western culture. But humans are not gods, and the messiah role, when a mere mortal assumes it, is one that typically disappoints both the leader cast as the messiah as well as his or her followers. The practice of groups in projecting all of their hopes and fears onto one of their members is inherently unreasonable and almost guarantees collective failure. It breeds dependency and relative incompetence while removing personal responsibility from group members for their own success.

2. *The Hero Fallacy.* This fallacy holds that a contest among heroes will reveal the true messiah. The Messiah Fallacy itself—and particularly the irrational need that groups feel to be rescued from their own incompetence by an individual erroneously believed to be endowed with super powers—flows from an unhealthy focus on individual heroes as the primary resource within groups for vision, strategic action and problem-solving. This focus on individuals and their acts of heroism creates destructive and wasteful behavior patterns within groups. Following these tendencies, aspiring leaders compete for power, influence and recognition within groups. The competition itself arises from the belief (the Messiah Fallacy) that group progress depends upon a savior emerging from the conflict among heroes: one who will lead the sheep to greener, safer pastures. The competition among heroes also often involves the creation of a crisis, or "quest," in which the competing heroes test themselves to see who deserves to be crowned as the messianic king. The aspiring heroes are often those who manufacture and perpetuate these episodes of crisis and quest, narratives that usually have little to do with meaningful progress for the group's real needs and desires. As a result, leadership processes that orbit heroes and prospective heroes within groups consume enormous amounts of time and energy unrelated to the group's vital work. Rather,

the hero-wars have to do with selecting who the group will test in the role of messiah. In this way, the process of leadership, and the cycle through which a series of leaders is publicly vetted, found wanting and finally rejected—even sacrificed—become wasteful distractions from real work and progress that would otherwise improve individual lives by engaging them in creative and collaborative efforts.

3. *The Fallacy of Leadership Nostalgia.* The third fatal flaw in the concept and practice of leadership involves the tendency in groups to mythologize and enshrine the ways and wisdom of past leaders. This is the fallacy that effective leadership can be understood through the study of what previous messiahs did or said to succeed, as opposed to our learning from their mistakes. Scholars combine subjective biographical research—with selective collection and editing of anecdotes—to reduce the life and works of former leaders to abstractions of dogma or recipes. Many such titles exist in leadership literature, usually in this form: *Famous Leader's* [fill in number] *Principles of Effective Leadership: Toward* [fill in promised success]."

The nostalgia for past leaders flows from the unsubstantiated belief that human communities obey universal laws. The concept arises from applying ideas drawn from the physical sciences (such as physics, chemistry and biology) to human communities, implying scientifically provable laws of human behavior similar to principles of motion or other physical laws. If this were true, then it would be possible to control the outcomes in any human situation simply by following the verified laws of human interaction. The thinking here is that humans must obey scientific laws in the same way for example, that water always freezes given certain temperatures and air pressures. On this basis, leadership researchers submit that producing desired outcomes within a group (profit, influence, growth) is like baking a cake. They maintain that, as in cooking, using particular ingredients and then rote following of specific instructions will necessarily produce the promised result:

Leader	Implied Thesis
Lincoln on Leadership: Executive Strategies for Tough Times, Donald T. Phillips (1992)	Copying selected practices of Lincoln (e.g., "Be a Master of Paradox," and "Master the Art of

	Public Speaking") will make you a great leader like Lincoln.
Leadership Secrets of Attila the Hun, Wess Roberts (1985)	Developing certain qualities that Attila the Hun allegedly possessed (e.g., loyalty and courage) will make you a powerful leader like Attila.
A Matter of Character: Inside the White House of George W. Bush, Ronald Kessler (2004)	Cultivating qualities purportedly exemplified by President George W. Bush (e.g., honesty, integrity and clarity of purpose) will make you a great leader.
A Higher Standard of Leadership: Lessons from the Life of Ghandi, Keshavan Nair (1997)	Adopting Ghandi's simple leadership practices (e.g., "Commit to the Journey," "Minimize Secrecy," "Focus on Responsibilities") will make you a transformational leader.

Countless works like these are available to the public, purporting to distill qualities, laws, practices and habits from the lives of leaders, suggesting that one can achieve greatness by mimicking certain aspects of their behavior.

There are two fundamental problems with this kind of nostalgia. First, lessons learned from the past in this manner usually have little to do with the reality of history and much more to do with particular ethical, moral or policy agendas advanced by the scholar. In the life of any leader there are as many counter-examples of effective leadership as examples themselves. In the afterglow of fame, the many failures experienced by leaders are forgotten and discounted. Rarely do such works document the intensive process of learning from failure. Instead, writers sort through the historical record for examples of practices that are acceptable and in sync with cultural values, and promote those. The omissions are revealing. We do not find leadership scholars writing about how one should emulate Ghandi's practice of sleeping naked with young girls (in some cases, relatives) in order to test his commitment to chastity. Nor do we find books explaining how young people should cultivate the melancholy and depression that afflicted Abraham Lincoln throughout his life and contributed substantially to his self-reflection.

The second problem is that human communities change so rapidly and pervasively that such guidebooks are really not worth much. We can learn from the past, but the lessons that time and experience afford, as far as communities are concerned, cannot be distilled into scientific doctrines that we can employ in the same way that principles of physics are used to understand the behavior of inanimate objects in motion. Human beings are alive and conscious; they have free will and are able to alter their behaviors voluntarily. Human beings make choices; they are not billiard balls. Scientific knowledge itself tends to expand human freedom, making behavior even more difficult to predict.

Suppose society establishes that a depressed person is more likely to commit suicide. Society could then respond by educating families and social systems to become aware of the symptoms of depression and to secure treatment for them. Over time, suicide rates associated with depression could decline, undermining the overall correlation. Knowledge offers to liberate humans from observed patterns because they are able to respond to them intelligently and disrupt the pathways observed in the original pattern analysis.

Assume society observes that people with a good high school education are able to better obtain jobs. Over time, more people pursue this education, so it is no longer a distinguishing characteristic for a job seeker; eventually, the link between a sound high school education (without more) is not a sufficient predictor of success in the job market. Knowledge of the pattern can be used by humans to change it.

Changing circumstances naturally undermine observed patterns. Before the invention of antibiotics, routine bacterial infections often led to death. Now, when antibiotic treatments are available, there is little correlation between routine infections and mortality. On the other hand, certain strains of bacteria have evolved resistance to antibiotics, making them more lethal than ever. These strains did not even exist in the past. They are the result of human intervention itself. Living systems change and respond to circumstances. For this reason, they are difficult if not impossible to predict over time.

Leadership Nostalgia also entails ascribing accomplishments and credits to the efforts of an individual that were actually performed by a group of human beings working together effectively, thus reinforcing the other core fallacies of leadership: undue focus on heroism and the search for a messiah.

These three deficits in the traditional concept and practice of leadership—the Messiah Fallacy, the Hero Fallacy and the Fallacy of Leadership Nostalgia—require organizations to develop strategies to succeed *despite* their leaders, not because of them. The most critical strategy involves the strength of genership, marshaling the creativity of the entire group even as a parallel process to the operation of the fallacies. Understanding how genership provides a different pathway requires full command of how the fallacies operate within organizations and communities.

Messiah in Chief

At the 1992 Democratic National Convention, New York Governor Mario Cuomo nominated Bill Clinton as the Democratic candidate for president. Clinton had been plagued by the kind of allegations of marital infidelity that later marred his presidency. Cuomo's speech, widely viewed as a key endorsement of Clinton, deftly framed him as the nation's new messiah.

"Bill Clinton... is our only hope for change from this nation's current disastrous course," said Cuomo to the enthralled convention audience, describing the nation as a ship headed for the rocks, about to founder. He urged that the passengers needed "a new captain and a new course, before it's too late." He then offered an image of the people en masse marching behind Clinton into the promised land:

> I'd like to march behind President Bill Clinton through cities and rural villages where all the people have safe streets, affordable housing and healthcare when they need it. I want to clap my hands and throw my fists in the air, cheering neighborhoods where children can be children, where they can grow up and get the chance to go to college, and one day own their own home. I want to sing proud songs, happy songs, arm-in-arm with workers who have a real stake in their company's success; who once again have the assurance that a lifetime of hard work will make life better for their children than it had been for them. I want to march behind President Bill Clinton in a victory parade that sends up fireworks, celebrating the triumph of our technology centers and factories, out-producing and outselling our overseas competitors. ... I want to look around and feel the warmth, the pride, the profound gratitude of knowing that we are making America surer, stronger and sweeter. I want to shout out our thanks because President Bill Clinton has helped us make the greatest nation in the world better than it's ever been.

Clinton's acceptance speech embraced the messianic motif, echoing Moses in offering the nation "a new covenant" and invoking a Scriptural reference to vision:

> Of all the things George Bush has ever said that I disagree with, perhaps the thing that bothers me most is how he derides and degrades the American tradition of seeing and seeking a better future. He mocks it as "the vision thing." But just remember what the Scripture says: "Where there is no vision, the people perish." ... We can seize this moment,

make it exciting and energizing and heroic to be an American again. We can renew our faith in each other and in ourselves. We can restore our sense of unity and community. As the Scripture says, our eyes have not yet seen, nor our ears heard nor our minds imagined what we can build.

George W. Bush was not shy about donning messianic robes. Contemplating a presidential run in 1999, he said to Richard Land of the Southern Baptists Convention, "I believe God wants me to be president." Evangelicals widely came to believe that Bush decided to run for president after listening to a sermon by Rev. Mark Craig describing how Moses had been called to service by God. The story goes that after the sermon, President Bush's mother turned to him and said, "He's talking to you."

This theme continued in Bush's two terms, with many evangelicals observing the work of God in Bush's reelection in 2004. "This was Providence," said evangelical leader and presidential adviser Chuck Colson. "Anybody looking at the 2000 election would have to say it was a miraculous deliverance, and I think people felt it again this year."

Throughout his presidency, many Americans retained the perception that Bush was being guided by prayerful communication with God and that he believed he was following and implementing divine will. In his book, *Plan of Attack*, Bob Woodward questioned Bush on whether he sought advice from his father on policy issues, particularly those involving the war, in view of the elder's experience as the 41st president. Bush's response was revealing: "He is the wrong father to appeal to for advice. The wrong father to go to, to appeal to in terms of strength." Then he said, "There's a higher Father that I appeal to."

In 2008, Barack Obama inherited the messianic mantle, despite his repeated efforts to remind the voters that "it's not about me" and "we are the ones we've been waiting for." Many Americans began to ascribe super powers to Obama, despite the fact that he had never held an executive position in the public or private sector other than running his own political campaigns. During the presidential primary, Mark Morford, a columnist for the *San Francisco Chronicle*, captured the sentiments of many Americans when he described Obama as exhibiting a "powerful luminosity," and a unique "high-vibration" integrity. "Many spiritually advanced people I know," continued Morford, "identify Obama as a Lightworker, that rare kind of attuned being who has the ability to lead us not merely to new foreign policies or healthcare plans or whatnot, but who can actually help usher in *a new way of being on the planet*, of relating and connecting and engaging with this bizarre earthly experiment. These kinds of people actually help us *evolve*. They are philosophers and peacemakers of a very high order, and they speak not just to reason or emotion, but to the soul."

On February 13, 2008, in a *Huffington Post* article, former Colorado senator and presidential contender Gary Hart described Obama in messianic terms:

> He is in fact an agent of transformation. He is not operating on the same plane as ordinary politicians, and this makes him seem elusive to the conventional press and the traditional politicians. His instinct for the moment and the times is orders of magnitude more powerful than the experience claimed by others. Experience in the old ways is irrelevant experience. In an age of great transformation, experience of the past is worthless because it is a barrier to the breakthrough gesture, the instant response in crisis, the instinctive bold decision in the face of totally new circumstances. Some see Barack

Obama as the long-awaited champion finally come to slay the awful dragon of race. And they are right. Some see him as a new start for the Democratic Party and national politics. And they are right. Some see him as the walking embodiment of internationalism, ready to restore an honorable and respected place for America in the world. And they are right. I see Barack Obama as a leader for this transcendent moment, the agent of transformation in an age of revolution, as a figure uniquely qualified to open the door to the 21st century and to convert threat to great new opportunity.

In words capturing the sentiments of so many voters, a political blogger named Gerald Campbell described Obama as "radiating truth and goodness" and possessing an extraordinary ability that could cure the great ills facing mankind:

For his part, Obama has the capacity to summon heroic forces from the spiritual depths of ordinary citizens and to unleash there from a symphonic chorus of unique creative acts whose common purpose is to tame the soul and alleviate the great challenges facing mankind. For their part, each citizen has within the potential to respond to such a heroic calling. When they do, noble qualities are unleashed from the very depths of the human spirit. When they do not, a politics of fear ensues. In either event, the choice is ours to make. Unlike other candidates, Obama is an inspired leader. He is authentic and truthful. He radiates truth and goodness. He possesses charisma and exercises sound judgment. For this reason, he serves as a catalyst to awaken the better part of ourselves.

Notably, in the aftermath of the presidency, each of these messianic figures fell to earth when the public inevitably discovered that they (being mere mortals without a direct line to the Almighty) could not, in fact, deliver the universe and a place to put it.

The Messiah Fallacy

The group's success depends upon the success of one extraordinary individual.

The Roots of the Messiah Fallacy

Infancy. Every infant who survives birth enjoys a short period in which someone else carries almost all the burdens of the child's existence. The experience is profound, leaving an indelible impression on the child's psyche. A successful and healthy early childhood gives rise to the belief, seemingly ratified in reality, that one or two people can make everything all right, no matter what happens. In the hands of loving, responsible parents, this experience can last well into maturity. The children of strong parents develop a robust faith that the universe will provide warmth, food, security and even pleasure through the work of one or two all-powerful parental figures. In many cases there is not a shred of doubt about this. The child offers up a complete suspension of worry and concern, knowing if the parental figure says that all is well, then everything will be so. What usually follows such reassurance is blissful slumber.

Maturity often arrives during a disconcerting moment when the painful world intrudes despite the best efforts of parental figures. The pain of maturity also breaks through when a parental figure intentionally allows some of that worldly chaos to enter, knowing that building resilience and self-sufficiency will make the child stronger. After all, children who develop self-reliance, who learn to manage and fend for themselves, can eventually provide security for others, even care for those very parental figures who once seemed all-powerful.

The uncertain moment when a child realizes that his parents either cannot or will not come to the rescue often produces indignant feelings and even anger. It seems unfair that parents should abandon young ones in their moment of need! Eventually children learn that their parents either wanted them to grow stronger or actually could not protect them from deprivation and harm. They learn that their parents are riddled with flaws and weaknesses. This bittersweet moment often leads children to appreciate their parents for the first time. It is one thing for all-powerful beings to take care of us, quite another for mere mortals!

Nonetheless, the initial experience that humans (at least those who survive) have of being well protected as infants, admittedly for a very short time, often takes up residence in the psyche as a deep longing to be in another's care. The concept is simple. Would it not be wonderful if someone was always out there, a mother or father, ready to step in and catch us when we fall, feed us when hungry, warm us when cold and scare away the monster under the bed?

Religion. In the struggle to explain to their children aspects of the world that they cannot control, many parents turn, understandably, to religion. Here again that all-powerful parental figure emerges, but this time in the form of the messiah. Such a figure appears in almost every religion, either as God, his messenger or as a person of extraordinary wisdom who somehow embodies an infinite spirit capable of ordering the mind so as to provide peace, comfort and security. The messiah's perceived actions often include healing people who have fallen into a state of helplessness or crisis. The relationship between the sick or helpless person and the messiah figure is to recognize the absolute authority and power of the messiah and to surrender in hopes of rescue. Of course, this is the same relationship prefigured between infant and parent.

The major monotheistic religions, Judaism, Christianity and Islam, involving nearly four billion people covering the majority of the world's population, all share deeply engrained messianic narratives following the same general form. The people are challenged, imprisoned, in a state of crisis, sick or beset with other difficult problems, and a prophet emerges from the group who is identified as God's messenger or manifestation. The messiah figure teaches, nurtures and leads the people to a new place where their fundamental condition is improved. Deep familiarity with these narratives causes people to believe that it is fundamentally rational to expect to be rescued by an all-powerful figure who will emerge from the group. People who study such religious narratives come to think of Abraham, Moses, Jesus and Mohammed, for example, as role models to be emulated. The study of religious narratives leads to deeply engrained expectations about the nature of leadership. Fundamentally, we learn to expect our leaders to be our parents and to take care of us. But our leaders are neither gods nor divine messengers, and because they are not our parents and cannot take on such a burden, to cast them in the role of parental saviors usually has disastrous consequences.

Groups. In our organizations and in our politics, groups often project the profound wish to be rescued, saved and protected by an all-powerful parent onto their leaders. Sometimes the leaders themselves encourage it. After all, it is quite a heady experience to be treated as some kind of all-powerful god. Sometimes leaders are the recipients of this projection even if they reject it and attempt to remind people that, after all, they are mere mortals just like those they lead. When the leader says things like, "It's not about me," the follower may respond and say, "The Great One is just being humble. And that humility makes him even greater." After all, it is scary and threatening to believe that "The Great One" is really just another human being with a full spectrum of flaws. Because if he or she is another fallible person, then who is going to rescue us?

A predictable pattern follows the Messiah Fallacy: The messiah figure lets us down. Think about this for a moment. If our own parents cannot always protect us as children, how could one person possibly rescue all of us? Unless the messiah is in fact God—and most people who believe in God also believe that there is only one—failure is not just possible, but inevitable. We cry and mom or dad does not appear to make it all right again. After the messiah's failure comes anger and outrage! Where are our parents when we call? Finally, rejection and the search for new parents to take care of us. "Well, if that's the way you're going to be, I'm just going to have to get some new parents to depend on!"

Some key elements of the Messiah Fallacy that deserve focus include:

1. *Helplessness.* The Messiah Fallacy is fundamentally rooted in a group's sense of its combined impotence and vulnerability. *A powerful and capable group does not need to be rescued.* If the group begins to feel lost or in need of resources, or feels fearful of an external threat, the perceived need for a messiah figure will emerge. A child who is busy playing, learning or eating does not need a parent, but a child who is alone, hungry or cold will begin to seek rescue.

2. *Search for "The One."* The Messiah Fallacy includes a deeply held belief that the group's needs can be satisfied by one special person who provides all that is required, or at least coordinates its delivery. The group does not attempt to resolve its own problems by calling forth its capacities or regulating participation among group members. Rather, the group abandons its activity while searching for a member (either existing or new) capable of handling it all. There is a strong belief that resolution of all the group's needs can be consolidated within one all-powerful parental figure, that failure to find the right person will lead to the group's demise.

3. *Omniscience, Special Powers, Reverence.* The messiah is revered by the group; its members circle around as if he or she were royalty or imbued with a god-like quality deserving reverence. The group justifies reverence for the messiah because of special powers, presumably relevant and necessary to group's work and often entailing a perceived kind of super-intelligence or omniscience beyond the group members' understanding. In some cases the reverence is justified as a result of some connection with the divine or the supernatural. In other cases,

reverence flows from the messiah figure's perceived unusual training and rare skill. The observation that groups sometimes treat leaders with rare skills and abilities as messiahs does not denigrate the possibility that individuals may really have certain special skills that develop through natural tendencies combined with experience.

4. *Loyalty, Fealty, Submission.* The messiah figure is deemed by the group to deserve loyalty, in part transactional. The messiah dedicates his or her life to the welfare of the group; in return, the group offers complete loyalty. This bond is critical to its functioning and the quality of leadership demonstrated by the messiah. In this context, questioning the messiah is deemed to be an insult, treacherous and even treasonous. Questioning the messiah is tantamount to betrayal of the leader and also the group. In this context, questioning the leader is the same as rejecting the group as a whole. The word "fealty" references the feudal concept that the group owes services and material goods to the messiah in exchange for his or her leadership. The messiah must be supported and protected by the group because of the dedication of his or her special powers to its welfare. The word "submission" describes the idea that, within the Messiah Fallacy, the group members are not seen as equals to the messiah, but almost as lesser beings incapable of contributing to the group's welfare except through service to the messiah or by following the messiah's instructions. In this way, the Messiah Fallacy promotes the development of group dynamics in which a group's members become extensions of the will of one person and in which its work becomes synonymous with the messiah's welfare.

5. *The Messiah Drama.* This refers to the group's focus on the struggles, accomplishments, failures, death and rebirth of the messiah. This drama becomes the central story that concerns the group rather than the narrative about the quality of life or aspirations of its own members. What does the messiah want? How is the messiah being tested? Has the messiah succeeded? How has the messiah suffered? Has the messiah failed or perished? If so, will the messiah return in a real or metaphorical resurrection? In American politics messianic figures such as Abraham Lincoln, John F. Kennedy and Martin Luther King, Jr., have been resurrected through memorials and nostalgic scholarship that remembers them almost as saints or civic demigods, tending to overlook or downplay their shortcomings, failures and flaws. The story of the

messiah is the group's story; it lives life—and by extension individual members live—through the messiah's life.

6. *The Inevitability of Failure.* The Messiah Fallacy entails a relentlessly predetermined outcome involving the messiah's failure and fall. This inevitability is rooted in several realities. First is the group's abandonment of action pending super powers to be deployed by the messiah. The group stands back, passively watching and waiting for the messiah to spring into action. Second is the reality that the messiah is not really imbued with any such powers, and is in fact closely related in skills and abilities to the group's members. Even though each member of the group possesses valuable skills that can be coordinated effectively to serve its needs, the group behaves as if the messiah's skills have a generally exalted nature rendering the group's input unnecessary or secondary at best. Because the group tries to carry out its work through only one member's lead, sidelining the majority of its members' own resources and abilities, the messiah experiences an intolerable burden, suffers and fails. Third, if the messiah confesses that he or she is not really the messiah, and requests help, the group will often choose to ignore or deny such statements. If the group comes to believe that the messiah has abdicated, it may then fall into a state of crisis, viewing this move as a breach of the fundamental bargain: the exchange of loyalty, fealty and submission in exchange for not bearing responsibility or having to think about the life of the organization. Even if the messiah has been protesting and calling attention to his or her humanity, the group feels betrayed because it has projected its needs and wishes upon the messiah figure.

Of course, these features of the Messiah Fallacy do not describe optimal group behaviors achieved through the work of genership; its central purpose is to understand the dysfunctional effects of the fallacy that genership must work to overcome.

The Hero Fallacy

A contest among heroes will reveal the true messiah.

Joachim Wtewael,
***The Battle Between the Gods and the Titans,* 1600**

The Roots of the Hero Fallacy

The Hero Fallacy is both prequel and sequel to the Messiah Fallacy. It operates within the narrative that involves the search for "The One." Groups with a failing or fallen messiah begin the search, which requires the establishment of a series of quests focused upon heroes. Heroes are those with the courage and strength to engage in the quests. They are meant to test the abilities of heroes aspiring to become messiahs. The qualities tested are designed to showcase the messiah's superpowers.

The Hero Fallacy narrative differs substantially from that of the Messiah Fallacy, which involves the work of the messiah to save the group from its crisis. In contrast, the Hero Fallacy involves the testing of heroes in combat against one another or a series of quests. It involves the group's belief that success in both combat and the quest means that the hero can function effectively as their messiah. In reality, this work is typically irrelevant to the group's needs and aspirations. The resources spent in attaining the status of messiah are not only wasted, they set both the messiah and the group back substantially because of the opportunity costs entailed in attaining messiah status.

Modern political campaigns offer a powerful example of the Hero Fallacy in action. Caught in the spell of the Messiah Fallacy, voters believe that only a person possessing extraordinary intelligence, wisdom and moral strength (a messiah) can rescue the people. They suspend work on solving their own problems and instead search for the messiah. To find such a person, voters create a system in which many heroes contend for nominations, battling one another in debates and through attack advertisements, competing to see who can raise the most money and endure extended media coverage regarding all aspects of their personality and personal lives. During this period, the contestants showcase (and in many cases, exaggerate) their abilities and personal qualities to prove to the voters that they can serve as messiah. This process of fighting one another is enormously expensive and drains them of energy. It often weakens whatever moral strengths they may have possessed as they make deals and compromise their principles in order to win the nomination. This often involves distorting their positions on a broad range of issues to gain the support of various factions. It also entails making incredible promises describing the rescue services they will provide once elected that will solve all the electorate's problems. Their combat with one another often has little to do with underlying issues facing the body politic. Does the fact that one candidate has more accomplishments than another mean a better exercise of judgment about public policy? Do qualities such as looking better on television or being more effective at raising money for attack advertisements have anything to do with effectiveness as a political decision-maker? Does a person's marital fidelity necessarily influence his judgment on issues of public policy? By the time one of the candidates wins, he or she may be substantially less able to perform effectively because of the distractions, compromises and deals endured during the campaign. This is an example of the opportunity cost that the Hero Fallacy imposes when the group selects a messiah.

Included among the dominant features of the Hero Fallacy:

1. *Transformation by combat or test.* Here the fallacy is that a mere mortal can obtain or demonstrate superpowers through the process of engaging in combat or a series of quests. The group behaves as if the process of surviving these challenges imbues the hero with magical or supreme powers. In reality, such combats and tests often destroy the

heroes before they are able to assume the doomed messiah role. Even the surviving hero—the one who prevails and becomes the group's messiah—is usually distracted and weakened by these contests. This process does not stimulate the development of magical or superior powers; it simply wastes the group's resources.

2. *Creation of combat or quest narratives.* Such narratives usually have almost nothing to do with the real issues facing the group, and thus may need to be invented solely to qualify someone to serve as messiah, so that the group can relax while all of its cares and concerns are believed to be addressed by its settled-upon messiah figure. Usually the organization's work is put into suspended animation while a variety of real or metaphorical battles play out among the competitors, along with various trials invented by the group.

3. *The formation of alliances and hero wars.* When groups are mired in the Hero Fallacy, their fundamental question concerns who will take charge to provide rescue. This may involve a complex and shifting arrangement of alliances and battles in which subgroups of heroes join together to defeat others. The demise of some subgroups may give rise to revenge plots and internecine disputes while the heroes compete to ascend the throne as the ultimate messiah. This can go on indefinitely, with the group's work and progress at a standstill as these battles are waged. The members of the group may feel themselves in a state of crisis while they try to determine who should deserve the emotions presumably reserved for the "true" messiah.

4. *The development of armies and bureaucracies and the purging of disloyalists.* During the hero wars, group members make preliminary promises of allegiance. The faithful are organized into armies and bureaucracies. The purpose of these institutions is not to advance the group but rather to guarantee messiah status to the hero once he is victorious. When a hero gains a strategic advantage against a rival or consolidates power by succeeding in a quest, he will begin to purge disloyalists from his followers. Those who survive inevitably seek to join the ranks of competitors.

5. *The rise of the heroes.* The heroes arise in response to a weakening or failed messiah, and they may actively contribute to his eventual

perceived failure in the group's eyes. In this part of the drama, the fundamental issue is whether the messiah has fulfilled promises made to the group about how he would provide rescue. The heroes gain power as their criticisms of the messiah mount. This behavior leads to a series of crisis episodes in which the messiah's strength is tested, eventually and inevitably resulting in failure.

The Fallacy of Leadership Nostalgia

Successful groups will enshrine the wisdom and ways of past leaders.

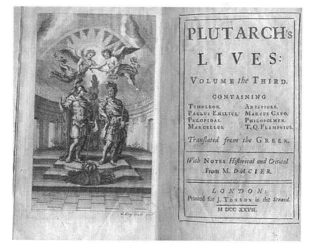

The Roots of the Fallacy of Leadership Nostalgia

Both the Messiah and Hero Fallacies are maintained in large part by the Fallacy of Leadership Nostalgia. Those who have witnessed the messiah's rise and fall, and who work closely with competing heroes, know all too well about their foibles. Nevertheless, to perpetuate interest in these fundamental narratives, this knowledge is pushed into the background. Edited versions of their exploits are then written and promoted. The purpose of these narratives is to reinforce the fundamental psychology behind them.

The nostalgia narratives that center upon the messiah figures purport to historically document their superpowers and attribute all-important human achievements from the past to their singular efforts. Any flaws that the messiahs struggled with are understood as additional burdens carried because of their superhuman capacities. When the nostalgia narratives focus upon heroes, they tend to describe their transformation to messiah status through combat and quest. Such episodes are imbued with a special religious, folkloric or magical significance, which is derived from a source located outside of rational dialogue. The fallacy underlying Leadership Nostalgia is twofold: first, that there is a referent of extraordinary behavior visible in the life of one person that becomes the singular prism for understanding historical human achievement; second, that this history can and should be successfully duplicated in the present.

The Fallacy of Leadership Nostalgia demonstrates these features:

1. *The resurrection of the messiahs or the heroes after they have fallen.* They are metaphorically brought back to life through stories and scenes attributed to them by a group of pseudo-scholars who study the historical record of their actions, relationships and words. The scholars are spurious researchers because their mission is not to determine the truth about the messiah but rather to glorify his or her actions and to make the study fit the messiah or hero narrative.

2. *The effort to fetishize the statements and actions of the messiah or hero.* With pseudo scholarship, what the messiah or hero said and did becomes imbued with extraordinary significance. In this process, words, actions and scenes are often attributed to the messiah or hero for which there is little or no evidence. In many cases, the messiah or hero is understood to have originated statements and ideas made by a broad range of individuals.

3. *Transfer of accomplishments.* These scholars work to associate the actions of the messiah or hero with accomplishments undertaken by teams of people over vast movements, as if the messiah personally coordinated widespread activities through leadership or personal influence. In this process, the work of teams and communities is revealed to have been coordinated by one person, who—like the Wizard of Oz—was supposedly coordinating all of their behaviors behind the scenes or in ways difficult for group members to understand at the time.

4. *Attribution of ideas.* The group works to attribute to the messiah or

hero the generation of ideas that actually found their development through many sources. New ideas generally emerge from dialogue between a number of practitioners grappling with a particular challenge; while there may be dominant voices, many individual thinkers contribute to the formation of ideas and theories within a learning community. The Fallacy of Leadership Nostalgia chooses to ignore this complexity, writing the history as if all of the ideas and insights emerged from one person acting alone.

5. *Creation of parables and codes.* This involves the group's work to systematize rules of conduct by generalizing from episodes taking place in one person's life. Leadership Nostalgia attempts to codify the life and learning of the past messiah or hero into a series of practices or steps that can be replicated in the present, as if the work of the messiah or hero is like a song that merely needs to be replayed to give rise to the same outcomes.

All Three Fallacies in Operation Together

Individuals and groups laboring under the Fallacies become paralyzed. Rather than creatively going to work on the challenges and opportunities confronting them, and having every member of the group taking part, they instead search for a messiah who can do this work for the group while they either stand back and watch, or participate without critical thought at the direction of the messiah figure. Once that person is found, instead of working together creatively, they begin to doubt whether their selected messiah is "the one" and mount criticisms against him or her. The question concerning the group members at this point is not "What can we each do?" but "Why hasn't the messiah fixed this yet?"

Rather than engage in creative work as the messiah begins to fail, group members organize trials of combat and quests that are usually irrelevant to their fundamental needs. These episodes dominate the group's psychology and imagination; the question then becomes "Who is the real messiah?" rather than "How do we make progress?" The group comes to see its fundamental work not in terms of achieving its overarching vision; instead, it remains one step removed by selecting a leader who will craft and achieve the vision while the hero wars and quests may go on in perpetuity. If one messiah emerges, the group shifts to the Messiah Fallacy, unreasonably heaping all of its work upon one member, and then passively awaiting that person's performance or failure. The group's focus on the messiah's identity and responsibility relieves its members from personal responsibility. The messiah will then become the group's savior or scapegoat.

In the background of these dynamics, the Fallacy of Leadership Nostalgia diverts the group's intellectual resources toward the study of messiahs and heroes of the past, looking for clues about how they developed their special powers and rescued earlier groups from crisis. These mythical histories present imaginary pictures of lost eras involving the work of individual messiahs who become a reference against which to judge the competence of the present messiah. The question is not "How should each of us bear responsibility for our future?" but "How should our leaders emulate the great and wise ones who came before us?"

Taken together, these Fallacies shamefully promote a specific worldview in which isolated individuals are actually responsible for all of human progress while the vast majority of people are understood to have been docile sycophants.

The three Fallacies are seen explicitly in the "Great Man" theory associated initially with Thomas Carlyle, who wrote, "The history of the world is but the biography of great men." Carlyle and his followers built a body of historical research suggesting that the progress of the world was attributable to work of great men and heroes. The Fallacies also find expression in the work of many philosophers, from Socrates and Plato advocating reliance upon a philosopher-king as the highest form of government in *The Republic*, to Nietzsche's idea of the Superman or Übermensch, expounded in *Thus Spake Zarathustra*. In 1896, Richard Strauss composed his famous tone poem with the same title as Nietzsche's work. Introducing the piece in Berlin, Strauss wrote in a program note:

> I meant to convey by means of music an idea of the development of the human race from its origin, through the various phases of its development,

religious and scientific, up to Nietzsche's idea of the Superman. The whole symphonic poem is intended as an homage to Nietzsche's genius, which found its greatest expression in his book *Thus Spake Zarathustra*.

These ideas were widely popularized in the literature of Ayn Rand, particularly in works like *The Fountainhead* and *Atlas Shrugged*. Rand's protagonists in these works are superhumans with extraordinary intellectual capabilities and creative powers.

Atlas Shrugged, for example, relates the exploits of physicist and philosopher John Gault, who has singlehandedly invented a machine that will produce infinite energy from static electricity in the air. Rand depicts Gault and other messiah figures revolting from the bond with sheep-like humans for whom they bear responsibility. Rather than questioning the fundamental thesis of the Fallacies, Rand reinforces them but asks the provocative question, "What would happen if the messiah abandoned the people?" Rand's answer—playing directly into the Fallacies—is this: The people would fall into a state of crisis and then perish. Rand's problem is not the idea of the Superman, but rather that these supreme beings owe anything to society. In Rand's view, they should be revered and allowed the spoils of their contributions to society through the mechanism of capitalism. Rand never questions the fundamental "Great Man" hypothesis. These words from Gault in *Atlas Shrugged* capture the concept:

> The man at the top of the intellectual pyramid contributes the most to all those below him, but gets nothing except his material payment, receiving no intellectual bonus from others to add to the value of his time. The man at the bottom who, left to himself, would starve in his hopeless ineptitude, contributes nothing to those above him, but receives the bonus of all of their brains. Such is the nature of the "competition" between the strong and the weak of the intellect. Such is the pattern of "exploitation" for which you have damned the strong.

Of course, Rand was concerned about collectivism and the idea that individual productivity should be sacrificed to the needs of a parasitic group, bleeding and milking its creative innovators dry, as if they were imprisoned livestock. What she objected to was the uncompensated sacrifice at the hands of the group implicit in the messiah narrative. What is fascinating about Rand's work is that it recognizes this narrative as untenable, that the messiah is a human being who would rather shrug and run away from the group if expected to carry all of its burdens.

What Rand failed to grasp is that the narrative rests upon a series of fallacies. In reality, there are no superhumans. The messiah who runs away typically does not do so because of a capacity to live grandly somewhere away from the flock, those dependent upon his sacrifice. The messiah runs away (or wants to) because he is simply not capable of satisfying the group's unreasonable demands. He recognizes that if he must act as a superman, then failure is inevitable. Without support from a network of innovators, John Gault is just another guy.

The Fallacies also work because they attempt to create stasis between competing individual and collective paradigms in understanding the work of groups. These Fallacies circle around group processes while ignoring their work. So a community could risk starvation, domination by an enemy or health epidemics while it obsesses about who will be the leader.

Enter Genership

Rather than describe something like a Zen koan, in which effective leadership is somehow seen to be its opposite, we can distinctly identify and explain a set of skills and practices observed within effective organizations and communities—often demonstrated by progressive leaders—clearly not associated with the core traditional concept of leadership. Genership (jen' er ship) aptly describes the practice in which humans collaborate with one another in generative processes— activities that foster creativity. Genership enables productivity; it brings into existence the desired materials, services, technologies and energies that benefit the group as a whole.

The Spectrum of Control Over Group Work—Individual to Collective

Group work generally falls along a spectrum from individual to collective. On the individual end, it would be at the command of one leader, and the group would essentially be an extension of personal psychology, the way the brain of one individual commands arms and limbs. At this end of the spectrum, what maintains discipline and order is complete submission to the individual who commands the group, which derives from the recognition of superior ability, fear of physical or economic violence, or forced exclusion from the group. Particularly within the prism of the Fallacies, these dynamics tend toward individual control that we associate with leadership.

At the collective end of the spectrum, group work tends toward increasingly less centralized direction, with each member acting freely and according to his individual will, but also effectively teaming with other group members. To understand this concept at a metaphorical level, imagine how a six-fold symmetrical snow crystal develops spontaneously in the air. Or watch a group of talented players in a basketball pickup game. In both cases, you will observe individual elements coordinating in parallel, simultaneous tracks that lack centralized planning but nevertheless arise from a common structure and realization of a shared objective. At the collective end of the spectrum, groups begin to manifest processes associated with genership.

As we look back through human history, the work of centrally organized social systems, particularly as they grow larger, has generally been coordinated through the credible threat of force and violence. Societal leaders in early human history generally maintained their control irrespective of the wishes of the collective through the use of actual or threatened force against those aspiring to interfere with their command. In such circumstances, the purpose of work is not the group's welfare but rather the leader's.

The messiah and hero narratives introduce a group moral assessment into the selection of leaders. It is the group itself that wields judgment about who are the competing heroes, about the nature of their combat and quests, about who is ultimately deemed the messiah and permitted to care for the group as their sovereign leader, and about whether the messiah rises to the challenge. The life of the group is what matters, rather than the life of the heroes and messiah. The evolution of leadership represents a progression away from the use of mere power. The Fallacies have thus functioned to mediate the legitimacy of the leader's use of violence to preserve authority. Indeed, the fundamental task of a hero or messiah may be to lead the group away from enslavement or oppression at the hands of a leader employing violence to maintain power. The quest narratives that we associate with leadership often entail this motif involving the group's escape.

We can liberate ourselves from these dynamics by understanding the historical role that they have played in human cultures, protecting the group from force and violence. As a further evolution of this trend, genership provides a vehicle through which the leader himself is transcended as the pathway to group progress. The group's well-being rests in the hands of group members themselves. They are capable of acting for their own benefit. They no longer need the messiah's protection or sanction.

Leadership and Group Dynamics Arising from the Nomadic Culture

Our fundamental ideas about leadership derive from the most primitive of human cultures: nomadic. Hunter-gatherer societies relied on travel for survival, following herds of animals and continuing to move in order to find new grounds to gather food from naturally occurring vegetation. Society based on following and finding food relies on moving together. Group members must know where to go next, leaving the barren lands behind and moving toward places with renewed potential. The leaders are those who move first and are followed. Those who stray from the group without being followed generally find themselves at significantly increased risk for having lost the company of their fellows. In this state, they may be weakened, injured or die unless they eventually return to the group as followers.

As human history unfolded, nomads who followed herds of animals eventually learned to control and exploit them, giving rise to metaphors (for example the motif of the shepherd) then applied between humans similarly controlled and dominated by others. Nomadic existence also gave rise to the possibility of conflict in which groups invade each other's territories to secure food and other resources. Battle between groups gives rise to leadership models in which certain members may plan attacks, defend against them and fight on the group's behalf. Battle also entails the concept of flight, to run away when being attacked and to escape when dominated. Flight contains the same fundamental metaphor of leadership; someone must know where to go, and that one is the leader.

Group dynamics in a nomadic context generally function where resources are discovered, not created. If there are food sources or other necessaries of life in the form of animals or plants, they are out there; the point is to find, dominate, use and protect resources from enemies and then move on once they are consumed.

The rise of agrarian economies altered these archetypal models of leadership by introducing the concept of renewable, expanding resources. With the introduction of agricultural technologies came a potent experience: surplus. While nomads take with them only what they can carry, farmers can husband crops and livestock to exceed their needs, storing the rest. Surplus production gives rise to leisure, which fosters technological development and trade. Centers of trade become cities and towns.

From these macroeconomic trends, new human capacities arose in addition to leadership in its nomadic form. The skill of increasing production through human specialization and coordination of function—key elements of teamwork—allows for steadily increasing agricultural production. The development of knowledge, tools and techniques to increase human productive power, and the transmission of these from generation to generation, also become critical skills. These new capacities eventually led to industrial revolution and also to modernity's steadily reinforcing spiral of productivity. The story of growing human population and production, along with increasing dominion over land, crops, animals and nature itself is the central story of human history.

Economic Measures of Creativity

Professor J. Bradford Delong, an economics historian at Berkeley, has written about the powerful research demonstrating the accelerating increase of total production in human society. Over the past 7,000 years, growth (measured in terms of total economic output) unfolded at a steadily exponential rate, doubling about once every millennium. Since 1800, however, output has accelerated dramatically, doubling every 15 years rather than every 1000, 60 times faster than the previous historical record. This explosion in growth is of course associated with the industrial revolution. Total productivity has dramatically outstripped population growth, which has also grown exponentially from approximately five million in 5000 BCE to more than six billion in 2000. Accelerating productivity has produced astonishing growth in per capita productivity during this time frame: measured in year-2000 international dollars, from $130 to more than $8,000.

Economists such as Robin Hansen of George Mason University have suggested that the rate of growth worldwide is accelerating further, approaching a cycle of doubling every six years, and that growth rates may stay on this trend line and produce unimaginable future wealth through the widespread deployment of robotics. Of course these projections do not predict a measure of equality or fairness in distribution of wealth. Economists together with other mainstream professionals attribute this unprecedented economic growth to technological developments driven by human ingenuity, first in agriculture, and later in industrial and information technologies.

There is a widespread misunderstanding about the source of the astonishing growth in human productive power, which has succeeded because of the underlying strength of genership, rather than as a result of messianic leadership.

Over these thousands of years of development, rapidly accelerating over the last several hundred, traditional leadership skills associated with the ancient, nomadic hero and messiah narratives have existed in increasing tension with the more recent group-process skills associated with agrarian, industrial and information economies. As agrarian societies flourished, they remained vulnerable to domination by nomadic hunter-gatherer societies willing to pillage the production of these more advanced societies. This resulted in the development of feudal social arrangements in which warrior classes emerged. They protected the emergent agrarian economy from invasion, guarded trade routes, respected property rights required for production and dominated the productive elements of human society, living despotically and parasitically from their surplus.

The warrior classes employed messiah and hero narratives to legitimize their power over production. In this effort, they were assisted by religious communities that perpetuated Leadership Nostalgia by claiming to relate the work of the warrior class to hero and messiah narratives drawn from religious and cultural texts and traditions. Because they relied on primitive violence, the warrior class remained primary within agrarian and even industrial societies. Nevertheless, the new skills at the heart of humanity's productive power existed (and exist today) in tension with the more primitive human narratives focused on an all-powerful messiah or hero who leads the people toward resources and away from danger, and who confronts and defeats adversaries.

The period of history that we think of today as the Enlightenment, followed by the rise of constitutional democracies and the concept of human rights, are the basis for genership practices designed to question and loosen the grip of messiah and hero narratives within human society. At the center of the Enlightenment is not divine power but rather human reason. The Enlightenment's focus is neither messiah nor hero imbued with magical or sacred powers, nor a God, nor even one unusual person, but rather the concept of humanity's power to shape reality through the application of knowledge that can be learned and transmitted through community dialogue and shared intelligence.

The new genership skills involved in increasing human productive capacity and inventing tools and resources to advance human welfare often existed—and still do today—in tension with traditional leadership ideas focused on concentrating power and influence in one person or small group. Humans engaged in creative work teams must collaborate in ways that spontaneously embrace and coordinate the input of many individuals according to their strengths. Inputs cannot be compelled through force or fear because people acting under duress will be distracted from their efforts and will flee at the first opportunity. The threat and reality of violence may be effective to organize destruction and oppression, but it cannot be used as an effective organizing principle to increase innovation and productivity. Moreover, since the messiah concept itself involves a fallacy (that he or she is endowed with superhuman abilities), collaborations engineered through force or violence do not harness the abilities of many individuals, but rather reduce them to subservience by one will. Such collaborations cannot ultimately hope to compete effectively with creative teams animated by genership, in which members are able to harness and leverage each team member's intelligence and energy, calling forth the gifts and strengths of each member.

The result is a seeming paradox when viewed from within the prism of traditional, nomadic, warrior-class leadership practices. In human communities focused on productivity and increasing human welfare, effective leadership exhibits a movement away from power consolidation, from belief in the supremacy of one individual or even a small group, and toward the qualitatively different capacity of genership. The new ability entails the skill of marshaling, coordinating and sustaining the creative powers of many. It no longer entails stepping out in front of the group, taking them to a new place or leading them from a dangerous area. Instead, genership involves stepping *into* the group, working to coordinate and increase the creative capacity of each member.

It is now time not just to move away from the old paradigm, but to let it go completely. We must recognize the messiah and hero narratives for what they are: irrelevant fallacies. We must understand that it is a waste of time to look back in history trying to resurrect fallen leaders or heroes in a revisionary process designed to distill the essence of messianic qualities that never existed in the first place. We can do better than this. We can advance a model that synthesizes the rejuvenating skills required for group work, and liberates those skills once and for all from their competition with traditional—and often antiquated—leadership narratives.

Distinguishing Genership from Leadership

Leadership and genership draw on fundamentally different models of human experience.

Leadership focuses on a journey in which one person leads a larger group of people who follow, walking behind. As described above, this model arises from the nomadic experience of travel through dangerous or barren lands to better surroundings. It is a metaphor focused on childhood experiences in which humans thought to be more powerful and wise led others believed to be smaller or less knowledgeable. It focuses mainly on hierarchy and power relations within groups. The primary metaphor that informs leadership fits comfortably with war and battle narratives in which a leader draws followers into violent battle in pursuit of victory.

In contrast, the vibrancy of genership focuses on creation and evolution, of people working together in innovative ways. These creativity advancements match society's extraordinary achievements in which humans working together in creative and collaborative settings are able to make hospitable and plentiful environments possible anywhere on earth. Genership describes the sometimes hidden and uncelebrated capacity of being able to create with others, and to enhance one's own creative ability through combined and collaborative action. Genership focuses on the results of the collaboration, not on the power relations and hierarchical positions of those involved in the creative process. While destruction, violent conflict and victory sit comfortably with narratives involving traditional leadership, they do not fit well within the overall framework and core practices of genership:

Listening
CoThinking (thinking together)
CoVisioning (envisioning desired futures together)
Building productive relationships
Learning from conflicting theories and from trial and error
Eliminating the employment or threat of force or violence
Mastering and ultimately transcending prevailing systems

In contrast, leadership in practice often focuses on very different skills:

Projecting
Arguing and persuading
Manipulating and politicking
Winning conflicts
Employing power, including force and violence
Problem-solving

While sometimes enlightened, evolving leadership theories attempt to capture the capacities listed above associated with genership, the following chapters will demonstrate that these capabilities stand in tension with the traditional elements of leadership. Mastering genership requires—demands—a completely new ideal. Through its fresh lens, the distinction from leadership can be seen quite clearly, while revealing the relationships among true creative practices.

Chapter TWO
The Cornerstone: Listening as the Foundation of All Creative Work

The Power to Be Still

Physics has something profound to teach us about the nature of listening. Between 1925 and 1930, quantum physicist Werner Heisenberg developed what would later be referred to as "the uncertainty principle." His insight involved physical properties within atoms: the position and speed of subatomic particles. He saw that measuring position interfered with assessing speed, and vice-versa. To know a particle's momentum entails obscuring its precise *location*. To know exactly where a particle is in space requires a measurement that interferes with its *momentum*.[iii] Buried deep within Heisenberg's idea about uncertainty is a profound insight: that observers influence their own measurements, not only through direct interaction with the observed world but by the very ideas they bring to the practice of measurement and assessment. We do not know the world in itself; we know it as it is for us, through the prism of our senses, ideas, instruments and actions. In the words of the ancient Greek philosopher Protagoras, "Man is the measure of all things." Just so, what we bring to our practice of listening deeply influences what we hear.

Philosophers and scientists have extrapolated from these ideas to generate a concept called the "observer effect," more intuitive to grasp than the uncertainty principle, offering important insights about listening. A person perceiving something affects what he or she sees through the effort to perceive. Relying on someone else's perception or even instruments still entails influence. Knowledge demands perception. At the most elemental level, one cannot perceive anything without bouncing light or sound waves or matter off of it. Perception involves interaction. Yet to perceive something under and through waves of light or sound or other apparatuses involves changing the object perceived substantially. Effective listening involves not only attending to reality, but also to the ways in which we ourselves influence reality through our efforts to comprehend.

Common sense tells us that an objective world exists independently of our minds, that if we listen carefully, we will hear the truth about reality in its pristine form, as it is without our influence. This simple approach induces us to believe and behave as if an independent reality influences our perception, rather than being subject to and shaped by our minds. We tend to have an idea about the world that is fundamentally wrong: That there is a world out there waiting to be known, and that knowledge of the world can be had that leaves the reality as it is, as if the world sits in a state of suspended animation to be studied by us at our leisure without entanglement with it. But the situation is much more complicated in ways that matter significantly. The world is evolving and our ways of knowing it are part of that evolution. When we study the world, we influence it and cause it to develop through that energy invested in knowing. To see how this happens we must recognize that the objects of our perceptions are always evolving and unfolding. They are part of our journey through time; a critical dimension of their reality involves not only what they are at the present moment but also what they have the potential to become. Everything that we perceive is in a state of changing and evolving into the future as in interacts with everything that surrounds it, including the minds that perceive it. This realization illustrates the profound role that our perceptions play in creating the world around us. Through our ideas, senses, tools and actions we can change the future potentialities of perceived reality, and thereby alter its essence. While reality surely has an independent voice, we are always in a creative dialogue with it, one capable of changing both the world and us. This means that in the broadest sense, when we listen to the world around us, we actively create that world as much as experience it. Listening is not a precursor to creativity; it is the seminal creative act:

> A man tries to find out if a woman is attracted to him. He calls her repeatedly to ask how she feels. She may have been unsure about her feelings, but now his behavior of investigating her emotions may make her think he is desperate and strange. Or perhaps she may have not noticed him initially, but now has become interested because of his persistence. The man's efforts to know her feelings may well affect them, positively or negatively.

> A consultant investigates a team to understand how its members interact with one another. He develops questions, sits down and interviews the team members, asking them how they interrelate. His questions stimulate the members to consider aspects of their communication that they had previously ignored. As a result of the interviews, the team begins to become conscious of its internal communications and members begin to change how they interact. The investigation has changed the team being evaluated; what the consultant came to study has been altered by his effort.

> A biologist wants to see how an animal behaves at night. She goes out into the field with a spotlight; what does she see? Animals reacting to her spotlight. Is this what they do at night? Suppose the biologist uses an infrared light to observe the animals. Animals still are capable of responding to her presence. We know that animals have powerful hearing and olfactory senses. The biologist will significantly influence the system she comes to observe through her simple presence, including her conceptual perspective.

Primitive humans studied and interacted with wolves. Scientists and historians believe that this interaction began as little as 15,000 years ago; in geologic time, moments ago. Yet this relationship has had profound effects on dogs, which have evolved through man's practices of selective breeding into a far more diverse and abundant species than their ancestors that first developed relationships with humans; the interaction with wolves, for example, transformed the species into something completely different. It is tempting to believe that man's efforts to study other physical systems are different and more objective than man's relationship with wolves. But closer inspection reveals otherwise. The human effort to understand the atom gave rise to nuclear power plants and weapons; likewise, research into crops and animal husbandry has given rise to genetically engineered vegetation and animals. There are countless similar examples that describe how knowledge influences the reality it sets out to know.

The ideas that we bring to the process of analysis alter our interactions and thus change our perceptions. Our ideas shape what information we regard as relevant and important. The information we possess influences our development of tools and actions. We are highly sensitive to information that supports or refutes our ways of thinking, while we barely notice information not central to our theories. We develop tools that help confirm what we already believe. Humans have built massive particle colliders to discover particles that they believe exist because their ideas suggest so, but one must also wonder whether the particles have been as much invented by these tools themselves as discovered by them. As Harvard biologist Ruth Hubbard has written, "Every theory is a self-fulfilling prophecy that orders experience into the framework it provides."

Knowledge is effective, creative and even destructive. Because it always involves selecting certain ideas over others, it entails foreclosing and limiting developments possible within the paradigms presented through discarded ideas. Some doors we open, others we entomb. In this way, knowledge is a dance with the world that leaves it fundamentally changed, an activity that is part of the world, not practiced upon a universe that somehow remains independent and pristine. We can only fully understand the role of listening within creativity when we come to grips with how the mere presence of our consciousness shapes the world around us. When we listen, we open those doors that our ideas, senses and related tools select from the much broader field of possible experience. This practice gives birth to some potential avenues for interaction and development and closes off others. Listening becomes the cornerstone of creative activity.

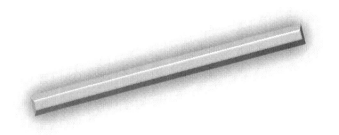

Eight Minutes

In 1994, I participated in a short training exercise that changed my life. The concept was simple. Be quiet for eight minutes while someone tells you his or her life story, then switch and tell your life story while that person is quiet for an equal length of time. The exercise had an important rule: no questions, no comments, no interruptions. Just listen.

In those days I was still practicing law, and the exercise revealed to me what a bad listener I was. As soon as my partner started to tell me the story, I wanted to ask a truckload of questions, directing the conversation to the places where I thought it should go. I wanted to follow up on certain details, ask about things the speaker hadn't mentioned, wanted to shortcut areas I thought I already knew, and learn more about what interested me, like someone fast-forwarding through a TV show. After about three minutes, however, something remarkable happened. That incessant voice in my head began to quiet, and for the first time I actually began to listen to what the speaker was trying to tell me. I observed body language, soaked in the selected words and stopped trying to control the conversation flow; in the remaining five minutes, I learned something profound about my dialogue partner.

Then it was my turn. At first the challenge seemed ridiculous. How could I tell my life story in eight minutes? Well, I could try to relate the salient details.

Off I went, and in approximately two and half minutes I was finished! How could this have happened? I started over again, and in the remaining moments experienced what it was like to speak in a conversation without being interrupted. My experience made me realize something crucial. I didn't really get to talk much, even though I was a practicing lawyer and talked all day. Importantly, most of the time, I didn't get to say what I was really thinking because someone was always waiting to pounce, cut me off, question me, redirect the conversation in some way that person thought was appropriate, which had been true in both professional and personal circles.

The exercise facilitator, a consultant for the Kellogg Foundation, encouraged us to go home and think about the role of listening in communications, particularly in our work as leaders. Fifteen years later, I think about the exercise almost on a daily basis.

In my leadership-development practice, I have helped literally hundreds of aspiring leaders through this exercise, and spent countless hours debriefing the experience, discussing with participants what it means. We use a quote from T.S. Eliot that comes from last of his Four Quartets:

> We shall not cease from exploration
> And the end of all our exploring
> Will be to arrive where we started
> And know the place for the first time.

I have watched many developing leaders work to come to grips with the meaning of these lines. The profound idea they convey is simply that we don't know what we think we know. We generally feel a sense of comfort at the place we start. This is home base. But after the heavy lifting of exploration, we come back to that place, and truly know it as if for the first time. This is the reward of deep listening: the opportunity to know something or someone again, and remarkably, as if for the first time. When we paradoxically *return to the first time*, we see that when we started, we were in a state of ignorance.

All that is created comes from what already is. This is not to say that there can be nothing new, simply that it must emerge from what is already present. For this reason, the creative process has no choice but to engage current reality. When individuals or teams attempt to create in a state of blindness about what is already there, frustration and failure quickly follow.

If I try to paint, I must know my canvas and colors, to sculpt, I must know the materials to create a form, to write, the words and grammar of the language at hand. By extension, when we create in teams, we must know the personalities, capacities and energies of those who compose the team.

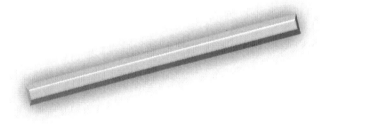

Ferruccio Busoni:
Listening to the Past; Innovating for the Future

Born in 1866, he became one of the most celebrated and innovative pianists and composers ever to emerge on the world stage. He devoted his prodigious mind and physical abilities to push previously cherished boundaries, and understood tradition as "a plaster mask taken from life, which, in the course of many years and after passing through the hands of innumerable artisans, leaves its resemblance to the original largely a matter of imagination." In *Outline of a New Aesthetic of Music*, he wrote that "the function of the creative artist consists in making laws, not in following laws already made. He who follows such laws ceases to be a creator."

Yet while Busoni greatly expanded upon the limits confronted by previous generations, employing cutting-edge compositional means with pioneering explorations of rhythm and tonality, here was a creative artist who ardently studied the music of Bach and Beethoven, realizing the futility of disregarding the sweat of his forebears. Busoni expressed that his *Fantasia contrappuntistica* "grew out of the attempt to complete J.S. Bach's last unfinished fugue. It is a study. Every self-portrait of Rembrandt's is a study; every work is a study for the next one; every life's work a study for those who come after." While redefining traditional tonality, Busoni incorporated Chinese, Persian, Turkish and Native American themes within many of his works; his compositional advances are akin to technological advances: Each new miracle is made possible by what has come before it. He also enthused about the potential of electronic instruments in as-yet undiscovered ways and perceived altogether new musical systems in ways that foretold the groundbreaking developments after his death.

Today's automobiles may have climate-controlled leather seats, global positioning systems, cruise control and hands-free phone capabilities, but they still have the Model T's four tires and a spare. Horse-drawn carriages and wheelbarrows were founded on the same principle of the wheel. Today's books may be audible and instantly downloaded, but the written word existed countless years before the Kindle. The iPod may have revolutionized how we obtain and listen to music, but recordings still begin with a microphone. With the spirit of the true explorer, Busoni wrote with profound simplicity, "There is no new and old. Only known and not yet known. Of these... the known still forms by far the smaller part." He saw all musical expression as ultimately interconnected, which he eloquently asserted in a widely discussed essay, "The Unity of Music." When composers or chemists, architects or artists, painters or poets attempt to create while blind to the past or ignorant about what already exists, frustration and failure soon result. Those individuals and teams who heed and learn from one another, while unafraid to display both humility and strong ideas, will continue to produce and prosper.

—*Robert Rimm*

In the paradigm created through leadership, listening becomes subordinate to the activity of advocating and presenting. In a leadership culture, we expect the leader to stand up and articulate the group's direction, reality and fundamental strategies. We expect the leader to gather information in a purposeful and efficient way. The leader asks targeted questions and determines what is relevant. Often he or she is perceived as a teacher; the group listens and asks questions, while submitting to the leader's greater knowledge and experience.

Leaders operating in this environment are generally poor listeners. They sometimes come to believe that those around them are stupid and incompetent, and consider conversations with team members to be a waste of time and energy. This behavior arises from the belief that the team members are there merely to function as extensions of the leader's ego. It is not important that group members understand what is happening and contribute intelligently; they must perform their discrete function, like parts in a complex machine that act without knowledge of the overall system that makes up the machine itself. What matters is that the members hear and understand the leader, not the other way around; the fundamental work of this type of leader is thus to project his personality and ideas upon a larger circle.

In this model, the leader is seen as the initiator and master over the created world. The relationship is unidirectional, as the leader feels he can dictate how reality will be. This unilateral concept of creation is captured well in the opening lines of Genesis:

> *In the beginning God created the heavens and the earth.*
> *Now the earth was formless and empty, darkness was over the surface of the deep, and the Spirit of God was hovering over the waters. And God said, "Let there be light," and there was light.*

God the creator brings something into existence from nothing; whatever may have been there can be transcended and reshaped. The primary urge to dominate—associated with traditional leadership—incorporates an agenda, which the leader sets, and others respond or react. As a result of the "observer effect," we can go further and say that the leader's agenda in fact shapes reality by establishing what the leader will absorb as information and considers relevant. While we can be comfortable with the idea of God as a supreme being capable of creating from the void, leaders who pretend to do so limit their creative potential. By contrast, humans create within a community, building upon those who came before and benefiting from the thoughts and perceptions of their colleagues. In traditional leadership, as the leader's creative agenda gathers strength, it generates the risk of obscuring these resources. Listening allows the agenda to remain open and to harness vital creative energy from others.

Listening

the
strength
to be
still
and
reflect

The Reflecting Pool and the Washington Monument

The leader's agenda functions—in the process of observation—like light and sound. Light both illuminates and hides, because it creates shadows and changes what we see. In thinking about listening, consider the physics of sound—molecules vibrating together in the air as a result of motion. No sound exists in a vacuum. When we make noise, we block sound waves from reaching us. This is precisely what noise-canceling headphones do: make sounds to block other sounds, just as a blinding light can stop us from seeing.

We can never completely eliminate our agenda to achieve total objectivity; knowing and observing affects what is known. But we can be sensitive to these effects. We can seek to create a dialogue with the world in which we strive for silence and let the world speak to us, while limiting our interference with what we observe. Our knowledge cannot eliminate the observer effect, but by minimizing it we gain access to critical understanding and awareness.

A Dialogue on Listening
(excerpted from actual classroom conversation)

Why is listening important? Why can't I just go into my study and create?
Creativity starts with two elements, vision and truth.

What is *vision*?
Vision is what you want to create. You picture a result—even if it's foggy at the start.

Can't I create by accident?
The creativity I mean cannot arise by accident. No great novel, symphony, painting, organization or achievement of human justice exists without intentional work. The work will not always be as you envisioned it; but you won't create something meaningful without intention.

OK, you said two elements. One was vision and the other was... ?
Truth. Another expression is current reality. This is what you have before you begin. If you're a sculptor, truth is the clay you start with. If you're a writer, the empty page in front of you. A painter, the blank canvas. Truth includes the tools, all the ways you have of interacting with the world. We call it *current* reality because we are going to *change* it.

What does this have to do with listening?
Listening lets you discover reality at the start. Listening allows you to *measure* your progress. Listening involves

interacting with reality as you shape and make it congruent with your vision.

Can you give me an example?
What do you want to create?

A beautiful relationship with my girlfriend!
Well then, current reality is the process of listening to how you interact with her now. If you don't see that clearly, you won't know how to shape it. Suppose you want good communication. What if the truth is that you don't communicate well? If you are deluded about that, then you can never change it. But here's something critical: What you perceive depends on what you want. If you want fun, you will see the amount of fun you have. If you want her happiness, you will see that. Intimacy, you will see that. You can't see your relationship with your girlfriend outside of what you want. That will be the lens, the headphones, through which you see and hear your relationship. It is your listening that begins the creative process.

OK, but what about something objective. What if I want to make... a bridge across a river? What does listening have to do with making something physical like that?
Building a bridge demands that you go to the site and observe reality in detail: the ground, the materials, the traffic that will cross, the winds that the bridge will have to withstand, the way that the construction elements— the steel and concrete and whatever—will affect one another. Everything that is part of a bridge already existed somewhere in the world before the bridge was assembled. So listening is always involved in locating and understanding whatever will become part of what we want to create.

What about math concepts? Do they exist without my listening? One and one is still two even if I don't listen to it, isn't that right?

You want to digress into metaphysics! One and one only makes two when you see that in the world. You can't even understand the idea of one and one without imagining something that you know of in the world, and then applying those concepts to it. *Two* is a mental category, an idea that you bring to the world, then you understand through that lens. *Two* means something when you find things and think about them as a grouping of two. That is listening to the world, and using the vision of two as your device to hear. You make two, you *create* the number two, by listening and perceiving objects in the world as a group of two. Your example *illustrates* what I mean.

Enemies of Listening

Identifying
    Amplifying
Branching
    Puppeting
Echoing
    Reframing
Drifting

Ron Adi, *Confusion*, 2005

The Enemies of Listening

There are a number of communications practices that interfere with effective listening.

The Identification Response. Identification is the simple urge to relate what we see or hear to something we already know from our own experience.

We are listening to someone tell us about his or her day. Here are some examples of identification responses:

1. Statement: "I started today by drinking a cup of coffee."

Response: "Me too, I love coffee. I buy Starbucks."

2. Statement: "I started today by brushing my teeth."

Response: "I brush my teeth at night."

3. Statement: "I started today by listening to the radio."

Response: "Me too. And then I watched the news on TV."

When we have an identification response to what we hear, we immediately attempt to relate it to our own experience. Suppose someone says he has a headache. If you have an identification response to that information, you will try to remember the last time you had a headache.

Why do we respond to communications with an identification response? One reason is that we are trying to identify with the person communicating. In this identification move, we attempt to say, "I am like you. I understand your experience." We may also want to encourage the person providing the information or to make him feel comfortable, which sustains the information flow from the person providing it. Ironically, the identification response tends to shut down dialogue.

1. Statement: "I have a headache."

Response: "So do I."

The identification response is a significant threat to listening. By immediately seeking to relate what we hear and observe to what we already know, or by drawing attention to ourselves, we substantially increase the likelihood of failing to hear effectively. This is because the process of identification discounts differences between what we know and the new experience we receive.

A 57-year-old woman feels a burning sensation in her chest intermittently over a period of months. The only similar experience she has had in her life is indigestion. Ah, she says, listening to her internal feelings, this is like indigestion. Soon she begins to interpret the sensation as a new form of indigestion. Unfortunately, she is actually experiencing the symptoms of heart disease. Eventually she has a major heart attack. The first unmistakable symptom of heart disease is tragically often death.

An American man is making a sales call on a devout Muslim woman from an Arab society. She does not look him in the eye during the meeting, but rather lowers her gaze, because in her culture, to make eye contact may be interpreted as immodest. If he understands her behavior through an identification response, he might draw the conclusion that she does not care about his presentation or is not interested in doing business.

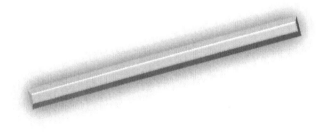

Listening to the Orchestra

Imagine working for a boss who has you under constant observation, who is closely attuned to your every mistake, who can make life quite difficult for you in the profession you love and for which you have studied for countless years. Consider the public face of your organization, someone who possesses enormous gifts and an equally enormous ego, who relates your input primarily to his own life and what he already knows, who is rigidly focused on his own way of doing things, who studies and learns tremendously complicated material in isolation rather than through community or dialogue.

This scenario was the norm for celebrated orchestral conductors of the past, publicly revered men such as Arturo Toscanini and Herbert von Karajan, whose stubbornness and pride remained in stark contrast to the glorious sounds they provoked and shaped. The situation is only somewhat better as the 21st-century calendar continues its relentless progression.

The first cellist suggests taking a slight pause just before a symphony's coda. "When I was studying in Vienna, the Philharmonic made an indelible impression on the audience by taking a ritenuto at measure 465. It literally makes the heart feel as if time has stopped. Surely that's what Mahler intended; can we try it this way?" The conductor's response is both quick and polite. "Ah, what a wonderful city, Vienna, a place of so many memories. The Vienna Philharmonic is a fine group, but as an associate conductor under Dohnányi, I learned that imitating other interpretations can lead to music-making that seems pasted on rather than really lived through. Do you all know his father's music? We really must program more of it for our subscription concerts."

Rather than addressing the specific question here, the conductor recalls his own memories of Vienna, posits a desire of programming and offers only the most general response to the cellist's question. This self-centered mixture of ego and lack of listening—offered with the icy smoothness of a well-blended piña colada—does little more than aggrandize the speaker's sense of importance. This kind of identification response virtually eliminates meaningful listening. By immediately relating the posited question to what he already knows, the conductor ignores a sincere and well-considered request from a gifted musician with decades of experience.

A new breed of conductors has begun to make their way in rehearsal and on the podium, men and women for whom leadership is synonymous with collaboration, extraordinarily gifted musicians with near-perfect ears and expansive brains that can memorize a 90-minute Mahler symphony with the same accuracy as recalling a Social Security number. The Canadian conductor Yannick Nézet-Séguin, Music Director of The Philadelphia Orchestra, belongs to a small but growing cadre of major talents with international careers who actually take the time to listen to fellow musicians, to consider their input and inspiration, to listen with the sole agenda of reaching ever-higher levels of human communication. In describing his work with the London Philharmonic, he is unafraid to acknowledge his gratitude. "I value so much the work in rehearsals, but the most important thing is to make it happen in concert, and these players have limitless emotional involvement and power in performance, which is a gift to any conductor." In an interview with soprano Renée Fleming backstage at New York's Metropolitan Opera, Nézet-Seguin speaks of always looking toward the singers and stage to create the most collaborative links that best serve the music with integrity. "For a conductor the most important thing is to be sincere." In discussing how much he values working with open-minded, collaborative musicians in an environment of true teamwork, he says with utter simplicity and enthusiasm, "I love that process."

—R.R.

The Amplification Response

Another enemy of listening is an amplification response, which takes an element of what we hear and attempts to inflate it:

1. Statement: "I went to the supermarket, the drugstore and the gym."

Response: "So, you went to the gym. Tell me about it."

2. Statement: "I believe in freedom, equality and taking care of vulnerable people."

Response: "Freedom is so important to American culture. Let's discuss your views on freedom."

3. Statement: "Abortion, healthcare and education are important issues."

Response: "What are your views on abortion?"

The essence of the amplification response is to focus on part of what is heard and then ignore the rest. The ignored part falls by the wayside as the dialogue unfolds. Amplification results in the inflation of certain subjects or themes in the dialogue, those of particular interest to the listener. Yet listeners can easily lose awareness of their role in shaping the dialogue by amplifying certain messages while discarding others. While possible to backtrack and focus on other parts of the message, the dialogue generally becomes distracted by the amplified subject and never returns to retrieve what was missed. Also, once something has been sufficiently amplified, it is often impossible to understand what has been heard as originally presented. When thinking through strategies to improve listening, we can overcome amplification by learning to suppress our agenda in the course of dialogue. By not inflating selected parts of what we hear, we can more clearly perceive the intended message, rather than as distorted by our interests and desires.

You are listening to sounds at night while in bed. Perhaps you hear people talking outside your home and one of them sounds like someone you know. Now your listening focuses on that person's voice, while the others fade into the background. This is the tendency toward amplification instigated by our own agenda. There are many voices, but you hear only one.

When combined with identification, amplification threatens to create even more severe distortions. Sometimes we inflate part of what we hear to find a point of identification. You are listening to someone speaking in a foreign language and then recognize one or two words in your native tongue. In amplification we focus intensively on those words, attributing special significance to them. In identification, we attribute meanings to those words based on our personal experience.

A person who doesn't understand Spanish hears the lyric in a song, "*Yo no soy marinero, soy capitan.*"

Using amplification, he might focus on the words "no," "soy" and "capitan" that are like the words used in English—"no," "soy" and "captain." Then by using identification, he might reason that the speaker is saying something like "No soy sauce, captain." Of course this would be ridiculous! But in real cases of listening, this is akin to how and why the mind creates distortions.

Amplification and Identification:
The Case of Laura and Whitney

On April 26, 2006, a van carrying nine people from a small evangelical Christian college in Upland, Indiana, suffered a head-on collision with a tractor-trailer on I-69 between Indianapolis and Fort Wayne. Five were killed on the spot. One survivor was airlifted to a hospital with several broken bones and serious head trauma.

Paramedics identified the critically injured woman as Laura Van Ryn and one of the dead as Whitney Cerak, on the basis of Whitney's pocketbook located near her body. Both Laura and Whitney were blond females, about the same size and with similar features. In possession of her pocketbook, Whitney's family was too emotionally devastated to view her remains and proceeded to plan and hold memorial services. "I was too emotional to have to see the body," Whitney's mother later told *Today*'s Matt Lauer. "So they just brought me back to a separate room and gave me her purse, which was horrible, even the sight of it. It smelled like gasoline and it was just dirty. And everything inside of it was snapped. They said that the purse was found next to the body." Meanwhile, Laura's family kept a 24-hour vigil going in the intensive-care unit. The medical staff had told them that Laura was not going to look like herself.

Laura's family suffered a terrible shock five weeks later when they discovered that the person in intensive care was Whitney, not Laura, and that Whitney's family had buried Laura's remains. A series of small inconsistencies (including for example, teeth that didn't look quite like Laura's and a pierced naval that Laura's family never knew about) came to a head when the patient, asked to scrawl her name, wrote "Whitney" and named her parents.

This case provides a powerful illustration of what happens when amplification and identification responses are combined. In this case, from a broad field of data rich with information, the authorities and Whitney's family amplified one data point involving the discovery of her pocketbook near the victim's body. That one piece became the totality of what was considered. Then, in an identification response, because they knew the pocketbook to be Whitney's, her family perceived that the body must also be what they knew:

the remains of their daughter. This striking story illustrates a common practice in listening, that of amplifying small portions of data and then working to relate them to our own experience. In the words of the philosopher and novelist Robert Pirsig, author of *Zen and the Art of Motorcycle Maintenance*, "We take a handful of sand from the endless landscape of awareness around us and call that handful of sand the world."

The Branching Response

Another obstacle occurs when we focus on one area of what we hear in order to create a new avenue of response. A good metaphor for branching is websurfing. An Internet page typically presents many links that can take us to entirely new bodies of information bearing only tangential relationships to that from which we depart. What drives us to follow a link is our own interest in what that link represents.

Another image that captures branching is to imagine being in a place with four doors leading to different rooms. When selecting a pathway, you close off all the alternatives. Once left behind, they are often difficult to recapture.

Branching creates a similar dynamic in listening:

1. "I was born in New York City in 1976 in Queens. As a child we used to play in the street and we liked to eat ice cream at a Baskin-Robbins on the corner.

Response: "That was an interesting year, 1976. Bruce Springsteen had some great songs that year. What's your favorite Springsteen song?"

2. "I have been thinking about healthcare in the United States. So many people are uninsured. Also it seems that the quality of insurance is going down. Each year, I pay more for less. I'm also worried about moving to a

new job and being able to take my insurance with me."

Response: "Tell me about your job."

3. "I haven't been feeling well at all lately. My feet are swollen by the end of the day and I'm having trouble breathing when I climb stairs. My stomach is usually upset. I can't sleep at night and stay up too late watching TV."

Response: "What late-night shows do you like?"

4. "The sales force just isn't getting the job done. We have 10% fewer accounts this year than we had last year. It seems like the clients just aren't accepting our projects like they used to. I was checking sales-call reports in the customer tracking system last night, and there are lots of complaints from existing customers on service quality."

Response: "I was using the system last night and it was really slow. Have you noticed a slow Internet connection lately?"

These examples share the phenomenon of changing the dialogue's fundamental course. It appears that some people listen because they take their cue from a word or phrase in what they heard. What they are actually doing is using what they hear to shift the subject to one that interests them or satisfies their agenda.

Branching is unlike amplification; it represents a change in the fundamental subject matter framed as a response. Nor is it identification; rather than translate an element of what was heard into the listener's experience, it changes the dialogue's substance and takes it in an entirely new direction.

The Puppeting Response

Another listening dysfunction is puppeting, when listeners take over the dialogue and reduce the speaker to an additional mouthpiece for their own ideas. In this circumstance, listeners behave as if receiving information from the speaker, but in reality, they talk to themselves.

Parent: "How is math going?"

Child: "OK, we're working on fractions."

Parent: "How are you doing? Do you get it?"

Child: "I think so."

Parent: "When I was your age, I had trouble with the relationship between fractions and decimals. I bet you are having the same issues."

Child: "I'm not sure. What are decimals?"

Parent: "I didn't understand them either. It's OK if you're not good at math. When I was your age, I had some real struggles, but I got through. You don't have to be embarrassed about it. I can see that it's worrying you. Just admit what you don't understand, then you can get help."

Child: "OK. Sure."

Parent: "You don't know where to go for help, do you? That's OK. I didn't know when I was your age..."

In this case the parent is filling in the child's conversation for him with elements of her own experience. The response goes beyond identification because the parent actually pretends that the information heard is originating with the child.

Now consider this example, a dialogue between a middle manager and her immediate supervisor.

Supervisor: "How are things with your direct reports?"

Manager: "Great."

Supervisor: "What are you doing to make sure they toe the line? Are you being tough enough?"

Manager: "They're highly motivated. Doesn't take a lot of prodding from me."

Supervisor: "Nobody gets motivated without leadership."

Manager: "I believe in leadership, but I also think it's important to hire strong people with talent. If you have a great team, the leader can step back."

Supervisor: "It's good that you're providing strong leadership; that's why your team members are motivated. That's why you don't have to push. That's excellent. I always say I'd rather lead than push. You never see the locomotive at the back of the train, if you know what I mean."

Manager: "You sure don't. I like self-starters."

Supervisor: "You really get it."

Manager: "You bet."

In this case, the supervisor provides an analysis that the manager agrees to, but after the conversation, the supervisor will likely believe that the manager provided it. Puppeting creates the illusion that one is hearing information from others. In reality, the puppetmaster is talking to himself, using others as mouthpieces.

This kind of dysfunction leads to the illusion that ideas are being externally validated, when in reality, the listener is planting ideas.

Puppeting: We Have Met the Messenger and He Is Us

After the Iraq invasion, when the United States military failed to find WMDs, the Bush Administration defended its actions by saying, essentially, that poor intelligence was at fault. "The biggest regret of all the presidency has to have been the intelligence failure in Iraq," Bush told ABC News shortly before his departure from office. "It wasn't just people in my administration; a lot of members in Congress, prior to my arrival in Washington, D.C., during the debate on Iraq, a lot of leaders of nations around the world, were all looking at the same intelligence."

In the eyes of many, this move could be interpreted as a classic example of puppeting. The administration wanted the public to believe that it was listening carefully to independent threat assessments of its intelligence agencies indicating that Iraq was hiding WMDs. What the administration ignores, of course, is that it had been pressuring and seeding those independent assessments to include information suggesting the presence of WMDs, putting words in the mouths of the intelligence analysts. The following is an excerpt from a letter published on August 19, 2010 in the *New York Review of Books*, written by Fulton Armstrong, a former U.S. intelligence officer:

> I was a member of the National Intelligence Council (NIC), as national intelligence officer (NIO) for Latin America, from 2000 to 2004. The NIC is the intelligence community's senior analytical group responsible for preparing National Intelligence Estimates (NIEs), including the Iraq WMD NIE. At the time, it reported to the director of the CIA, George Tenet, in his "intelligence community hat" and was located at CIA headquarters. Although the NIC is an interagency body, the CIA has always dominated its staff and work.
>
> The first congressional briefing I ever took part in as an NIO, along with my colleagues, included

discussion of WMDs, and it started with 15 minutes of paeans of praise by Jesse Helms and other Republicans on the Senate Foreign Relations Committee, for our intelligence work. Several of the NIOs were praised for having embraced the findings of the Rumsfeld Commission, which pressed upon the Clinton administration a hyped analysis of the missile threat (and rationale for an accelerated "missile defense strategy"). The NIOs clearly knew what was going on in that room. Intelligence officers are all trained to remind the recipients of their reports that they are never to take sides in a policy debate. These NIOs, however, said nothing and were clearly happy with the praise by the Republican committee members.

The National Intelligence Estimate produced by these NIOs on weapons of mass destruction in Iraq, with the participation of the CIA and other intelligence agencies, was not subjected to the customary "peer review" of the National Intelligence Council because, after delaying the project for months, the NIOs didn't have a spare hour for the discussion and debate that the council's review would have provided. But we knew what they were up to. During our closed-door council meetings, they would eagerly report their progress in dividing the 15 coordinating agencies that had contributed to the NIE. They boasted how, after an obviously extensive search, they finally found an Energy Department employee willing to contradict his agency's consensus position that Iraq's missile tubes were not, as the administration and the NIOs asserted, centrifuge tubes.

The NIOs who were preparing the NIE also boasted how they found an Air Force analyst to dissent from his service's position that Iraq's little unmanned surveillance planes could not be armed. They were happy that challenges to their and the administration's assumptions about Iraq's chemical weapons and biological weapons capabilities were minimal; after all, who's going to try to prove a negative?

The most back-patting, however, was reserved for their success in forcing the State Department's intelligence shop, the Bureau of Intelligence and Research (INR), to take a "footnote"—a dissent at the bottom of the page—on a lesser judgment in the paper rather than on the overarching judgment that Saddam Hussein had WMDs. One of the NIOs smiled when he reported that INR couldn't prove that Saddam did not have WMDs and that no one wanted to be seen as defending Saddam anyway. That was exactly the Bush administration's political strategy as well. Instead of allowing INR to develop an alternative analysis in the main text of the NIE— the proper form for a different view when the information is so obviously weak—the NIOs humiliated the only agency at the table, the State Department's INR, that dared to question the administration's preordained conclusions.

When we on the National Intelligence Council finally got a full read of the National Intelligence Estimate on WMDs, after its publication, a couple of us expressed grave reservations about the fatally weak evidence and the obsessively one-sided interpretation of what shreds of information it contained. (We were not told at the time that "Curveball" was a solitary source of obviously questionable credentials, nor that contradictory evidence was actually suppressed from the intelligence collection and dissemination process.) One colleague said it was clearly a paper written to provide a rationale for a predetermined policy decision to go to war. When I challenged the lack of evidence and the lack of alternative explanations, including forcing the questions raised by the INR into a lowly footnote, one of the WMD-promoting NIOs leaned forward and bellowed: "Who are you to question this paper? Even *The Washington Post* and *The New York Times* agree with us." The irony was complete: previously respected reporters, spoon-fed by Bush administration officials, were now being used to provide cover for the NIOs' similar compromise in accepting the administration's view.

The National Intelligence Council and director of central intelligence, George Tenet, gave the NIOs concerned with WMDs big cash awards for producing the NIE, and seven years later and 17 months into the Obama administration they remain in the same or equivalent jobs. The Bush administration left office, and its defenders still claim that the errors in the WMD debacle were innocent, just as the hyperventilation about "yellowcake" from Niger in a State of the Union address—cleared by a careerist in a CIA line office who worked closely with the administration and the NIC on WMD issues— was said to be innocent. Intelligence community spokesmen are rolled out to deny allegations of politicization, even though at least one of them, a former analyst who threatened to resign several times because of political pressures when he was working on Cuba, has witnessed it close up and paid a short-term career price for resisting it.

Covering up or ignoring the problem of politicization won't make it go away. US intelligence will continue to fail again and again until we resolve it.

What is striking about this description of the intelligence process is the way that the administration made its conclusions known to the investigators, and then behaved as if those conclusions where coming independently from those same investigators. This is the essence of the puppeting response in listening: the process of casting information in a circle and then "hearing" as it returns to the point where it began.

The Echoing Response

Another barrier to listening is called "echoing": responding to what someone hears by repeating back parts of it to signify that the message has been received. This can be done by using the same language but without receiving any sense of what is meant. Observe this conversation between a computer technician and a client.

Client: "My computer won't start."

Technician: "Could be an operating-system defect."

Client: "A *system defect*, I see."

Technician: "Yes"

Client: "So what should I do?"

Technician: "You need to use a boot disk."

Client: "I should get my *boot disk*."

Technician: "Yes, you've got it."

Client: "OK, I find my boot disk, then what?"

Technician: "System scan, system restore, maybe reinstall the operating system."

Client: "I need to *reinstall the operating system.*"

Technician: "If the scan and restore doesn't work, yes."

Client: "If nothing else works, *reinstall the operating system.*"

Technician: "Yes."

In this conversation, the user gives the impression of having listened to what the technician is saying but may be just echoing words and phrases. A lot of the modern world's communication takes this form, the mere repetition of words substituting for actual listening. This can only result in time delays and frustration.

Consider this conversation between an investment broker and his client:

Client: "The market has been very volatile lately. It seems like the Dow is up and down every day by hundreds of points."

Broker: "I understand your concern. Remember though, there are always opportunities in times of crisis."

Client: "Gold is going through the roof. I read somewhere that people see it as a hedge against inflation."

Broker: "That's right. You could also go with TIPS."

Client: "TIPS. Sure. Wait... Can you remind me what TIPS are?"

Broker: "Treasury Inflation-Protected Securities. They protect you against inflation."

Client: "Inflation-protected? That sounds good. How does it work?"

Broker: "Well, if we have inflation, the TIPS pay additional interest to protect you."

Client: "How do they measure inflation?"

Broker: "They use the CPI."

Client: "Oh, the CPI."

Broker: "The Consumer Price Index, they check a basket of goods."

Client: "A basket of goods."

Broker: "Yes, and that determines inflation levels."

Client: "So they measure inflation using the CPI?"

Broker: "Yes."

In this exchange, unless the investor is a student of economics and investing, he will have little sense of the real mechanics involved in Treasury Inflation-Protected Securities. Yet his ability to repeat the words uttered by his broker creates the illusion of understanding the mechanism. In this case, repeating words layered upon words creates the illusion of understanding. If this kind of interaction seems unlikely in the real world, consider the thousands of sophisticated investors duped through money manager Bernard Madoff's now infamous Ponzi scheme, the largest in financial history. When investors inquired how he was able to achieve breathtakingly consistent high returns, he explained that his firm used a special "split-strike" options trading strategy that also employed a computer "algorithm." This statement was not simply a lie (there were no such trades); words that conveyed no real meaning masqueraded as an explanation. Anyone who fathomed Madoff would have realized that the alleged technique could not have produced his firm's atypical returns, comparable to a gambler never losing at roulette and simultaneously playing on all the available tables. Nevertheless, the ability to echo a string of words offered highly intelligent investors the illusion of comprehension.

This conversation between two spouses at the end of the workday illustrates the dynamic in another arena:

Spouse 1: "How was work?"

Spouse 2: "OK, I guess."

Spouse 1: "Yeah me too. OK."

Spouse 2: "Well, that's good. How do you feel, darling?"

Spouse 1: "A little off."

Spouse 2: "Ah, a little off?"

Spouse 1: "Yes. How 'bout you?"

Spouse 2: "Tomorrow will be better."

Spouse 1: "It sure will."

Echoing leaves the reassuring impression of communication because we are able to repeat words and phrases, even if there is little understanding of what underlies them. In this exchange, the partners to the communication may be employing mental projections to fill in the substance of communications, substituting a detailed narrative for the expressions, "OK," "good" and "a little off." Such projections are usually based on detailed prior communications and longstanding experience. Yet over time, reliance on the shorthand can cause massive communication failures as the experiences and situations evolve and begin to diverge from what was previously understood.

Consider the case of John Rapp, who owned up to consciously employing the technique of echoing as a tool in his conversations:

Here's a trick I have used throughout the years, and it really works.

Next time you're in some boring conversation you do not wish to be in, but you don't want to start a fight when the person realizes and calls you out on not listening, do this:

Space out while the other person yammers on about whatever useless nonsense they feel the need to vomit out onto you.

Wait for them to stop talking.

When they finally shut up, just repeat one of the last major events or things they were talking about, but put a question mark at the end of it.

Example:

Boring Person: So I was driving to work the other day and I realized I forgot to look in the... blah blah blah... so the guy says, "That was yesterday!" And I was like, "What?"

[PAUSE]

You: It was yesterday?

Boring Person: Yeah! I can't believe it, you know? Yammer blah blah...

Get the idea? Sounds stupid but it totally works. You can also try adding things like, "that's crazy" or, "I can't believe it."

Believe me.

I've done this for years and I have yet to be busted.[iv]

John is likely well aware that his technique is exploited in conversations across the globe within relationships and organizations.

Echoing is part of a larger trend in organizational dialogue that substitutes memorization and rote repetition for understanding. Every day in schools around the world children are called upon to memorize words and lists of phrases and asked to repeat them on command when provided with an appropriate prompt. In geography, for example, we ask children to name the capitals of nations and states. In biology, we ask them to name the bones in the skeleton and parts of a cell. Experienced teachers well understand that the ability to recapitulate, to echo what has been said, does not imply comprehension of the underlying concepts. The deficiency of echoing in listening is equivalent. A recorder can play back exactly what has been said but without understanding its meaning. In his seminal essay, "The Four Pillars Upon Which the Failure of Math Education Rests (and what to do about them),"[v] Matt Brenner (Ed.M. Harvard University), a math teacher at Phillips Exeter Academy and Sidwell Friends, compellingly describes the consequences of recapitulation without understanding and insight:

> Kids are taught math as pets are taught tricks. A dog has no idea why its master wants it to perform. With careful training many dogs can be taught to perform complex sequences of actions in response to various commands and cues. When a dog is taught to perform a trick it has no need or use for any "understanding" beyond which sequence of movements its trainer desires. The dog is taught a sequence of simple physical movements in a specific order to create an overall effect. In the same way, we teach children to perform a sequence of simple computations in a specific order to achieve an overall effect. The dog uses its feet to move about a space and manipulate objects; the student uses a pencil to move about a page and manipulate numbers. In most cases, the student doesn't know any more than the dog about the effect he creates. Neither has any intrinsic motivation to perform nor any idea why the performance is demanded. Practice, practice, practice, and eventually the dog can perform reliably on command. This is exactly how kids are trained to perform math: do a hundred meaningless practice problems, and then try to do the same trick on the test.

To combat this trend, Brenner created a new method—Computationally Augmented Approach to Math and Problem Solving (CAAMPS)—that draws heavily on scientific research while focusing relentlessly on students' understanding and explicit metacognitive skills development.

The implications of echoing behavior in dialogue across our culture are profound. When we agree to policies, practices and contracts we may echo words with little sense of their content or meaning. This often creates the appearance of true understanding and agreement when it is nonexistent in reality.

The Reframing Response

Another technique in listening that can result in lack of understanding is "reframing," which occurs when we purport to recapitulate what is heard, but with substantial differences designed to influence the meaning. We alter the frame of reference—the system of beliefs, values and assumptions that inform the meaning of what we have heard. Reframing may also influence its emotional context, changing the overall tone and the perception of those in the dialogue about the possibilities for action. While reframing is often intentionally employed as a strategy in negotiating, it is nevertheless critical that we understand how reframing can interfere with listening, and thus effective communication.

Consider this conversation between two team members working on a building construction project.

Contractor: "We don't have enough funds to purchase the materials we need for this job; we're going to have to pull the plug on this."

Manager: "Well, we're working through a financing challenge. We need to explore some options on reducing our materials cost to keep the project viable."

Contractor: "We made a lot of stupid mistakes in the planning; we should have done a much better job of predicting our costs. Our mistakes are going to result in the complete failure of the project."

Manager: "It's true that the actual conditions for the project are deviating from our projections. Many of our assumptions need to be changed to reflect our actual experience. Our ability to move forward will depend on whether we can make adjustments quickly and effectively to accomplish the build in a way faithful to our design."

Contractor: "Whoever made this plan should be fired. That person was incompetent. He doesn't know how much it really costs to build something."

Manager: "We need to think through whether we have engaged the best possible players in the design portion of the work, particularly in cost accounting. Some adjustments there might help us to execute our builds more effectively and efficiently in the future."

In this conversation, what is heard is reflected back but intentionally distorted in the process. Specific frustrations and negative feelings are heard and recast in a way that generalizes and neutralizes them.

In a different sphere, consider this exchange between two spouses.

Spouse 1: "I'm so exhausted lately. I just feel like I'm on a treadmill and can't stay up. The inbox at work just keeps getting bigger and I am so behind on my home projects."

Spouse 2: "You do look tired. I wonder if you have a bug or something. Maybe you should get a checkup."

Spouse 1: "I just can't seem to stay on top of it all and it's wearing me out because I feel like I'm losing ground. No matter how much work I do, my to-do list keeps growing and growing."

Spouse 2: "You know I just read a book about time management that might really help. The author has a great system for setting priorities."

Spouse 1: "I just feel really drained... when am I going to find time to read a book on time management?"

Spouse 2: "You might be drained because you're not managing your time well."

In this exchange, Spouse 2 attempts to reframe Spouse 1's situation as a problem that can be solved through personal intervention that changes the latter's response to the workload. In this reframing, Spouse 2 is obscuring Spouse 1's expression of frustration and exhaustion, and also the possibility that unreasonable external demands are being placed on Spouse 1's time.

The Drifting Response

Another problem in listening occurs when the listener actually ceases to hear what is said as attention drifts to other matters. The result is to actually block or repress received information. Drifting occurs when two people talk to each other without listening to what the other says. People in dialogue may spend substantial time drifting. The impact is for two or more participants to end up talking to themselves while in each other's presence. This creates the illusion of communication. Because the dialogue participants have shared a common physical space, they each believe that communication must have occurred. This is not necessarily so when drifting sets in.

Consider this conversation between a college president and a program director:

President: "Can you give me your report on adjunct faculty recruitment?"

Director: "We're getting very strong candidates. A number of them have doctorates. One from Columbia."

President: "I visited Columbia last weekend after my daughter's wedding. My old friend Jack from high school is teaching there..."

Director: "Yes, we also have some ABD resumes. Some from very strong institutions. And we have quite a few working professionals with master's degrees."

President: "... he and I played football together. And then he went to get his doctorate in anthropology from Arizona."

Director: "Some of these have teaching experience. Some don't. I have a few qualified high school teachers, how do you feel about them?"

President: "I wonder if Jack might know some people in our neck of the woods interested in teaching for us... he really has a good eye for talent."

Director: "I've had mixed experiences with high school teachers... teaching adults is so different from teaching a teenage population."

President: "I really think we should give Jack a call."

Director: "These are pretty good resumes as a group. We've got some good prospects here."

President: "Good. Now what about our full-time faculty..."

In this exchange, quite typical of workplace communications, two parties to a conversation are speaking in each other's presence but thinking alone, not actually listening and responding to what each other says about the topic at hand, instead drifting within their own conversational frames. These may overlap thematically but do not foster the exchange of information or ideas.

Challenge	Alternative
Identification—relating what we hear to our own personal experiences and concepts.	Exploring and investigating how what we hear may differ from our own personal experiences and concepts.
Amplification—selecting part of what we hear and placing extra emphasis on that part.	Paying attention to all parts of what we hear and maintaining proportionate focus to the information as presented.
Branching—selecting part of what we hear and using it as a point of departure to introduce a new avenue of	Staying focused on the information and the context originally presented.

conversation.	
Puppeting—putting words or ideas into the mouth of the person with whom we are talking.	Retaining ownership of our own words and ideas, and drawing forth those of our dialogue partner.
Echoing—pretending to listen by repeating what has been said without a sense of its meaning.	Retaining focus and asking questions to clarify meaning and context.
Reframing—restating what has been said but changing the frame of reference in ways that affect the meaning and/or the emotional context of the communication.	Striving for fidelity to what has been communicated. Maintaining transparency illuminates assumptions, beliefs and values that form part of the context. Asking questions to make explicit unclear aspects of the frame of reference.
Drifting—losing focus on what has been said and responding instead to messages that are interior or independent of the dialogue.	Retaining focus on what has been said while ignoring distractions presented by interior or independent messages.

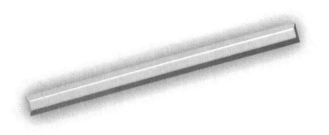

Listening and Letting Go

Over many years of working with leaders on listening skills, I have come to understand the relationship between listening capacity and the work of quieting the mind and letting go of our agendas. The best metaphor I have heard to describe this process employs the imagery of water reflecting the sky. When disturbed by wind or a current of some kind, water cannot reflect well. On a still and peaceful day, however, water becomes a pane of glass, a mirror reflecting everything that surrounds it. The mind is like this. When we work to quiet our minds and let go of agendas, to the extent that we can, what is around us becomes more comprehensible. We must recognize that it is impossible to do this consistently. We will always bring some agenda, some seeking, to the process of listening, and that will distort what we perceive.

To some, letting go may sound like a passive activity, but it actually requires significant energy to suspend desires and goal-seeking behavior to listen more effectively. Think of how much energy would be required to shield a large body of water from winds and currents so that it could perfectly reflect the sky. This is the kind of concentrated energy expenditure required to be still and listen effectively. Letting go requires us to marshal energy because we are predisposed to seek and strive. To be still requires mastery over the fundamental tendencies of moving and wanting. We find one of the key differences between leadership and genership in this choice. Traditional leadership processes tend to remain forward-leaning and agenda-focused, while genership frees energy to open external, emergent potential.

We can associate this idea of letting go with the Zen concept of Beginner's Mind—to strengthen our capacity to see the world the way a child sees it, with as few judgments and preconceptions as possible. As they mature, children begin to lose their innocent quality. As adults, we often lose our capacity to discover and instead seek to develop our ability to know—to have mastered the world and to become experts. But when doing so, we can lose our openness to new learning. In the words of the famous Zen Master Shunryu Suzuki, "In the beginner's mind there are many possibilities, in the expert's mind there are few." This is why artists who exhibit extraordinary creative work find it hard to remain fresh and open in their thinking.

One of the most counterintuitive aspects of learning to let go of our agenda is that it becomes more difficult as we build intimacy with a relationship or organization. We might imagine that we can become most unguarded and most other-focused when we are with those we know well or care deeply about. The reverse is true. When we build intimacy, we begin to develop deep attachments, longings and expectations of one another. We experience these expectations and needs as an ingrained, almost preconscious agenda. To quiet these needs and expectations so that we can hear and see what is happening with a Beginner's Mind requires discipline and focus. It may be impossible without help from others to surface our agendas so that we can at least keep them in our consciousness.

Why Do We Listen?

We belong to a culture that celebrates the individual and often acts as if the purpose of groups is to enhance individual power. Thinking about the great accomplishments of mankind, however, we will quickly see all those that appear to be the work of individuals have actually come about because of their participation in teams. In many cases the teams are composed of individuals interacting contemporaneously; in other instances, team members are distributed throughout history.

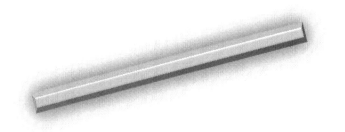

No Genius Works Alone

What is the nature of innovation? Do deep thinkers and diligent scientists toil in isolation, conceiving their discoveries without tending to the fertile histories that preceded them? Would the name Einstein appear in every textbook, and grace hospitals and centers, without Newton and his work with mathematics and theoretical physics several centuries before? Einstein's discoveries—in common with that of most scientists, including those of Newton himself—began with the observations and theories of others. Would James Joyce remain the subject of intense debate—whether in early 20th-century Ireland or throughout the world today— and would subsequent novelists write in their stream-of-consciousness ways, without the epic Greek poetry of Homer?

And what of the singular tools—so easy to take for granted—that populate our lives today, the products of anything but single thinkers? Vast teams of scientists, engineers and visionaries regularly come together with the aspiration of innovation, men and women who could achieve little without the cornerstone of true listening and the skill that derives from receptive ears.

Consider the airline industry and the first passenger-reservations system, well before yesterday's travel agents and today's Expedia et al. Put into public practice in 1960, the Semi-Automated Business Research Environment represented an extraordinary advance for airlines in a crucial, manually intensive area. With ever-increasing numbers of flights and the intense complexities of scheduling, pricing, crew management, baggage handling and competition, this system greatly streamlined the world's transportation requirements and facilitated periods of unprecedented global growth, commerce and relationships.

An unplanned meeting between the president of American Airlines and a senior IBM salesman, on a coast-to-coast flight seven years earlier, led to the light-bulb discussion of an instantly accessible reservations system that elevated data-processing to its next logical step. In today's age when 25,000 CDs can be stored and manipulated on a device lightly grasped within two fingers, how easy it is to take for granted the huge and then-unwieldy requirements of SABRE, the world's first software and hardware application (and the product of 400 man-years) that enabled real-time business to take place across a network. This became possible only through the eager collaboration—the ardent listening between people working toward a purpose larger than themselves—of airline and computer expertise in a well-integrated hybrid of diverse industries.

Their results directly led to productivity advancements, search capabilities, price optimization, consumer involvement and automation across a wide range of industries. SABRE's breakthroughs also made possible our social-media landscape half a century later in ways that those pivotal executives during their 1953 encounter could not then have conceived, in a portrait of bona fide innovation.

—R.R.

Many leaders approach listening as a morally correct or polite thing to learn how to do. Some leaders think of listening as a form of public relations. Leaders go on "listening tours" to showcase their listening ability. The mistake here is to view listening as a way to develop buy-in for one's own ideas. The unhelpful concept involves reciprocity: "If I listen to you, then perhaps you'll listen to me."

This approach to listening defeats its fundamental connection to creativity. Listening is essential; it provides the only way to engage the power of more than one mind. Effective listening allows many minds to coordinate like computers in a network, creating exponential increases in creative power. When listening falters and ultimately fails, however, people become less and less effective, incapable of realizing their visions in reality.

Effective listening opens up the listener's mind to three critical information pathways. The first is to see current reality through the eyes of another mind. How we think about the world shapes what we see in it; when seen through the eyes of another thinker, elements revealed by those unique perspectives become available to us. Each mind brings to the world its own light. The differences between perspectives do not need to be reconciled; they must be integrated to provide a complete set. Failing to shine the light of many creators upon a project annihilates their perspectives and contributions.

Consider, for example, an individual's sense of identity. He has ideas about his own personality, skills, tastes and other characteristics, but when seeing himself as others do, he discovers differences between his viewpoint and theirs. It is not that the external perspectives are correct and his are not, or vice versa. The process does not entail choosing among competing perspectives; rather, a full appreciation of individual identity must account for all perspectives, the way that understanding the geometry of a three-dimensional object involves seeing it from all sides and perhaps even as it unfolds in time as the fourth dimension. Multiple perspectives made available through listening exponentially increase the possibilities for learning and understanding.

A second critical information pathway involves exploring the potential of any situation that confronts us. The world is not only as it is, but always becoming. For this reason, diverse thinkers see different aspects of its potential and the myriad ways in which it can manifest going forward.

Think of a simple event like a birthday party. People planning it may have a complex spectrum of images about how such an event could unfold. When one person plans alone, only one potential concept is actualized. When a group listens effectively to a diverse set of participants interested in planning the party, numerous possible outcomes are observable that go beyond what any one person could have imagined. Now the potential for the event has been exponentially expanded. Listening radically increases the potential for creativity and, to be sure, conflict in any human situation. Genership harnesses the energy within conflict to advance collaboration.

Listening allows for the coordination of spontaneous collaborative work. Without effective listening, the possibility for impromptu action is reduced or eliminated. Instead, actions are then coordinated through one mind only, without effective feedback.

If a sports team had to function with only one player deciding what actions the team would undertake at the moment of a play, it would fail. One player attempting to centrally direct the others during the game without processing any independent feedback from them simply could not respond effectively. A successful team is one in which all the players are in tune, responding to one another and collaborating spontaneously. And effective coaches encourage players to "stay in the moment" because they well recognize that listening and open perception are the foundational skills for this kind of decentralized and dynamic interaction.

In the evolution from leadership to genership, listening becomes the cornerstone of a foundation; when listening weakens, the creative process within individuals and teams deteriorates. But when the capacity to listen becomes more focused and flexible, creative work gathers momentum. In the words of the celebrated American psychiatrist Karl Menninger, "Listening is a magnetic and strange thing, a creative force. The friends who listen to us are the ones we move toward. When we are listened to, it creates us, makes us unfold and expand."

CHAPTER THREE
COTHINKING: *SHAPING REALITY BY THINKING TOGETHER*

The impetus to seek out a friend and to think together about a matter of importance provides a concrete action that takes us away from all three of the leadership fallacies. To engage others in critical dialogue about the problems and decisions we confront transcends both the egoism we may associate with leadership and the dependency that ceding leadership to others may imply. Seeking dialogue demands humility in that we recognize we can learn through interactions with others. But true dialogue also expresses belief in our capacity and confident willingness to invest thought and action to shape our circumstances. We are not mere spectators.

Under the misguided spell of the Messiah Fallacy, it is not for us to think; our goal is rather to find the true messiah who will think for us. Under the misleading spell of the Hero Fallacy, it is not for us to think; rather, for us to allow heroes to compete and reveal their superpowers. Under the deceptive spell of Leadership Nostalgia, it is not for us to think, but to recapture the great thoughts of those messiahs and heroes who came before us.

Buried beneath the Fallacies is a dysfunctional way of thinking about truth itself, as if the truth lay hidden like buried treasure waiting to be discovered. Think about the metaphor of discovery itself, that fully formed insights arise when we uncover secrets or valuable materials. In this erroneous view, the truth is something valuable and scarce that could be found by one person and then kept—perhaps exploited for gain—like a natural resource. The truth is something believed to exist in a pre-articulated state, written out like an ancient book discovered in a cave, needing only dusting off and translation.

According to this concept of reality implicit in the leadership construct, what matters in the transaction between two thinkers is the explanation and teaching that flows from one who understands to another who understands less well. In this view, the world that we encounter is the ultimate textbook. One simply has to know how to decipher its code; secrets can then transmit from the world to the wise, and from the wise to those seeking wisdom. Thinking is essentially understood as a form of observation. Truth is understood as correspondence between thinking and reality, the ultimate professor. What we know must be derived from an ultimate source, which itself reigns over mankind like a king.

To paraphrase Aristotle's *Metaphysics*, error is ascribing existence to *what is not*. Truth is faithfully describing *what is.* Acquinas concurs in his assessment: "A judgment is said to be true when it conforms to the external reality."

In this view, reality simply is. The true mind is one in which reality forms an equation with the intellect.

In contrast to the practice of CoThinking, the search for the messiah, heroes and their forgotten wisdom—with its religious overtones—entails some fundamentally limiting concepts about both the future and truth. We might expect these concepts to govern within the domain of faith and religion. Those who are devoutly religious sometimes understand the future to be something directed by the will of God. They also tend to see moral law (defined as conduct that humans should strive to realize during their lives) as something handed down fully formed from heaven, not invented by men. But the Fallacies extend this religious prism into the secular world, apply these ideas about the future and what constitutes good behavior to organizational life. This move severely limits the group's ability to influence its future. The die is cast, and the future is a drama already written out somewhere in the heavens. The messiah and heroes, with their superpowers, supposedly have the ability to know what is already written in the "Book of Time." This transcendental knowledge allows them to prepare the lesser beings that surround them for the inevitable. Fate is what hasn't happened yet but must. Those with insight and foresight see what must happen before it unfolds.

This unproductive worldview associated with the Fallacies does not allow that thinking together is how the world makes progress. Existence (the future itself) is seen to be wound up like a clock and now has no choice but to run down. Thinking together within this context may provide us with some understanding of what is happening, but cannot change what is destined to happen.

The effective practice of CoThinking will reject this view of reality associated with the Fallacies, overthrowing this tyrant. By embracing the practice of CoThinking, we come to see reality as something more malleable than fixed—something changeable that can become the raw material from which our visions are constructed. CoThinking allows groups to overcome the egoism (and often fraud) perpetrated by the messiah and heroes who wish to shroud their decisions in the language and costumes of infallibility.

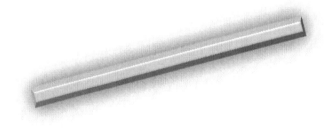

Two Ways of Knowing

One approach adopted within Western culture tends to associate knowledge and understanding with observation. This involves the scientific method, invoking observation in the development of questions, hypotheses and experiments designed to test predictions about the future. The body of knowledge that results from this way of knowing is a set of hypotheses that remain reliable in the face of ongoing efforts to test them through falsification. This confirms a deterministic worldview. The idea is simple: If we acquire a complete set of scientific laws, we will be able to predict the future with absolute certainty. In this view, the challenge of understanding and controlling the future becomes equivalent to amassing knowledge from observation of experiments. A hypothesis that cannot be tested and thus falsified through an experiment is outside the bounds of scientific knowledge. For example, the hypothesis that God plans the future cannot be tested through experiment because no matter what happens, we may say that God planned it. There is no test case to prove that God did *not* plan the future. On the other hand, the hypothesis that water being boiled will evaporate can be tested by boiling it. If water did not evaporate, we would see that the boiling process left the same amount of water we started with. The fundamental method for expanding scientific knowledge is to use what we know to attempt to make new predictions that can be tested through experience, and to accumulate and add these to the patterns of which we are certain. This strategy also relies on reductionism, the practice of analyzing complex behavior by breaking it down into component parts, and then attempting to master the patterns that govern each aspect.

Imagine an observational, scientific approach to knowledge of chess. Researchers would study games and eventually discover chess' laws. They would notice that certain pieces only move according to certain patterns: The king, with the exception of being castled, can only move one square at a time, and each bishop can only move diagonally to squares of the same color as that from which the piece originates. Moreover, beyond allowing one player to move first, chess involves no element of chance: There are no dice to throw or coins to flip. Scientific knowledge of chess derived from observation allows for countless valid predictions about every play and every game. And yet, all of the accumulated science derived from observing chess would still not allow any researcher to predict with certainty what would happen in a single game. This is not simply a matter of lacking information or processing power, although that is also a problem as there are more theoretically possible games sequences in chess than there are atoms in the observable universe.[vi] But the fundamental problem is different; chess as a game actually played (rather than a collection of rules or an abstract set of mathematical possibilities) is determined as much by the free choice and will of its players as by its rules. Those rules create parameters for action, but the game is created by its participants. It emerges in the present moment in a way that cannot be predicted. It does not exist according to a regular pattern the way the laws of gravity or the speed of light exist. Similar problems confront science in predicting human behavior across innumerable domains. To understand something like a game of chess requires knowledge of a different kind.

From the perspective of a player, rather than observer, it is possible to know the game of chess in a different way. A person very skilled in chess can use such knowledge to influence the outcomes when competing against other players in real games. The game cannot be known scientifically as if determined by essential physical laws, but it can be played to win, and does not involve any dimension of randomness or chance. The kind of knowledge required to play the game of chess well is like that required to write a compelling novel or to compose a beautiful piece of music or to paint a lifelike picture. It is knowledge derived from conscious, intentional and creative engagement outside of oneself.

Philosophers and scientists have used the word

emergence to describe this other way of knowing. Dr. Peter Corning, Director of the Institute for the Study of Complex Systems, using chess as his referent, describes emergence in this way:

> Rules, or laws, have no causal efficacy; they do not in fact "generate" anything. They serve merely to describe regularities and consistent relationships in nature. These patterns may be very illuminating and important, but the underlying causal agencies must be separately specified (though often they are not). But that aside, the game of chess illustrates precisely why any laws or rules of emergence and evolution are insufficient. Even in a chess game, you cannot use the rules to predict "history"—i.e., the course of any given game. Indeed, you cannot even reliably predict the next move in a chess game. Why? Because the "system" involves more than the rules of the game. It also includes the players and their unfolding, moment-by-moment decisions among a very large number of available options at each choice point. The game of chess is inescapably historical, even though it is also constrained and shaped by a set of rules, not to mention the laws of physics. Moreover, and this is a key point, the game of chess is also shaped by teleonomic, cybernetic, feedback-driven influences. It is not simply a self-ordered process; it involves an organized, "purposeful" activity.[vii]

CoThinking within genership involves an evolution from the kind of observational, deterministic and reductionist thinking at the heart of the scientific method to the self-ordered, end-oriented, purposeful thinking associated with emergence. When CoThinking, we recast roles. We are no longer passive observers documenting reality from the sidelines of experience. We are not seduced to believe that we can solve problems merely by diligently studying and reflecting upon reality. Instead we are deeply connected to reality, residing proactively within it; we are part of its evolving and unfolding. We are creators on the field of play. We *are* what we observe and we are *doing* as much as thinking.

CoThinking

We engage with others in reflective dialogue about our desired future, our present circumstances and the possibilities for strategic action.

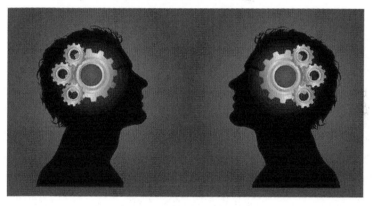

CoThinking and Reality

Genership explicitly rejects the worldview associated with the Fallacies in favor of one profoundly different. Future possibilities are understood to be radically altered by a group's chosen ideas. The future is not found, but made. The shared mind developed by a team of creators possesses a transformational relationship with what it encounters. Mind is not subordinate to reality, not a mere instrument to reflect it. Mind is the most critical force in the world. When the mind changes, so does its relationship with the world; reality itself is not seen as something fixed, other, external to the thinker, but rather transformed by and profoundly connected to human will. The future is not a preexisting story, but an ongoing series that we compose as we go along. We cannot, of course, control everything in the future, but we can influence some part of it; by definition, we can alter the totality.

In this view of the relationship between the mind and what it encounters, we do not *understand* the world we see, we *see* the world that we choose to understand. By developing our understanding, we can literally give life to a new world—a function of the interplay between experience and the ideas brought to it.

Because genership envisions thought itself as not merely reflective, but also as exerting and releasing a creative, transformative power, it engages multiple thinkers in the development of ideas, which is where creativity begins. Ideas are not passive. The practice of linking minds together in such creative work exponentially increases the mind's power; a team of minds thinking together possesses the potential to become the most powerful force in nature.

The reality of nuclear power provides a vivid example of this capacity. Seen through the prism of the Leadership Fallacies, nuclear power would be viewed as a preexisting, natural force discovered within an atom. But seen through genership's kaleidoscopic lens, nuclear power is understood as the force arising from the human mind itself. Without the mind, there is no nuclear power. The atom itself as a concept is a product of thought. We cannot experience atoms with our immediate senses. What is required to access the atom is a complex set of physical tools used to interpret information created by them, which can only be understood within a preexisting theoretical matrix, itself the product of thought. As Einstein reminded us:

> Physical concepts are free creations of the human mind, and are not, however it may seem, uniquely determined by the external world. In our endeavor to understand reality we are somewhat like a man trying to understand the mechanism of a closed watch. He sees the face and the moving hands, even hears it ticking, but he has no way of opening the case. If he is ingenious he may form some picture of the mechanism which could be responsible for all the things he observes, but he may never be quite sure his picture is the only one which could explain his observations. He will never

be able to compare his picture with the real mechanism and he cannot even imagine the possibility of the meaning of such a comparison.[viii]

In this way, the features of the created world, including the capacities of nature developed through technology, are nothing less than the collective mind itself made manifest. The powerful creations and tools surrounding modern life—buildings, computers, telecommunications, vehicles—are products of the collective mind. This is true not only of machines but of vast elements of the natural world in which man's intentional, conscious interaction with nature has given rise to new species of plant and animal life. We take all of these features of existence for granted as part of the universe we inhabit, yet they stand as examples of extensions of human thought into reality. To master CoThinking is to tap the vital power that informs the creative and created world.

How exactly does the mind become manifest in the world? By three domains of CoThinking: Think about the desired future, about reality in light of that future, and practical planning, executing and evaluating shared action.

CoThinking and the Desired Future

Our understanding of the future determines our approach to the practice of thinking together.

A fundamental activity of the mind is to observe patterns—repeated sequences within our experience. A pattern does not exist without the concept of repetition. A singular instance of something cannot give rise to a pattern, which is an experience repeated in time. Think of the shape, texture and color of an apple. Once learned, we can use those factors to recognize apples in the future. We can predict with a fair degree of certainty that buying something in the market that looks and feels like an apple will taste like one. Our knowledge of the pattern allows us to replicate or avoid it in future experience.

This is the fundamental reason why living beings seek to master patterns. Those recognized as reliable can be replayed or avoided in reality. The concepts of mathematics and logic that inform rational thought are nothing other than the fundamentals of pattern analysis. Take the elemental "if... then" statement:

> If a person consumes more calories than burns through activity, he will gain weight.

> Also, if a person burns more calories than consumes, he will lose weight.

These statements describe patterns that have been repeatedly confirmed through experience. The awareness of these patterns allows humans to control their weight through diet and exercise. If we consume more than we burn, it *follows* that we will gain weight, and vice versa.

When we approach the world from the dysfunctional perspective of the Fallacies, we tend to see the future as fully determined for us, nothing but an extension of existing patterns of experience. In this view, everything that will happen in the future, properly understood, is determined by what has happened in the past.

To illustrate this mindset, think about the sunrise and sunset. These events happen with such regularity that by studying the past, we can predict with utter certainty what will happen in the future. Moreover, the forces involved are so enormous that there is little, perhaps nothing, that can be done to alter the future in this regard. The same is true of the universal pattern of life and death, giving us certain knowledge that at some point our physical bodies will die.

On the other hand, there are aspects of the future that cannot be predicted with certainty no matter how much time is invested studying previous experiential patterns. Think, for example, about the weather, including exact precipitation, wind speed and temperatures. We may know these variables within ranges, but not with absolute precision. There is little we can do to control the weather. This reflects our experience of complex human systems. We cannot know with great certainty what will happen in the stock market, no matter how much effort is applied to studying the patterns of past experience. This is in part because of the self-reflexivity involved in such knowledge: As we know more about future trends, we respond to them, which influences the trends themselves. The uncertainty principle continues to come into play: Our ability to anticipate the future allows us to change it. What we can change is inherently unpredictable, because it responds to human will.

Billionaire's Poker

The history of the stock market continues to be littered with stories of artificial gains and multiplied losses, of investors and speculators stuck in a perpetual battle of supremacy in a zero-sum game. The market phenomenon of selling short involves borrowing stock for the sole reason of selling it. A speculator who believes shares in XYZ have nowhere to go but down will want to sell at $20 and buy back at $10 (or at pennies when the company files the hoped-for bankruptcy) when the rest of the planet comes to grips with the enterprise's true value. Regardless of the flawless logic and inevitability that such a trade may possess based solely on fundamentals, the downside can be brisk and brutal: If for any reason the stock rises, the losses multiply as those shares must eventually be bought to return to the party that initially lent them.

In October of 2008, the drama surrounding trading in automaker Volkswagen captivated the markets, starkly illustrating the intersection of greed and reality. After weeks of price declines to around €200 per share, the stock did not just double or triple in value, it quintupled to almost €1000 within a 24-hour period, making this

German manufacturer the world's most valuable corporation. The stock then quickly dropped by half.

The German state of Lower Saxony owned 20% of the company and Porsche had been buying to increase their stake to about a third of all shares outstanding. That activity, combined with decent sales increases from Volkswagen dealerships, led to large rises in its share price that appeared to make it impractical for Porsche to continue buying and ultimately take over their German counterpart. Hedge funds and other speculators thus determined that those prices were unsustainable. If Porsche did not follow through, the company would be worth a lot less on its fundamentals. The canny Porsche understood this dynamic and bought those selfsame borrowed shares. The Economist reported that a Morgan Stanley stock analyst warned its clients against playing "billionaire's poker" with Porsche.

On that wild day, Porsche released the news that they had increased their ownership position to 74%, which meant that just 6% of Volkswagen remained available to trade. Yet short-sellers had already sold more than 10% of the company. Their panicked attempts to cover those positions led to losses in the billions, and drove the price up exponentially more than the company had been or would ever be worth. Porsche could ask essentially whatever price it wanted for its shares, made huge gains in a startling transfer of wealth and found itself in the driver's seat in a classic example of a short squeeze.

—R.R.

Beyond these boundaries—futures we know with great certainty but cannot influence, and futures we cannot know nor can influence—there is a third domain involving patterns that we can determine or at least influence substantially. Within this sphere, we can rationally introduce the concept of desire. Some writers and thinkers on the subject of leadership use the word "vision," but genership explicitly avoids this word because it risks a perhaps unintended connotation of seeing a future that already exists in some sense. When we express desire by imagining the future, what we wish for does not presently exist. In this sense, to want something is to imagine what *does not* exist. Desire is extinguished when reality conforms to our wishes.

We often speak about vision in the same context that we use the word "visionary." Within the domain of leadership, when we describe leaders thus, we often mean that they have some unusual powers of foresight, such the ability to foretell the future as if looking within a crystal ball. In this mindset the future is deemed to actually exist somewhere in time, as if reality existed along a trajectory coming from the past, with us in the present moment and then projected into the future. Within this concept, we are traveling inexorably down the road of time to a place that already exists further up the road from where we are. There is no doubt that upon arrival we will see the world as it appeared within our crystal ball. Arthur Schopenhauer succinctly describes this view as entailing "the conscious certainty that all events are bound firmly together by the chain of causality and thus occur with strict necessity, so that the future is already totally fixed and precisely determined, and can be no more altered than the past can."

The concept of the future associated with genership differs substantially from this crystal-ball approach. It contains the belief that the future is susceptible to influence and might be determined through our efforts. The future is not preordained; it is created out of energy and matter available in the present. This idea that the future flows from the raw stuff of creation wrestles with the reality that while we cannot control all elements within future time (for example, the weather, the fact of our mortality, the movements of celestial bodies) and perhaps not most, we can control some of them completely. For example, a composer determines the music in a symphony. A painter determines the scene in a landscape. A novelist determines characters and plot. An architect determines designs of windows in a house.

Through the worldview presented within the Leadership Fallacies, we must answer all questions about the desired future for ourselves and our communities by consulting the messiah's crystal ball, his supreme vision of necessary destiny. The fundamental question is this: What does the messiah see as our true future? Confusion about who the messiah is devolves into the Hero Fallacy: Who should we select to tell us our true future? This mindset implicitly rejects the concept that the messiah's view of the future could be indeterminate. After all, a messiah lacking the superpower of foreknowledge would be no messiah at all. Under the spell of the Fallacies, if we remain in doubt about the future, the problem can only be in our understanding of the messiah, of what he sees, of clearly understanding his true desire. The essence of the relationship is to have the messiah explain our destiny. If we believe there is a true messiah, then we really possess only one choice: striving to understand or choosing to remain ignorant.

Genership calls for a new approach. Within this paradigm, we no longer attempt to understand the messiah's brilliant insight into a necessary, inescapable future reality, but rather to understand our own will for the future as it emerges in dialogue with others. CoThinking is the pathway to such understanding. Another important freedom arises from letting go of the concept of necessary destiny. As long as we cling to the idea of a predetermined future, even the most collaborative dialogue will be restricted as it searches for one possible future deemed to be true. In such a view, the framers of the Constitution did not create it through their dialogue and shared thinking, but rather discovered it as a sort of platonic ideal, a true version that was out there in the ether somewhere among a myriad of possible false articulations. Consider these words of Joseph Smith, founder of the Mormon religion, to describe the United States Constitution:

> The Constitution of the United States is a glorious standard; it is founded in the wisdom of God. It is a heavenly banner; it is to all those who are privileged with the sweets of liberty, like the cooling shades and refreshing waters of a great rock in a thirsty and weary land. It is like a great tree under whose branches men from every clime can be shielded from the burning rays of the sun.

Genership—innovation, human creativity, acknowledgement of the power of learning through mistakes—casts aside this worldview holding that there are true articulations of the future and that the cause of dialogue is to discover and reveal their transcendental nature. Having let go of the idea that there is a single, true destiny, we can work collaboratively to develop our own concept of the desired future, constrained by nothing but our collective imagination. Previous patterns of experience do not limit, and in fact open up, our sense of what is possible. We do not judge whether a desired future is right by asking whether existing patterns of experience can be deemed consistent with it.

The creative work of delegates to the Constitutional Convention illustrates CoThinking in action. Hundreds of years later, it is easy to forget that the Convention gathered not to create a new government out of whole cloth, but to address the weaknesses in the Articles of Confederation. The participants had no grand ideas about their charge at the start of the proceedings. The Convention proceeded loosely, without strong centralized control or a disciplined process of drafting and deliberation. There was no limit on the number of delegates from the states who could participate. Seventy were appointed but only 55 attended; there was never an occasion at which all were present at the same time. Rhode Island did not participate in the Convention at all; the body had trouble initially establishing a quorum; New Hampshire delegates arrived weeks late in the midst of the proceedings.

Deep division and argument characterized the meeting. An extremely diverse group populated the convention, representing small and large states and drawn from the divergent interests of the day, including commerce, farming and law. It is quite clear that there was no unifying vision at the outset of the convention and certainly no single leader who forged consensus from the different visions and interests represented by the participants. While George Washington was unanimously elected as chairman of the proceedings, he did not play a significant role in the deliberations, nor did he align with any of the factions or direct the group to a result.

Virginia's George Mason refused to sign the Constitution because it lacked a Bill of Rights. Two of the delegates from New York left before the document was signed and the third, none other than Alexander

Hamilton, declined to sign because his colleagues had not.

That so many delegates remained in doubt about the Constitution's viability is not surprising given the significance of the controversies confronting the delegates, including the balance of power between large and small states, questions involving slavery such as how to count slaves in measuring a state's population and whether the slave trade should be abolished, and the nature of the presidency, among many others. In all of these matters, the delegates worked together to frame rules that represented innovations in design that either forged compromises or transcended differences among the members. The delegates did not resolve their differences by appeals to power but rather by working to create new structures and thinking together.

The clash between the Virginia and New Jersey plans provides a specific example. The Virginia plan called for a bicameral legislature, with the people directly electing the lower-chamber representatives, who would then elect the upper-chamber members. The number of representatives in the lower chamber would be proportional to the state's population, creating an advantage for large states. The alternative New Jersey plan favored small states, staying closer to the original Articles of Confederation, providing for "one state, one vote" in a unicameral legislative body. Rather than force a decision between the two plans, the Convention members framed what would come to be known as the Great Compromise, adopting the bicameral legislature from the Virginia plan, including one house with representatives based on population, but with the other house providing two votes per state. This unprecedented formulation satisfied the needs and interests of both the large- and small-state factions.

A century after the Convention, in a case of Leadership Nostalgia, William Gladstone said that "the American Constitution is, so far as I can see, the most wonderful work ever struck off at a given time by the brain and purpose of man." But at the time the framers were working on it, the Constitution seemed all too human, a work that contained flaws and reflected the limitations of those who had drafted it. On September 17, 1787, James Wilson delivered remarks endorsing the Constitution composed by Benjamin Franklin, who could not make the speech in person because of age and infirmity. Franklin's words are a pure articulation of genership, especially his recognition of doubt and confidence in the power of collective imagination, located specifically in his observation that wisdom involved rejecting certitude and paying "more respect to the judgment of others."

Ben Franklin:
Genership and the Constitutional Convention

As recorded in James Madison's notes of the proceedings, Franklin had this to say:

Mr. President:

I confess that there are several parts of this constitution which I do not at present approve, but I am not sure I shall never approve them: For having lived long, I have experienced many instances of being obliged by better information, or fuller consideration, to change opinions even on important subjects, which I once thought right, but found to be otherwise. It is therefore that the older I grow, the more apt I am to doubt my own judgment, and to pay more respect to the judgment of others. Most men indeed as well as most sects in Religion, think themselves in possession of all truth, and that wherever others differ from them it is so far error. Steele a Protestant in a Dedication tells the Pope, that the only difference between our Churches in their opinions of the certainty of their doctrines is, the Church of Rome is infallible and the Church of England is never in the wrong. But though many private persons think almost as highly of their own infallibility as of that of their sect, few express it so naturally as a certain french lady, who in a dispute with her sister, said "I don't know how it happens, Sister but I meet with no body but myself, that's always in the right — Il n'y a que moi qui a toujours raison."

In these sentiments, Sir, I agree to this Constitution with all its faults, if they are such; because I think a general Government necessary for us, and there is no form of Government but what may be a blessing to the people if well administered, and believe farther that this is likely to be well administered for a course of years, and can only end in Despotism, as other forms have done before it, when the people shall become so corrupted as to need despotic Government, being incapable of any other. I doubt too whether any other Convention we can obtain, may be able to make a better Constitution. For when you assemble a number of men to have the advantage of their joint wisdom, you inevitably assemble with those men, all their prejudices, their passions, their errors of opinion, their local interests, and their selfish views. From such an assembly can a perfect production be expected? It therefore astonishes me, Sir, to find this system approaching so near to perfection as it does; and I think it will astonish our enemies, who are waiting with confidence to hear that our councils are confounded like those of the Builders of Babel; and that our States are on the point of separation, only to meet hereafter for the purpose of cutting one another's throats. Thus I consent, Sir, to this Constitution because I expect no better, and because I am not sure, that it is not the best. The opinions I have had of its errors, I sacrifice to the public good. I have never whispered a syllable of them abroad. Within these walls they were born, and here they shall die. If every one of us in returning to our Constituents were to report the objections he has had to it, and endeavor to gain partizans in support of them, we might prevent its being generally received, and thereby lose all the salutary effects & great advantages resulting naturally in our favor among foreign Nations as well as among ourselves, from our real or apparent unanimity. Much of the strength & efficiency of any Government in procuring and securing happiness to the people, depends, on opinion, on the general opinion of the goodness of the Government, as well as of the wisdom and integrity of its Governors. I hope therefore that for our own sakes as a part of the people, and for the sake of posterity, we shall act heartily and unanimously in recommending this Constitution (if approved by Congress & confirmed by the Conventions) wherever our influence may extend, and turn our future thoughts & endeavors to the means of having it well administred.

On the whole, Sir, I can not help expressing a wish that every member of the Convention who may still have objections to it, would with me, on this occasion doubt a little of his own infallibility, and to make manifest our unanimity, put his name to this instrument.

The spirit of genership can also be located in George Mason's refusal to sign the Constitution, because that work—wonderful though it was— lacked what many have since come to view as its most critical part, the Bill of Rights. The Constitution, with its 27 amendments, stands today as an archetypal example of the power and promise of CoThinking.

Seeing Reality Through the Prism of Desire

From within the worldview of the Fallacies, the quest for truth—a search for ultimate reality—becomes the central focus. In thinking about desire and the future, the Fallacies imply that we can ascertain our one true future by understanding ultimate truth in the present moment. A major quest of the human experience thus becomes the search for objective truth in the present moment—truth that will be judged, like the speed of light, to be the same for all observers, no matter their frame of reference.

Knowing such present truth would tell us with certainty what to strive for, how to achieve it and what role to play. It is as if we could discover how to live and act at each moment of our lives if only we had access to Plato's world of the forms, in which the ideal form of everything is contained within it right now, awaiting nothing but our understanding. This notion includes the belief that there is a correct and incorrect answer for every decision. Life is something we can get right if we study the answer key.

The truth in this context becomes a proxy for the messiah or hero. Objective, indisputable knowledge becomes a source of security upon which we can depend like the loving arms of a nurturing parent. The idea that such truth could exist seems comforting, even if we do not understand it for ourselves. All we need is for the messiah or hero to understand it, then he will take care of us. So our faith in such knowledge can become a proxy for our own knowledge of objective truth.

This perspective would have us believe that the existence of one unified truth must mean that there will be a particular part for all who know the truth. To know how our part must play out relieves us from the creative struggle of having to invent it.

Genership rejects this worldview about reality, looking at it from an entirely different perspective, not as something fixed and certain, but as something inherently dependent upon both perspective and motive. Genership recognizes that values frame facts and deeply influence not only how they are perceived but their intrinsic nature. Within the creative mindset, desire does not merely provide a different lens through which to see the world, it opens up entirely new vistas that otherwise would remain not simply invisible but nonexistent. Genership perceives desire as a provocative force that calls forth and gives life to new realities that did not exist at all before their encounter with the creative mind. This is not to say that reality yields to the mind whatever it wishes, without work, as if reality itself were nothing but a blank screen upon which to manifest dreams. But over time and through creative effort there is no limit to what can be manifest through the mind's work upon the world. Of course, there is no way to prove that something is impossible for all of eternity as we the living have not yet seen eternity. Nor is there a way to prove that something is possible other than to attempt and achieve it.

We can look to the example of nuclear power, not as a preexisting force within nature, but rather one that arose from the creative encounter between mind and matter. If man did not set out to investigate reality for the purposes of unleashing its power, would that power exist today? What we discover in the world reflects what we seek in it through our creative process. Genership recognizes that the process of invention creates the contexts that birth discovery.

Consider the study of human psychology and illnesses. Many such studies are funded and performed by drug companies. Desiring to increase the market for pharmaceuticals, they perceive the reality of mental illness from the perspective of individual consumers, with a view to those aspects of the mind that can be impacted through pharmaceutical approaches—namely, through brain chemistry. As a result, we are developing a conception of the human mind as an idealized chemical state, comparing the brains of functional, productive people with those "suffering" because they cannot become productive, successful or happy within modern society. For this reason we are adapting brain chemistry through chemical intervention to the prevailing societal norms. We are *creating* what is regarded as normal brain chemistry as much as we are *discovering* it, because we have selected highly functional, idealized individuals as exemplifying what is normal. We are *creating* this pharmacological reality of the human mind, one susceptible to chemical intervention, as we discover it through the fundamental prism of one specific desire: to build a humanity dependent upon pharmaceuticals.

Proceeding from an alternative set of desires might give rise to an entirely different reality of the mind. A community desiring to understand human psychology with reference to social organization might view the individual not as optimal brain chemistry, but rather as an autonomous being within a social network; we may well develop knowledge about how humans interact within communities and how they can be influenced through social contacts. This understanding could be as rigorous and predictive as that developed within the psycho-pharmacological account of the human mind. It would likely result in different measures of normalcy and varied interventions grounded in social interactions rather than ingesting pills.

Understanding necessarily entails privileging a selection of observations from experience as relevant information; from this the mind constructs patterns. But the information selected and the patterns observed in reality invariably relate to the desires and motivations of the person or company observing; there is no universal data set.

Consider a physicist and a musician studying the violin. The physicist may make a series of observations designed to reveal information about the nature of the instrument's materials and how they bond together. The musician will pick up the instrument and know it with her hands, arms and ears. The data sets are incommensurate; each is true but they differ enormously because the investigators bring radically different desires and objectives to their study of the object; that referred to as "violin" in the consciousness of the musician bears little relationship to the same object in the physicist's consciousness. These kinds of perspective disparities exist in our knowledge of everything.

For this reason, a diversity of investigators working together, each bringing their unique desires and perspectives to the task of considering reality, reveal it in a substantially more powerful way than even a brilliant investigator acting alone. Motives and goals are not functions of intelligence (defined as the ability to recognize patterns); even people who lack understanding and experience can reveal critical new perspectives on reality when they bring new desires to bear upon it.

Genership entails the critical skill of CoThinking, allowing for diverse thinkers to work together to understand current reality in light of their conflicting—even initially incompatible—desires.

CoThinking and Strategic Action

Strategic action is infused with intention, designed to manifest a specific desired result. Under the Leadership Fallacies, there is one person who knows how to bring about desired results: the messiah. We are to put our faith in him and follow his commands about what we should do, no matter where the course of action takes us. In the presence of the messiah, the group's belief is that there is one true quest and path to satisfy it. If there is any doubt about the viability of the messiah, the Hero Fallacy takes control. The group has only one strategic action: to find and anoint the true messiah.

The belief that there is only one right way of proceeding is crippling to group progress, because the group, rather than beginning to move toward its goals, often becomes paralyzed. This blockage arises from the belief that if there is only one way to achieve something, then any false move must—by definition—lead to failure. In this mindset, being right acquires more value than making progress, because only one path leads to success. Other roads are believed to lead to dead-ends, no matter how initially promising. If the Constitution's framers had believed that there was only one true guide for the American people, they would have become paralyzed in their efforts to create it, feeling that a mistake could lead them to a kind of existential disaster in which the truth of human nature failed to actualize itself. To the contrary, the framers saw that there were numerous possible strategies to achieve their goals; they felt free to experiment and even fail, then change their course if necessary based on experience. The very presence of Article V, allowing for amendments, shows their underlying awareness that there was no single correct way to proceed, and that the Constitution would have to adapt as the nation evolved in the future. The framers saw themselves and any others who would purport to lead as entirely fallible. To accept fallibility liberates organizations to experiment and learn from failure in their work on tasks that are mundane but nevertheless critical to progress: developing mission, building teams, strengthening performance.

Genership rejects the journey metaphor—the idea that there is one true path—and focuses instead on the group's underlying shared creative activity. There are infinite ways to create what is desired. Enabled by genership, a collaborating team of minds is able to devise more efficient, effective methods than one person acting alone. There is no one right way toward success, with many competing ways presenting combinations of strengths and weaknesses that only the group as a whole can assess. Groups practicing genership are not paralyzed; they are flexible and opportunistic, gaining ground whenever possible, discovering new resources and methods as they progress.

CoThinking: Levels Within Groups

Sheep

Groupthink

Debate

Dialogue

Ascetic Bodhisatta Gotama with the Group of Five

Competing Models of Thinking in Groups

Comparing approaches to group processing, and considering the three elements of CoThinking (thinking about the future, thinking about the present in the light of desire, and thinking about strategic action), four evolutionary stages emerge in group dynamics: Sheep, Groupthink, Debate and Dialogue. In defining these stages, genership relies not on the traditional definitions, but frames a special vocabulary to understand the practice of CoThinking within the larger context of genership.

1. *Sheep.* Members do not participate consciously in the group's

strategic thinking. The messiah and heroes think for the group, but its members do not have awareness of this process. They are unaware of danger, of the machinations required to preserve and give quality to their lives. The messiah is a benevolent shepherd who cares for the flock but does not engage it. Participants are aware of their comfort and discomfort, but they have no conscious desire for a different state of affairs by thinking critically about current reality and forming plans. Disagreements with the messiah are not perceived; indeed, the group does not perceive the messiah as such. Blissful ignorance precludes dissent. At the level of sheep, group members are driven by the primal emotions of pleasure and fear; they live almost entirely within the present moment.

2. *Groupthink.* The messiah thinks for the group, which has consciousness of this reality and accepts his thinking without questioning or reflection. The group accepts the messiah's foreknowledge of the future, assessment of reality and directions with regard to strategic action. People who disagree with the messiah are regarded as deluded, mentally ill or enemies of the group.

3. *Debate.* Here an important evolution in consciousness occurs. For the first time, group members perceive themselves as fully engaged in the development of ideas about the desired future, current reality and strategic action. In debate, however, they are still committed to the idea of a singular truth, often grounded on an appeal to immutable authority; i.e., that there is one right answer to the group's inquiries, and that this definitive answer can be achieved through intellectual combat among participants. Debate entails the idea that certain truths will win and prevail over others. The messiah may be viewed as a powerful competitor within the dialogue itself or as a judge over the debate who determines winners and losers.

Most importantly, within the paradigm presented by debate, ideas are accepted or rejected, but generally not shaped or reframed. This is in part because of the idea that the truth serves as an objective reference point. Since truth is thought to be immutable, correct ideas must be immutable as well. If an idea is one percent incorrect, it is entirely incorrect because it does not fit the truth. If ideas succeed in a debate contest, advocates become loyal to them in the way that one is loyal to a messiah. To abandon such victorious ideas is almost like a being a traitor to a cause and may even be viewed as a character flaw. This is because of the belief that truth is fixed and eternal; the messiah and truth become consciously bonded.

4. *Dialogue.* This entails a breakthrough. When groups are engaged in dialogue, ideas are no longer viewed as winning or losing but rather as tools that refine the key elements to stimulate creativity: the desired future, reality in light of that desire and strategic action. *Dialogue as a process does not view obtaining a singular truth as its goal.* Genership transcends the concept of a singular truth in favor of a dynamic concept of truth, one that sees reality as evolving and therefore subject to human creativity. The goal of dialogue within genership is not to discover immutable truth but rather to shape reality in accordance with creative desire. Dialogue strives to achieve a desired future state: something that can only become true if it succeeds in becoming manifest in reality. From the perspective of the present, the future state of affairs is thought of as true if it accurately reflects the group's current desires. For those grounded in genership, the true future is not predestined or somehow determined by fate, but rather reflects the group's evolving desires. The group understands that right and wrong, good and evil, emerge from its creative desires, understanding that even its most deeply held convictions about what to create, and how to do it, represent choices for which there are viable alternatives. The group perceives its creative work as unnecessary in the sense of being inevitable, understanding that creativity always entails such freedom. The group that achieves this level of authentic dialogue knows that creativity can only operate within those spheres of existence open to the will and determined through choices that express the group's desires.

Within dialogue, reality is not treated as a constraint, but rather as the raw material from which visions are crafted and made manifest in experience. The group in such dialogue does not measure the value of ideas by whether they accurately depict reality, but by whether they work to shape and change reality so that it becomes congruent with vision. The group does not concern itself with the truth of ideas but rather with their usefulness and evolution.

Approach to…	vision (desired future)	truth (reality in light of desire)	strategic action	Those who disagree are…
1. Sheep (no thinking)	No choice / no awareness of choice	No understanding of reality / a belief that there is nothing to learn	No action to take / there is no choice about action	… not perceived.
2. Groupthink	One choice	One reality	One action	… insane, ignorant or evil.
3. Discussion and debate	Possibility of diverse choices / the best choice prevails	That proven to be right or correct	The best action proven most effective	… wrong.
4. Dialogue	Possibility of diverse choices / potential of new choices emerging from dialogue	Many diverse truths depending on goals and perspectives / new truths may emerge	Many ways to achieve goals	… valuable resources for future learning possibilities.

CHAPTER FOUR
COVISIONING: *THE FUTURE MADE, NOT PREDICTED*

Within the practice of CoThinking, CoVisioning involves the unique domain of thinking together about those elements of reality capable of changing. We may think together about the past and present as observers who can respond to what they see but not alter it. Yet when we think together about the future, we explore tangible possibilities for creating change.

Whether something in reality can change depends literally upon how we think about it. The art and practice of genership depends upon CoVisioning, which involves explicitly thinking with others in a way that enables us to change the present according to our desires.

The Limits of Change

The famous American theologian, Reinhold Niebuhr, penned one of the most popular modern prayers:

> God grant me the serenity to accept the things I cannot
> change, courage to change the things I can change,
> and wisdom to know the difference.

Niebuhr's appeal for wisdom recognizes that the boundary between what can change and what is immutable may not always be clear. Particularly at this moment in human history, we have witnessed many miraculous accomplishments in which humans working together have changed the world in ways that, before, would have seemed impossible even to the courageous. Such changes include not merely scientific breakthroughs in atomic energy, communications, information technology and medicine, but also social transformations such as the civil rights movement and the end of the Cold War.

Genership expresses an adventuresome willingness to test the boundaries of change, and recognition that thinking and working together has the potential to create change where previously it may have been thought not possible.

In coming to grips with our power to change reality, we begin by working to explore features that we believe cannot change, entailing boundaries to creative work.

Usually when presented with this challenge to test the limits of change, people begin to ruminate about facts and truths. We tend to think about them as those features of our experience that remain constant.

Many people regard history as unchangeable; the future contains possibilities, but as they move into the present, they become defined. Once in the past, they are fixed for all eternity.

But think deeply about the concept of the past, then ask this question: Where does the past exist? There is no place to experience the past as such. We have no access to the past except through the artifacts that it leaves in the present: video, pictures, notes, memories and other impressions. The past by definition does not exist now beyond these records; if their source were fully available to us in the present moment, we would no longer define that period as being past.

We interpret the past based on the record that it has left behind in the present. For example, we understand the history of human evolution by interpreting bones that remain in the present from creatures that we believe, based on our latest scientific theories, lived millions of years ago. The past is obviously not visible except through the theories that allow us to perceive such evidence. The past does not necessarily tell itself; it requires narrative reconstruction based on layers upon layers of interpretation. We create narratives of the past out of whole cloth by interpreting the fragments that persist into present moment.

Think of the Zagruber film of the Kennedy assassination; although a visual record of what happened the day Kennedy was shot, it has been understood through inconsistent ideas that yield multiple interpretations. To this day there remains controversy about whether more than one gunman was involved in the murder, notwithstanding that the event was captured on film and a thorough autopsy conducted.

Even something as concrete as a birthdate may be reimagined. We think of ourselves as having been born in a particular year. But in a different culture, marking time from a different place, we would understand our birth year as being different. In Western culture, one might believe that he was born in the year 1961. But in Islamic culture, the year 1961 was the year 1380, marking time from 622 CE, the year of the Islamic prophet Muhammad's emigration from Mecca to Medina.[ix] Also, in our culture we define birth as an event that occurs at a specific moment in time. Yet suppose we think about birth differently, defining it as when people first acquire consciousness, self-awareness. When did that happen? Now it is not so clear.

Westerners tend to think of time as linear, beginning in the past and extending infinitely into the future. We see ourselves positioned on a straight timeline; some events preceded our birth, some follow. But the Hindu perception of time is circular, so that culture understands the past as a recurring cycle. In that sense, what happens today might be seen as *older* than the past or contemporaneous with it.

Creating the Past

Those not trained as historians may find it difficult to come to terms with the idea that we create the past. But modern psychological experiments speak powerfully to this concept. Mental models or mind maps exert a palpable, constructive influence on perceptions of the past; we tend to *see* evidence that conforms to our mental maps while we discount or omit whatever does not. An experiment conducted by

Brewer and Treyens (1981), one among many, asked each participant to wait in an office for about 35 seconds for another laboratory room to be prepared. They were then moved to another room and asked to recall everything in the office. Participants showed a strong tendency to recall the presence of objects consistent with the contents of a typical office. Nearly everyone remembered a desk and the chair next to it. But only eight of the 30 recalled a skull visible in the office, few recalled a wine bottle or the coffee pot, and only one called up the picnic basket. Some recalled items that had not been there at all: Nine remembered specific books not present in the office. These findings, consistent with many others on the subject, show that people tend to project their ideas onto the record of the past, thus creating narratives and imagined incidents consistent with their mental models and beliefs. We construct the past in this way.

If history is an understanding of patterns that occurred and are now gone, then how we think about them changes what patterns we observe in history. If we think of history using psychological ideas, then we may well see different patterns than when looking at history using ideas from economics. To observe the past through the prism of Freudian psychology will likely yield focus on information relating to psychological relationships. Studying the life of Hitler, a psychologist might focus on the German's relationship with his father and mother. The psychologist-historian looks for narratives that circle Freudian theories. How did Hitler resolve his Oedipus complex? A Marxist will see something else entirely, focusing perhaps on the economic forces that allowed Hitler's rise to power. The economist-historian sees history through economic principles. How did the rise of German industrial power enable Hitler's war efforts? In the past, we see the narratives that we choose to focus upon because of our current worldviews, and may become blind to those beyond our landscape of ideas. We are susceptible to project as much upon the past as the future.

What about abstract principles? Do they change? What of the mathematical idea that the circumference of a circle is about 3.14 times the radius, otherwise known as the mathematical constant, pi. Some would maintain that it can never change.

But with genership, pi can change depending upon how we view the nature of space itself. If one assumes that space is perfectly flat (as in Euclidean geometry) and envisions a perfect circle, then the approximate 3.14 definition of pi holds up. But if space itself is distorted (curved), then it doesn't. On a curved surface, the ratio changes. And in nature, no perfectly flat surfaces exist and neither do any perfect circles, so pi really only exists in the mind.

Einstein's work on the nature of gravity arose through exactly this process: thinking that employed new mental concepts beyond standard Euclidean geometry. The geometric context within which we see the world deeply impacts our perceptions of space and time. If we ask someone who has stayed in bed for 24 hours how far he has traveled from the perspective of the bedroom, the answer is nowhere. But ask the same question from the vantage point of outer space, and we see that the individual who has stayed in bed has traveled one complete rotation of the earth and one day's distance in the earth's orbit around the sun, a distance of over 400,000 miles.

Einstein's creative work involved a similar mental exercise; he exposed new perspectives by altering the concepts he brought to bear upon understanding the world. In his theory of general relativity, he introduced the novel concept of space-time, the idea that space and time are one fabric that can be distorted like a rubber sheet stretching and curving. This idea is difficult to conceptualize because in common experience we think of space as a medium distinct from time. The difficulty also lies in not being able to imagine a physical place that is itself outside of space and time, the kind of vantage point supplied by an extra dimension allowing one to observe curvature. Despite the impossibility of visualizing this curvature in the Euclidean three-dimensional space of everyday life, Einstein—using mathematics—came to think of gravity as the curvature of a new concept associated with the presence of matter. Before Einstein, gravity was understood using Newton's physics in quite different terms, as a force operating between objects in space related to their mass and distance from one another. As Newton wrote in *Principia*, "Every particle of matter in the universe attracts every other particle with a force that is directly proportional to the product of the masses of the particles and inversely proportional to the square of the distance between them."

This is not to say that there is nothing immutable in the world. Of course there is, if we choose to think of it in a way that makes it so. A person born a male might view his gender as being unchangeable. But another person might see sexual identity as something that can change through hormone therapy, a sex-change operation and behavioral adjustments, understanding gender as something that can change within one being's lifetime.

Why is this meditation on the nature of change so central to the practice of CoVisioning? Because groups practicing genership expand the boundaries of what they see as being capable of change. They are able to take elements of reality that appear to be immutable and reframe them, creating opportunities for change through the application of thought and action. Think of Moore's law, describing the long-term trend in the history of computing hardware. The law states that the number of transistors that can be placed on an integrated circuit doubles approximately every two years. This trend has continued since the late 1950s. At any given moment since then, there was a real-world constraint governing the density and speed of microprocessors, yet there have been forces of genership at work expanding that constraint. Reality is in motion and creativity is in the driver's seat.

One might reasonably ask at this point, "Is there anything in experience that cannot be changed by CoVisioning?" Genership and the practice of CoVisioning specifically address this question.

Freedom and Playfulness

In normal usage the word *playful* signifies frolic and humor, and suggests a context of recreation. Genership, however, focuses on a particular definition of the verb *to play:* to move or function freely within prescribed limits. Within genership and CoVisioning, the word *playful* conveys commitment to free experimentation and movement, in the sense that someone might play with a control panel or software package to learn how it works and discover its full potential.

To play and be playful in this sense means to explore and exploit a situation's full potential. The opposite of such an orientation is one bound by rules and limits, or by reality itself. Imagine how a person with severe arthritis in the hands might be limited in her ability to play a piano. Or how a basketball player performs when his coach imposes strict limits on what he should do within the game, threatening to bench him if he goes beyond set boundaries.

Genership promotes enthusiastic playfulness, whereas the leadership paradigm tends to restrict it. Inherent in the Leadership Fallacies is a sense of servitude, of being bonded and indebted to the messiah. This kind of relationship limits creativity because our individual creative will is discounted.

Liberated from the Fallacies, something new emerges: a playful orientation toward the world. Genership requires just such a mindset; from within that perspective we see the world as something subject to our will and desire. The essence of playfulness is the ability to dominate something, take it apart, reconstruct it, use it at will. To play with a ball, for example, is to throw it around the environment, to observe it flying and bouncing in all directions. To play a game is to enter into it and explore everything that can happen within its environment as we move and manipulate its features. The opposite of a playful orientation is one that sees the world as given and something with which we *should not* interfere. When someone tells us, "Don't play with that!" what he admonishes is *Don't touch it, don't manipulate it, let it be only as you find it.* A critical part of the creative orientation required for genership is to explore the environment together, testing the application of the will to all parts of it in a playful way—manipulating, risking and examining what happens when we attempt to make changes.

Playing together in groups expands our ability to explore the potential environment for change. One person playing alone can only apply his personal thinking and activities. A team of people creates the opportunity to apply a spectrum of ideas and abilities to the world, yielding infinitely greater potential for change.

When we suffer under the Fallacies, we cease to play with the environment, instead allowing the chosen one to do so, while we watch passively from the sidelines. Under the spell of the Hero Fallacy, the game itself is being played only to discover the messiah, the one whose true game will reveal ultimate reality and the right strategy. The Fallacy of Leadership Nostalgia involves studying the playfulness of a messiah from the past. It is only when we liberate ourselves from the Fallacies that we begin to enter into the state of playfulness that informs effective genership.

Any Googler Can

Inherent in the Fallacy of Leadership Nostalgia is a sense of employee indebtedness for the job itself and then ongoing servitude to the messiah. These circumstances remain distinct from gratitude and humility, twin emotional realities that should ideally be displayed from both sides of the paycheck. By contrast, workplace rules and reigns engendered by the Leadership Fallacies severely limit creativity; individual creative will is buried under prevailing service to the messiah. What matters is not what employees can create, but what the messiah desires. Workers become tools of the messiah with the sole purpose to adhere to the messiah's "true" vision without deviation. The messiah decrees and employees follow, while watching, paying homage and, at most, assisting.

Many companies—especially the more freewheeling technology-oriented enterprises—offer a variety of perks to supplement the standard benefits; on-site extras tend to keep employees in the office longer and thus increase productivity (a fact not lost on savvy executives). Need a haircut? Schedule a freebee on campus. Crave a workout? Head over to the company gym and swimming pool. Want some down time between meetings for hands-on fun? Pop into the rec center for Ping-Pong or video games. Feeling sick? Make an appointment with a doctor upstairs. What would happen, though, if those on the payroll could devote one out of every five working hours to push their own creativity to limits not otherwise possible under the heavy hands of managers?

Along comes Google.

Its celebrated 20-percent time program permits employees to pursue pet projects beyond their normal responsibilities, a "crazy" perquisite that yielded Gmail and Google Earth, together with other key innovations and patents. Picture a workforce eager to arrive at the office, stimulated to use their obvious gifts in service to ideas beyond job descriptions and quarterly earnings goals, high on the natural endorphins that come with genuine human creativity. Is it a coincidence that Google consistently ranks among the best companies to work for in widely quoted national surveys? Is it a fluke that the company possesses thousands of patents? Is it an accident that its quarterly earnings are measured in the billions?

As the company works to foster an inspired and motivated employee base, its 2012 job description for engineers speaks for itself:

- We work in small teams to promote spontaneity, creativity and speed.
- We listen to every idea, on the theory that any Googler can come up with the next breakthrough.
- We provide the resources to turn great ideas into reality.
- We offer our engineers "20-percent time" so that they're free to work on what they're really passionate about. Google Suggest, AdSense for

Content and Orkut are among the many products of this perk.

While Google's challenge will be to maintain its open culture of creativity, to retain its quirks and perks as it becomes evermore entrenched as a public company beholden to stockholders, here is a stunning refutation of the Fallacy of Leadership Nostalgia—backed up with smiles, satisfaction and summits of cash.

—R.R.

Experimentation

The root of the word "experiment" is experience, meaning knowledge from skill. While experimenting, we know the world from having tested it ourselves, with our own senses. Genership prioritizes experience over other forms of knowledge, primarily that received from others as accepted wisdom. The Fallacies suggest to us that knowledge should be received or revealed through others with superpowers. We cannot achieve knowledge ourselves, only the privileged super-beings can know and then teach us. Experimentation, by contrast, offers a commitment to learn by doing and through direct observation of the way in which one's will interacts with the environment. The essence of experimentation is first to act and then to observe.

Under the Leadership Fallacies, experimentation has come to be understood as a vehicle to reveal immutable, scientific truths of nature. But the sense of experimentation that lies at the root of genership is quite different, designed to expose hidden potentials for change in the world. The fundamental question asked in this kind of experimentation is not "What is truth?" but "What is changeable?" and "How can the world be influenced?" Note that asking "What is truth?" seeks that which *cannot* change.

Do flint and steel together make a spark? Only if one strikes the other in a specific way. It is the action of striking—as much as the raw materials—that causes the spark, which is created as much as discovered. The spark is not truth per se; it is a way in which human action upon the world can change it.

Think of a composer experimenting with a sequence of musical notes, a poet with a sequence of words, a painter with a colorful palette. In each case, the artist may discover and select a sequence from infinite potentialities. Do such sequences exist before they are created? The compilation of notes in Beethoven's Ninth Symphony has been theoretically possible since the dawn of time itself, but it did not become real until Beethoven gave it life. So also with Shakespeare's sonnets and DaVinci's *Mona Lisa*. Our creations become manifest through experiments of a different kind: those that immortalize the possible rather than illuminate the inevitable.

CoVisioning
We think with others about desired changes to reality.

Thomas Cole, *The Dream of the Architect*, 1840

Practices of Invention

The practice of CoVisioning often finds its roots in shared exploration and observation of the creative environment. During this phase, people exercising genership analyze the world and events around them, dissociating and isolating factors into smaller parts. Understanding such patterns involves grasping the elements that comprise them. When studying the color green, for example, we learn that it becomes visible when we mix the primary colors yellow and blue.

A similar process of analysis is used to understand anything. Think about how people understand a narrative in terms of setting, character, plot, conflict and resolution. Or how someone may employ ideas from physics to understand the flight of a bullet, focusing on mass, speed, trajectory, force and resistance; the ideas employed to analyze something affect what patterns are observed. When people CoVision, however, they bring a diversity of ideas to the process of dissociation and isolation, with a broad spectrum of possible approaches. Imagine a team working to understand patterns within a human situation; the group that includes a sociologist, political scientist, psychologist and theologian will have a broader potential range of analysis than a team that includes only one approach. Consider the team working to design of Apple's iPhone, which combines component elements of computers, mp3 players, telephones, GPS systems and personal digital assistants. The product's creative vision required a team that could bring all of these analytical elements together in a single unit. In a different arena, picture the early development of the World Wide Web, among the most transformational technologies in human history. The Web was developed by envisioning how the functioning of networks, Internet protocols and computer languages could be combined to create a new language (HTML) that would allow for the development of a network that used uniform resource locators (URLs) to create a web of interconnected documents stored on diverse computers. The kaleidoscopic theories and knowledge frames brought to bear upon the visioning process allowed these elements to be marshaled in unprecedented ways.

In contrast to this open and dynamic approach, the generation of ideas for analysis is ceded—within the prism of the Leadership Fallacies— from the group to the messiah, the heroes or a messiah from the past. The result is that the thinking applied to analyzing any situation becomes impoverished and stunted. This has significant consequences for the creative process because the work of dissociating and isolating components provides the building blocks for new visions.

Consider the work of CoVisioning in greater depth by exploring specific strategies:

Reframing

Simple CoVisioning often involves changing the context and reframing. In doing so, two people practicing genership work to take an identifiable pattern and change the setting for it, or alter the wrapper in which they find the pattern. Think of the CoVisioning entailed in creating the first laptop, which involved taking the components of a desktop computer and reframing them to form one portable unit. Or imagine taking a piece of classical music and having the themes played by a rock-and-roll band. The chord progression in Pachelbel's Canon has been reframed in many modern popular songs including Green Day's "Basketcase," and Aerosmith's "Cryin" and Bob Marley's "No Woman, No Cry." In another context, imagine taking a stage play like Hamlet and making it into a motion picture. In these and countless other cases, we take fundamental elements of the pattern and change the context—the frame—in which we observe the pattern.

Construction and Recombination

Another kind of CoVisioning involves construction and recombination that takes pieces of patterns and combines them in new ways. Think of a smartphone, which today integrates elements of phones, cameras and personal computers. Think of a dinner theater, which combines elements of a theater and restaurant. Or an infomercial that embeds advertising within TV programming. The distinction between reframing and recombination is obviously not precise. Recombination takes parts of patterns and combines them so that the original is no longer clearly observable. To the extent that we can observe one of the original patterns, it will appear to us as having been reframed. Iced coffee could be thought of as coffee reframed into a cold beverage or as recombined with ice.

Iteration and Variation

Another core practice of CoVisioning involves iteration and variation;

members of a group practicing genership take a pattern and then work to repeat it, intentionally varying certain elements the way one might vary notes in a melody. Variation has perhaps infinite possibilities but several dominant forms. One involves sequencing: A meal might involve an appetizer, main course, dessert and coffee; imagine a variation such as dessert, main course, coffee and appetizer. To eat such a meal would definitely provide a different experience merely as a result of varying the sequence. Similarly, varying the sequence of melodic notes creates an entirely new theme. Another common variation in iteration involves substitution, in which one element of a pattern is swapped for a new one.

In the Articles of Confederation, the United States government included essentially only a legislative branch—Congress—that provided each state one representative with one vote. In this context, the President of the Continental Congress lacked any real executive power and no federal court system existed whatsoever. During the Constitutional Convention, the framers varied this pattern through several iterations embodied within competing plans:

Plan	Legislature	Executive	Judiciary
Virginia Plan	Bicameral congress with one house selected by direct election at the state level and the second house selected by the first	One-term executive selected by congress	Judiciary function composed of supreme tribunals plus a council of revision that would include the executive, with members selected by congress
New Jersey Plan	Unicameral congress composed of two to seven members per states, who would vote together (one	Executive selected by congress with possibility of more than one executive	Judiciary appointed for life by the Executive branch

	state, one vote)	member	
Hamilton Plan	Bicameral congress with lower house elected by the people and the upper house elected for life by electors (in turn selected by the people)	Life term for an executive called the "governor" selected by electors chosen by the states, and congress would also appoint the state governors	Twelve-member judiciary appointed for life (unclear who would have power of appointment)
The Constitution (as ratified)	Bicameral congress with one house selected by the people within states and the senate selected by state legislatures (two per state)	President elected to four-year terms by electors selected by state legislatures in the manner prescribed by them, with electors for each state equal to the total number of senators and representatives	Judiciary selected to life terms by the president with advice and consent of the senate

As this table shows, the convention members did not select among the competing plans, but rather adopted concepts from each and created a new synthesis. This demonstrates the practice of CoVisioning, in which creators become adept at testing both variations in sequence and substitutions in elements of patterns.

Another common variation involves changing timing and intensity. Think of a basketball team that plays the game by varying the timing and speed of its passes to confuse the opposing team, or a baseball player varying pitches.

Depending on context, there are infinite ways to vary any pattern in human experience.

As a group becomes adept at CoVisioning, it will begin to employ all of these techniques. The group will experiment with and test the results of this process, evaluating what is produced as a result.

The history of the U.S. Constitution's development provides a prime example of a broad range of participants effectively practicing CoVisioning. The Bill of Rights, consisting of the first 10 amendments, was developed after the Constitutional Convention in Philadelphia. The general public does not typically understand that the Bill of Rights—containing perhaps the most sacred provisions of the Constitution to Americans today—did not come into legal effect until more than two years after ratification. The development of the Bill of Rights represented a recontextualization and recombination of many ideas expressed in the Magna Carta, the English Bill of Rights of 1689 and Virginia's Declaration of Rights written in 1776.

The history of the airplane's invention tells a similar kind of story. Wilbur and Orville Wright did not invent air flight from scratch. They spent years studying previous attempts at controlled flight and then began experimenting and systematically reframing, recombining and varying patterns of design employed by previous inventors. The Wright brothers invented the propeller, which was actually a rotating airplane wing employing the force of lift that they had observed in developing the plane's fixed wings. This is a classic example of the recontextualization and recombination employed in CoVisioning. The Wright brothers' sensational initial creation naturally continued to be reframed and varied in successive iterations of the flying machine.

CoVisioning and Shared Ownership

Within the Leadership Fallacies, vision is the special province of the messiah; group members must tread respectfully if at all. The group understands the messiah as a messenger or custodian of the vision, seen as somehow transcendent and perhaps even beyond the group's ability to understand, shape or question. The messiah may imply that the vision has a divine origin. The result of this posture is to freeze or severely limit creativity, binding it to the capabilities of one person's mind. The messiah owns the vision and everyone else should keep quiet and keep their hands away from it.

The practice of CoVisioning rejects this premise, viewing the vision as living, present, subject to change and development, constantly to be revised and updated in the light of experience. It sees the creative work of mankind as something that will be developed and actively created in the light of experience rather than handed down from above. CoVisioning is democratic and participatory while holding itself open to the potential that what has been created will change and evolve as the future unfolds.

CHAPTER FIVE

RELATIONSHIPS: *FUELING CREATIVITY BY GIVING LIFE TO EMOTION AND MOTIVATION*

Anyone attempting to accomplish something ambitious faces the challenge of managing human energy. Unlike machines, humans cannot sustain significant levels of activity without sleep. Resting, replenishment, healing and playing form critical parts of productive cycles. This is true of individuals and teams at both the physical and psychological levels.

As individuals and group members, we possess a visceral experience of critical energy— motivation—that ebbs and flows. Like the tides, at times we feel full and high, at times low and distant, waiting for restoration. We observe the level and intensity of motivation in teams and other individuals, knowing that those with high motivation are much more likely to succeed. Yet within most organizations, the underlying complex nature of that motivation is poorly understood and managed; business tends to rely on the blunt lever of money. Cash becomes a crude adrenalin pump, promised to spur action and either threatened or subtracted to quell it.

Essential to every creative process, motivation flows from emotional dynamics much more intricate than can be influenced through simple rewards or threats. Motivational complexities arising from personal identity, relationships, culture and social networks are often obscure within individuals, groups and organizations. In many settings within cultures focused on productivity, emotions are disregarded as being irrelevant or not appropriate to discuss publicly. In such settings, reason often maintains a significant priority over emotion, and members of groups are taught to hide or suppress their emotional responses. There is widespread agreement among people familiar with Japanese culture that displays of emotion there are much more restrained than in American society. Researchers have also observed stark differences in display of emotion within Western cultures. French employees dealing with American service professionals invented the expression "la culture Mickey Mouse" to describe what they perceive as an unduly repressive approach to expressing feelings in service situations. Transcending primal carrot-and-stick approaches to the development of motivation within individuals and teams depends upon gaining a deep understanding of such emotional dynamics.

Mastering Emotion, Motivation & Relationships

- Emotions and Movement
- Relationships as Emotional Incubators

Aljaz Zajc, *Rainbow Gathering*, 2007

Emotions and Movement

What exactly are emotions and how do they relate to motivation? The

Latin word *movere* that serves as the root of emotion means 'to move.' Emotions are closely related to movement. When we feel something deep within, we say that we are moved, sensing fundamental forces of attraction and repulsion within our consciousness and physical being. Within the realm of genership and leadership, emotions fall into two fundamental categories: desire (moving toward) and rejection (moving away). Every emotion—love, hope, joy, relief, fear, jealousy, hatred, anger, shame—can be described in terms of an urge to move toward or away from something, someone or some state of experience.

To feel love is to want to move toward what or whom we love, to be near, to spend time together. To hate something or someone is to want to get away. Jealousy is the desire to move toward that possessed exclusively by another. Shame is the desire to move away from a condition or state of being associated with one's identity. Even an explicitly complex emotion such as schadenfreude can be described as being attracted to (wanting to dwell upon or think about) the misfortune of a person whom we dislike. Millions of years of evolution have programmed humans to be adept not only at reading emotions but also at sharing them. If our empathy is well developed, we feel the happiness of another's laughter and the sadness of her tears. We also carry innate biological sensitivity to group boundaries and status changes. We feel something when people enter and leave our groups, and we intuitively measure our prestige within social hierarchies. Over millennia, our psychologies have become specially evolved and adapted in this way because those lacking such capacities did not survive and reproduce. Thus we can feel complex emotions such as jealousy and schadenfreude in which our emotional response runs counter to empathy, producing negative feelings when a competitor succeeds and positive feelings when we perceive his failure or frustration.

Emotion deeply informs motivation; strong emotional intensity provides the energy for action. Weak intensity manifests as low energy, producing ineffective or meaningless responses. Individuals and teams may learn to mask their emotions, expressing feeling only through movement toward what they desire and away from what they detest. In some cultures, direct displays of emotion are not common and may be viewed as wasted opportunities for action. Expressions such as "Don't get mad, get even" and "Still waters run deep" exemplify this recognition that powerful emotional responses may remain hidden while they animate action from beneath the surface.

Emotions serve as critical regulating mechanisms over the energy levels of individuals and teams, providing infusions of energy when matters of great importance are unfolding, and allowing for periods of rest and recovery when they subside. Substantial opportunities and threats produce strong emotional reactions, while those judged to be less important produce lighter responsive energy. Someone who notices a $100 bill lying in the road will have a much greater emotional reaction than one who sees a $1 bill. Spotting a burglar outside one's window at 2 a.m. would produce a stronger emotional reaction than seeing a raccoon or cat. Emotions provide creative energy to meet the positive and negative circumstances confronting us on a daily basis. Successful teams learn to harness this emotional energy. Such responses may occur spontaneously and organically or may be engineered by leaders within a group who manage or manipulate perceptions to influence emotional drives.

Relationships: Incubators of Emotion and Motivation

Relationships between individuals form the nucleus of emotional—and therefore, motivational—power in human communities. Relationships serve as the generators and pressure valves for our emotional responses. At the heart of every human aspiration to create is a relationship. We never create in a vacuum. Our creations always have an audience, even if that consists only of our own reflection upon what we have created. Through the practice of self-reflection upon our own creative choices, we develop the power to think about what others have created and to collaborate with them. Our relationships are deeply impacted by what we create in our own lives, and how we reflect upon and share creative projects with others.

Across all human cultures, relationships develop over lifespans. We enter the world through the primary dialogues formed with ourselves, parents or caretakers. They become the model for relations with relatives, friends, other members of the community and those whom we learn to dislike or even to hate because they threaten individual or group creative projects. This foundational network of relationships prefigures those that develop within and between organizations and more amorphous social groups as one enters maturity. Through religious education and experience, many individuals also experience a relationship with God not as an abstract being but as an individual personhood possessing a consciousness, manifesting desires and expressing emotions about our creative choices. Any and all of these relationships can become the generators and regulators of emotional and motivational power.

The impact of relationships upon creative motivation is something we understand intuitively and with a great sense of immediacy but not necessarily insightfully and with precision. We tend not to appreciate fully the extent to which our individualized identity is a psychological illusion. Because we cannot understand ourselves except through the lens provided by our relationships, even our self-reflection is itself an expression of our personal networks. Of course, the reverse is true also; through dialogue, we construct the sense of individual identity that others experience. Others learn to see themselves as we see them. Modern telecommunications has made this dynamic of interconnected human identity even more profound. We are constantly plugged into this network via television, cellphone, Internet, email, text messaging and other emergent technologies, as well as being physically surrounded by those in our family, workplace and community; relationships are the means through which we understand our identity and help others comprehend theirs. Modern social networks like Facebook and LinkedIn are not simply ways of connecting with others; they also define and develop how we see the reality of our own consciousness along with that of our constantly evolving network.

Relationships are able to serve as emotional generators and regulators because they provide the primary medium through which we develop our individual and group sense of vision and current reality. We cultivate our sense of personal vision through the dialogue that we sustain with ourselves, God and those around us. By definition, our desires encompass what should be avoided in the future as well as what is sought. For example, our relationship with God, combined with a parental relationship, may cause us to develop a personal vision to live within the bounds of moral and legal laws. This may well attract us toward creations that are lawful—creating a successful business or philanthropy or marriage—and revulsion from those that are unlawful.

Beyond serving to develop the content of our personal visions, relationships also deliver a particular emotional charge—the level of energy we bring to pursuing our vision. We may be strongly impassioned or feel something less dynamic. Every aspiration holds a specific emotional charge, not all of which are equal across diverse situations and cultures.

A person's network of relationships may create a series of aspirations related to personal health, family obligations, accomplishments at work and community projects, among many others. For a particular person, the intensity of the emotional charge associated with caring for a child may exceed those associated with physical appearance or personal health. Such matters naturally depend on the individual and interpersonal networks involved. The crucial observation here is that visions are not simply tactical and pragmatic, like a to-do list, but stem from at least two factors.

The first involves centrality to an ideal personal identity, a detailed vision of who one hopes to become. One who sees himself as a devout Christian will experience a strong emotional intensity surrounding life purposes that closely relate to faith and morality. A professional basketball player who dreams of one day entering the hall of fame likely carries within him an idealized vision of his identity as a successful athlete, imbuing related aspirations—to win an NBA championship—with emotional intensity.

If a person's central vision of identity—a picture of his or her ultimate positive potential— lacks a powerful emotional charge, then other secondary aspects building from it may also suffer. To understand the departure of genership from traditional leadership, we must recognize the role of empathy in developing our sense of idealized identity. Empathy allows us to feel and adopt someone else's emotional state as our own, to feel the emotional charges that others carry initially. If our parents or teachers hold a key vision that a person should be honest, we may first experience its emotional power through empathy, understanding the associated emotional charge they have connected to this specific identity.

The second factor related to emotional intensity involves our assessment of current reality. When we perceive that we are moving *away* from an aspiration holding a strong emotional charge, our intensity increases. On the other hand, as we move *toward* our vision, intensity diminishes and we experience this release of tension as pleasure, a release of dopamine into the brain that gives rise to euphoric feelings. An opposing dynamic appears with respect to negative visions, those that we wish to avoid. Approaching them, our emotional intensity increases, and then diminishes as we move away or they become less likely to manifest. Our sense of current reality defines our awareness of whether we approach or retreat from the visions we love and those we fear.

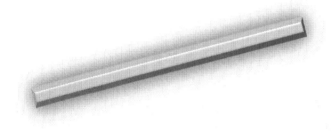

Beethoven:
Emotion and Motivation in the Life of a Creator

"Ah, it seemed to me impossible to leave the world until I had brought forth all that I felt was within me. So I endured this wretched existence...."
—Beethoven's *Heiligenstadt* Testament, 1802

By age 31, Beethoven was already an accomplished composer, having completed his first symphony, several piano concertos and many of his most beloved works of chamber and piano music, including the famous "Moonlight" sonata. Unfortunately, he had begun a physical decline that plagued him for the rest of his life and included the steady erosion of his hearing, yet doubtless contributed to the deepening progression of his art. In October 1802, living as a recluse and approaching a nervous breakdown, he poured his heart into a letter that he kept hidden until after his death more than 24 years later:

[S]ix years ago I was attacked by an incurable malady, aggravated by unskillful physicians, deluded from year to year, too, by the hope of relief, and at length forced to the conviction of a lasting affliction (the cure of which may go on for years, and perhaps after all prove impracticable).

Born with a passionate and excitable temperament, keenly susceptible to the pleasures of society, I was yet obliged early in life to isolate myself, and to pass my existence in solitude. If I at any time resolved to surmount all this, oh! how cruelly was I again repelled by the experience, sadder than ever, of my defective hearing! — and yet I found it impossible to say to others: Speak louder; shout! for I am deaf! Alas! how could I proclaim the deficiency of a sense which ought to have been more perfect with me than with other men, — a sense which I once possessed in the highest perfection, to an extent, indeed, that few of my profession ever enjoyed! Alas, I cannot do this! Forgive me therefore when you see me withdraw from you with whom I would so gladly mingle. My misfortune is doubly severe from causing me to be misunderstood. No longer can I enjoy recreation in social intercourse, refined conversation, or mutual outpourings of thought. Completely isolated, I only enter society when compelled to do so. I must live like an exile. In company I am assailed by the most painful apprehensions, from the dread of being exposed to the risk of my condition being observed. It was the same during the last six months I spent in the country. My intelligent physician recommended me to spare my hearing as much as possible, which was quite in accordance with my present disposition, though sometimes, tempted by my natural inclination for society, I allowed myself to be beguiled into it. But what humiliation when any one beside me heard a flute in the far distance, while I heard nothing, or when others heard a shepherd singing, and I still heard nothing! Such things brought me to the verge of desperation, and well-nigh caused me to put an end to my life. Art! art alone deterred me. Ah! how could I possibly quit the world before bringing forth all that I felt it was my vocation to produce? And thus I spared this miserable life — so utterly miserable that any sudden change may reduce me at any moment from my best condition into the worst. It is decreed that I must now choose Patience for my guide! This I have done. I hope the resolve will not fail me, steadfastly to persevere till it may please the inexorable Fates to cut the thread of my life. Perhaps I may get better, perhaps not. I am prepared for either. Constrained to become a philosopher in my twenty-eighth year! This is no slight trial, and more severe on an artist than on any one else. God looks into my heart, He searches it, and knows that love for man and feelings of benevolence have their abode there! Oh! ye who may one day read this, think that you have done me injustice, and let any one similarly afflicted be consoled, by finding one like himself, who, in defiance of all the obstacles of Nature, has done all in his power to be included in the ranks of estimable artists and men. ... So be it then! I joyfully hasten to meet Death. If he comes before I have had the opportunity of developing all my artistic powers, then, notwithstanding my cruel fate, he will come too early for me, and I should wish for him at a more distant period; but even then I shall be content, for his advent will release me from a state of endless suffering. Come when he may, I shall meet him with courage. Farewell! Do not quite forget me, even in death; I deserve this from you, because during my life I so often thought of you, and wished to make you happy. Amen![x]

Most striking in Beethoven's misery is his deep emotional longing to create, his art being the spiritual energy keeping him from collapsing into despair, his incredible will not to "quit the world before bringing forth all that I felt it was my vocation to produce." From the depths of this despair, his creative vision impelled Beethoven to continue on through deafness and painful illnesses (a combination of chronic nervous and gastrointestinal maladies) while composing his greatest symphonies and experimental works that would change the nature of music for all time. Beethoven's testament stands as a monument to the power of emotional and spiritual energy—and motivation—in the face of continuous physical decline. The testament also shows the primal quality of Beethoven's relationship with his own spirit and the sense in which he served as an audience for his own works, art that he could no longer experience with his ears but nevertheless profoundly with his imagination.

Zones of Emotion and Motivation

The Vision Dimension

We can think of vision as the feature of our imagination that allows us to project our desires, hopes and fears into potential future states of being and experience. As we engage in this active imagining, we have the power to choose from and combine potential elements, creating aspirations that satisfy our deepest desires while avoiding outcomes that we dislike, fear or despise.

Vision falls along a spectrum from highly favored states of being to those that are loathed. Within particular cultures, there are obviously shared aspirations and fears. Most people wish to avoid illness, deprivation and death, while they long for health, life and wealth. Many desires and fears are by nature intensely personal. A particular person may hold a deep aspiration to climb Mt. Kilimanjaro and a simultaneous terrible fear of spiders. What provokes a deep passion for one person may leave another cold or unmoved. One might feel a strong desire to take a vacation in Hawaii, but remain neutral about traveling to Atlantic City.

We can picture visions falling along a vertical spectrum. At the base are strong fears, states of being (negative visions) that we passionately want to avoid (e.g., death, illness, deprivation). At the spectrum's center fall states about which one feels neutral. At the top are positives, states of being that we ardently wish to attain (e.g., health, prosperity, love).

The Reality Dimension

Current reality falls along the spectrum from states that we feel very certain are true, to those shrouded in doubt or ignorance, to those that we know are false. This comports with our common-sense awareness that there are some things we know with great certainty (the current time and date) while other matters clearly are not true (humans cannot fly under their own power, nor are they capable of telekinesis). On the other hand, there are some things that we cannot know with certainty (next week's weather, the worth of our investments in the extended future or our health).

At the far left of the Reality Dimension fall matters that we know with certainty are not true. In the center we would find situations that we do not know with certainty. What we are sure about rests at the far right. This spectrum may vary considerably across different people and contexts. An investment banker focuses on key economic indicators, knowing some facts with great certainty. These form the opposing poles of the spectrum—those that are clearly true and not so. A banker also generally holds a certain set of observations in doubt; there are some realities about which he or she would be currently unsure or lack information despite their concrete nature: the center of the spectrum. The economic growth rate for a market is a tangible variable affecting valuations, yet we only perceive it in hindsight and its measure fluctuates when observed through diverse economic indicators, including changes in the gross domestic product and inflation rate.

When we lay the vision (vertical) over the reality (horizontal), four quadrants emerge:

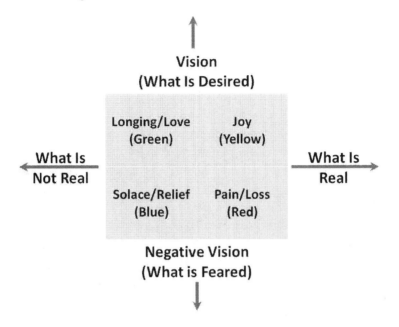

**Vision
(What Is Desired)**

Longing/Love (Green)   Joy (Yellow)

What Is Not Real   **What Is Real**

Solace/Relief (Blue)   Pain/Loss (Red)

**Negative Vision
(What is Feared)**

1. Red Zone (lower right)—something we do not want to happen (a negative vision or fear) has actually become true. Picture a gambler placing all his winnings on the roulette table and betting on red. As he sees the ball fall into a black space, he feels "red" emotions: anger, frustration, loss. What he did not want—to lose—has now become reality. Or imagine a politician seeking reelection and seeing his shortfall in the final vote count.

2. Blue Zone (lower left)—something we do not want to happen has actually not happened. A worker fears being fired after having made a mistake. He is called in to see his supervisor and advised that he will be given one more chance. He feels a sense of relief. This emotion and its related feelings all concern the sensation of deliverance, respite or solace felt when we avoid something detested or feared.

3. Green Zone (upper left)—we do not presently have something that we want. Imagine an NFL receiver running a route in the middle of a championship game. As he chases the pass, catches the ball and heads

for the goal line, he is solidly in the green zone, animated with the emotion of striving and longing for his yet-to-be-achieved vision of scoring a touchdown. Or a man who longs to marry a particular woman. When he buys an engagement ring and prepares to make his proposal, he is animated by green-zone emotions: hope, anticipation, longing and love.

4. Yellow Zone (upper right)—we have obtained something we desire. Picture the above man at the moment he is married, the receiver running into the end zone after catching a pass, or a woman who seeks to climb a mountain as she scales the summit. This emotion and its cousins (joy, happiness, elation) represent the pleasurable release of tension that we experience upon achieving our vision.

The emotional quadrants defined above provide an evocative rather than definitive guide to understanding the creative dynamics that underlie emotional states. Real emotions blend and traverse these quadrants, reflecting the complex motivational currents that inform productive activity. An unemployed executive who obtains a job that she has been passionately seeking may feel a diverse set of emotions that intermingle yellow-, blue- and green-zone feelings: joy in obtaining the position desired, relief at avoiding the problems of lacking income and hope about future promotions. Similarly, someone recovering from a serious illness may experience a range of red-, blue- and green-zone emotions: pain in confronting persistent symptoms, relief as the symptoms retreat and hope about energies and abilities that the healing process will soon restore.

Women often surpass men in perceiving and understanding both their own and others' feelings. Daniel Goleman, author of the internationally best-selling book, *Emotional Intelligence* (1995, Bantam Books), explains why:

> Women tend to be better at emotional empathy than men, in general. This kind of empathy fosters rapport and chemistry. People who excel in emotional empathy make good counselors, teachers, and group leaders because of this ability to sense in the moment how others are reacting. Neuroscientists tell us one key to empathy is a brain region called the insula, which senses signals

from our whole body. When we're empathizing with someone, our brain mimics what that person feels, and the insula reads that pattern and tells us what that feeling is. Here's where women differ from men. If the other person is upset, or the emotions are disturbing, women's brains tend to stay with those feelings. But men's brains do something else: they sense the feelings for a moment, then tune out of the emotions and switch to other brain areas that try to solve the problem that's creating the disturbance.[xi]

Emotional Intensity

We can also use the diagram formed by the Vision and Reality axes to understand emotional intensity, defined as the area measured from a particular coordinate to the center of the axis. This focus arises from strongly charged visions and fears, combined with clear knowledge that these states of being either exist or have not yet come to pass. So one might greatly fear being murdered, but if blown up instantly without any knowledge of the impending doom, there is no emotional response to this event; fear did not manifest on the Reality axis, so emotional intensity remained at zero.

On the other hand, suppose one is told that a company is considering layoffs, causing a great fear of being unemployed. This possibility appears on the Reality axis, against a substantial fear producing significant emotional intensity. Notice that emotional intensity can be drained on either spectrum. If a person being terminated did not care about his job, then it does not register on the Vision spectrum and not much intensity is generated from the job loss. Intensity can also be drained by illusion about reality. If a person who cares about his job is told falsely that layoffs will be delayed for a long period of time, his emotional intensity will diminish in the interim.

A person planning a gathering learns that a recent acquaintance will definitely be five minutes late to the event. The planner does not have a strong emotional response to this situation because even though he has a clear sense of reality (the guest will definitely be late), this assessment is related to someone he does not know well (low on the vision/desire meter), and further, the deviation from vision (a event that proceeds as scheduled) is quite minor.

It is through our ability to engage in a dialogue with ourselves, as well as through our network of relationships, that we learn to develop and accurately assess aspirations and fears. If we strongly desire to be a good parent and our self-assessment is that we are failing to achieve this, emotional intensity will increase; similarly, if we aspire to avoid association with criminals, we will suffer strong feelings if we learn through dialogue that someone within our network is engaged in criminal activity. Such emotions arise through relationships that imbue visions with an emotional charge and then influence our perception of movement toward or away from that desired or feared.

Steve Wozniak's Creation of the Personal Computer

Steve Wozniak's memoir, *iWoz*, stands as a compelling testament to the creative process. By his own account, Wozniak's creativity did not stem from pursuit of fortune, fame or power, but rather from the sheer joy of invention and tinkering. During his development of designs for the personal computer, he worked as an engineer for Hewlett Packard, in the division of the company that produced calculators.

While Wozniak loved his job at HP, it was his hobby with the Homebrew Computer Club—an informal association of computer hobbyists—that inspired his personal-computer designs. His fascination with electronics and interest in computers dated back to his childhood, and most importantly to a loving relationship with his father, an electrical engineer at Lockheed Martin who taught Wozniak the fundamentals of math and electrical engineering as a boy.

Even though Wozniak had already founded Apple Computer with Steve Jobs, he loved HP; his sense of duty to the company impelled him to offer HP his personal-computer design before attempting to proceed with its development at Apple. In a legendary failure to recognize creative genius, HP rejected Wozniak's design, leading eventually to his departure from the company and Apple's launch of the PC industry.

Wozniak had this to say: "In my heart, I wanted to be an HP employee for life." What is most striking about Wozniak's motivation and passion is its primal source in his sense of identity as an engineer within a community of engineering professionals. His almost limitless energy for design sprung from the connection between his idealized identity as an engineer and his personal vision to create designs that would delight his own sensibility as well as those of immediate friends and colleagues. His generosity inspired him to share these designs and even to attempt to give them away. Remarkably, when Apple went public, Wozniak insisted—even in the face of company disapproval—on sharing some of his personal stock with a number of line-engineering employees so that they could benefit financially from the company's extraordinary success.

These dynamics apply with equal force in thinking about groups, which develop visions and invest them with emotional energy in the same way as individuals. A group's motivational state arises not only from the network of dialogue unfolding within it, but also from what develops between the group and outsiders.

Think about an elementary school. Individual teachers and administrators collectively form a vision and sense of current reality regarding the school, further developed through dialogue with the parents, students, board of directors, regulators and members of the larger community. Similarly, sports teammates have both internal and external conversations that inform their sense of vision and reality, shaping these elements not only among themselves but through dialogue with spectators, family members, coaches and members of other teams.

Within organizations today, leaders recognize the importance of motivation to organizational performance, but often lack coherent ideas and practical tools for developing it. Many leaders rely on the bluntest of instruments, focusing primarily on increasing financial rewards and social recognition in exchange for performance. There is little understanding or awareness within most organizational dialogue about the strategic impact of emotion, emotional energy, motivation and relationships. When leaders undertake this work, they often attend to it using their intuition, relying on instincts developed from experience. Lacking an explicit conceptual framework, this approach yields inconsistent and sometimes inexplicable results. Consultants steeped in organizational psychology may rely on concepts borrowed from psychoanalytic theory involving the satisfaction of drives, while those steeped in sociology and group psychology seek to explain motivation descriptively with reference to the process of obtaining status within social groups. These theories generally fail to capture fundamental elements of motivation as it relates to creativity.

Relationships serve as the primary medium through which emotions and motivations are shared and shaped among groups of individuals. At times, individual emotions are magnified and inflamed by social networks; at other times, modulated and suppressed. The impact on emotional states arises from manipulation of the vision/reality dimensions described above. Individuals are capable of reading and responding to the emotional states of others depending on the nature of their relationships. One strong measure of intimacy and emotional bonding is the extent to which we experience the emotions and motivations of others as our own. The capacity of empathy allows us to understand and feel the emotional states of others, serving as shorthand for the more complex assessment about what happens in groups. If one enters a group that is in a state of crisis and panic, one will feel these emotions before understanding their source.

We know that humans are capable of extraordinary blindness to others' perspectives and feelings. Nevertheless, our capacity to perceive and share (in the sense of actually feeling) another person's emotions should not surprise us. Empathy, defined as the capacity to feel what another feels—to imagine another being's experience as if it were ours—is a capacity honed through countless millennia of evolutionary forces. As primatologist Frans de Waal argues persuasively, empathetic relationships forged in collaboration are as fundamental to the survival of life as competitive behaviors. De Waal's insightful exposition, marshaling not only anecdotes but laboratory science, comports with common-sense observation of cooperation within species and families. Across mammals, mothers are able to read and respond to the emotions of their offspring. This happens not simply intellectually as abstract knowledge but through feelings that create powerful motivations. Survival from generation to generation clearly requires it. Such capacities run deep into our evolutionary biological heritage. Even social insects such as ants and bees demonstrate complex cooperative behaviors that imply action based on understanding, concern and motivation about the fate of others.

Genership sharply diverges from conventional leadership in the management of emotion, motivation and relationships within groups. Given a culture steeped in leadership rather than genership, groups fall under the spell of the Fallacies. Members begin to experience and be moved by what they imagine is the messiah's state, a dynamic that suppresses their individualized experiences. In this way, the aspirations and fears of one person, or of a small leadership group, take on supreme importance; group members begin to live vicariously through the lives of their leaders.

In this setting a subtle but critical transformation may take place. Individual group members sometimes cease to explore their subjective vision and do not make a personal assessment of current reality. Instead, through an empathic process, they adopt those of the messiah. They also may cease to explore his perspective and instead simply begin to respond to his emotional state; group members become extensions and replicators of the messiah's emotional energy. If he is energized, the group is energized; if relaxed, the group is relaxed; if despairing, the group despairs. An almost mystical psychological and spiritual connection between the group and its leader becomes manifest.

Being Hillary Clinton

The 2008 Iowa Democratic caucus vote placed Hillary Clinton third, an unexpected outcome that found the candidate in a must-win situation going forward if she were to have any chance at her party's presidential nomination. Her main challenger's strength belied his standing as a youthful, somewhat inexperienced candidate and first-term Illinois senator. She, on the other hand, was for decades in the center of power first through her husband and then her own capture of a New York Senate seat. While expecting somewhat straightforward primary victories, she instead witnessed the momentum shift toward Obama. In the day before the New Hampshire primary, a middle-aged woman asked, "How did you get out the door every day? I mean, as a woman, I know how hard it is to get out of the house and get ready."

Clinton became clearly emotional, with voice and tears on tap; whether purposely or spontaneously she replied, "I just don't want to see us fall backward as a nation. I mean, this is very personal for me, not just political. I see what's happening. We have to reverse it. Some people think elections are a game: who's up or who's down. It's about our country. It's about our kids' future. It's about all of us out there together."

After adding a number of aspects from her more standard speech, Clinton reintroduced the personal element: "This is one of the most important elections we'll ever face. So as tired as I am and as difficult as it is to keep up what I try to do on the road, like occasionally exercise, trying to eat right... It's tough when the easiest thing is pizza." She then finished her speech in a quiet voice (for effect or genuine reaction?) that listeners strained to hear. "I just believe... so strongly in who we are as a nation. I'm going to do everything that I can to make my case and then the voters get to decide."

The state's electorate became moved by Hillary Clinton's personal drama as much as the policies she advocated, and responded with a 39- to 36-point win over Obama; the candidate declared that she had found her own voice on that Portsmouth day. The media, however, had other ideas, much of it negative. Her tears, finding her voice, humanizing herself... Was this the Clinton they had known all those years or a carefully calculated effort at pulling the clichéd heartstrings? Maureen Dowd—the experienced *New York Times* columnist—reprinted the observation of a fellow reporter: "That crying really seemed genuine. I'll bet she spent hours thinking about it beforehand." Was it her hiring of drama and vocal coach Michael Sheehan that set the stage for this new, improved, accessible and vulnerable Hillary Clinton? The more conservative commentators clearly did not buy the tears and had fun indignantly knocking her down.

In those few New Hampshire days, at least, the cold, calculating candidate had indeed changed to someone more emotional, more open, more ready to acknowledge humanity. Under the spell of the Fallacies, people seem to have ignored their own previously demonstrated reluctance to support her. Could she be the new messiah? Had her own aspirations and fears taken on supreme importance to New Hampshire voters, through whom they could live vicariously? She may have endlessly debated gender norms versus projecting a presidential visage in a male against female internal drama. As Secretary of State rather than presidential candidate, however, there is little room for such interplay; the world takes for granted the toughness of her outward life and she appears happy to oblige.

—R.R.

Living Vicariously

Given this underlying connection between the leader and followers, the central questions that confront a group's emotional and motivational status no longer relate to the content of its vision and judgments about reality. Instead, the group's emotional and motivational states become deeply connected to the messiah's personal narrative. As the messiah fails, the group psychology becomes bonded to the narratives of the competing heroes. The question about the group's performance is understood through the lens of the messiah's status. So, for example, as a proxy for measuring the nation's economic prospects, the Gallup organization measures how the public feels about the president's performance. During the election season, measurements about the public's view of presidential competitors also take the stage. Rather than think about the national aspiration for the economy and current economic indicators, the question becomes reframed when we labor under the Fallacies: How does the messiah feel (in this case, the president of the United States)? If there is low energy in the economy, it is because the messiah has failed to galvanize the emotional energy of the nation. Stepping back from this example and assessing clearly, it is astoundingly silly to think that the emotional energy of one person could impact the economic reality of a nation composed of hundreds of millions of individuals and billions of economic transactions. Nevertheless, the group and leader behave as if this were true. Management of the nation's emotional energy is thought to be a responsibility of leadership.

Leadership and the Fisher King

A figure drawn from Arthurian legend and Celtic mythology, the Fisher King—or the Wounded King—appears within the Holy Grail narratives. In variations of the stories, the king is always wounded in the legs or groin, and incapable of moving on his own. He is mysteriously linked with the land and people. Through his injury, his kingdom suffers, with his impotence affecting fertility and rendering his domain a barren wasteland. Little is left for him to do but fish in a nearby river. Knights travel from far and wide to heal the Fisher King, but only the chosen one can accomplish the feat: restoring the King, and thereby the kingdom, to health.

In early 1979, the Islamic revolution in Iran led to an oil crisis, causing gas prices in America to rise sharply in the wake of shortages, sowing the seeds of a painful recession that would take hold during the 1980 election year. Long lines at the pump across the nation fomented deep-seated anger, which was directed at the nation's leader, President Carter. As messiah-in-chief, many felt that it was his responsibility to fix the problem. His approval rating dropped to 25%.

In July, the president huddled with a team of advisors at Camp David, grappling with how public opinion had turned against him, holding him responsible for the nation's economic woes. Carter's pollster, Patrick Caddell argued that the negative years leading to Carter's presidency—dominated by war, political scandal, economic decline, and the violent deaths of inspirational leaders such as John and Robert Kennedy and Martin Luther King—had rattled American confidence. Buying into the idea that the president could and should be charged with the emotional and motivational leadership of the people, Caddell urged Carter to make an inspirational speech.

On July 15, 1979, Carter delivered his famous "Crisis of Confidence" speech to the nation. He began by emphasizing the deep connection between himself and the people: "I promised you a president who is not isolated from the people, who feels your pain, and who shares your dreams and who draws his strength and his wisdom from you."

But then the president departed from the messiah narrative. Rather than heaping the problems of America on his own shoulders and telling the people that he would fix everything, he decided to tell them that the fault lay in their own moral choices and values:

> But after listening to the American people, I have been reminded again that all the legislation in the world can't fix what's wrong with America. So, I want to speak to you first tonight about a subject even more serious than energy or inflation. I want to talk to you right now about a fundamental threat to American democracy.

> I do not mean our political and civil liberties. They will endure. And I do not refer to the outward strength of America, a nation that is at peace tonight everywhere in the world, with unmatched economic power and military might.

> The threat is nearly invisible in ordinary ways. It is a crisis of confidence. It is a crisis that strikes at the very heart and soul and spirit of our national will. We can see this crisis in the growing doubt about the meaning of our own lives and in the loss of a unity of purpose for our nation.

The president then urged the people to take charge of their own circumstances, looking not to Washington, but rather, into the mirror:

> First of all, we must face the truth, and then we can change our course. We simply must have faith in each other, faith in our ability to govern ourselves and faith in the future of this nation. Restoring that faith and that confidence to America is now the most important task we face. It is a true challenge of this generation of Americans.

> One of the visitors to Camp David last week put it this way: 'We've got to stop crying and start sweating, stop talking and start walking, stop cursing and start praying. The strength we need will not come from the White House, but from every house in America.'

> We know the strength of America. We are strong. We can regain our unity. We can regain our confidence. We are the heirs of generations who survived threats much more powerful and

awesome than those that challenge us now. Our fathers and mothers were strong men and women who shaped a new society during the Great Depression, who fought world wars and who carved out a new charter of peace for the world. . . .

We are at a turning point in our history. There are two paths to choose. One is a path I've warned about tonight, the path that leads to fragmentation and self-interest. Down that road lies a mistaken idea of freedom, the right to grasp for ourselves some advantage over others. That path would be one of constant conflict between narrow interests ending in chaos and immobility. It is a certain route to failure.

All the traditions of our past, all the lessons of our heritage, all the promises of our future point to another path, the path of common purpose and the restoration of American values.

The president concluded his speech by pointing out what Americans could do as individuals in local communities to tackle the nation's energy crisis while outlining dramatic policy goals pointed at reducing American dependence on foreign oil.

At first Carter's speech was hailed as unprecedented straight talk to the American people and he enjoyed a significant bump in his approval ratings, which quickly rose more than 10 points. Soon, however, political pundits began to spin Carter's departure from the expected messianic narrative as a failure of leadership. Ted Kennedy, who challenged Carter for the democratic nomination, complained that "the people are blamed for every national ill, scolded as greedy, wasteful and mired in malaise." The aspiring messiah Ronald Reagan piled on as well: "I find no national malaise. I find nothing wrong with the American people."

In the fall of 1979, as Carter's administration became embroiled in the Iranian hostage crisis while a recession took hold, it became all too easy to suggest that the nation was weak because Carter was weak, like the Fisher King, and that America's problems could be fixed by electing a new messiah, one capable of rescuing the people. As in the legend, the leader and the land were seen to be inexorably linked. Reagan famously remarked, "Recession is when your neighbor loses his job. Depression is when you lose yours. And recovery is when Jimmy Carter loses his."

Decades later, the themes in Carter's speech have proved to be among the most important to American character and prosperity. Many have also commented that the fundamental points made in Carter's speech are inherently conservative in locating the solution to the nation's challenges in the people, rather than their government. Hendrik Hertzberg, author of Carter's speech, later commented incisively that while Carter "turned out to be a true prophet, he turned out not to be a savior." Carter's departure from the messiah narrative led directly to his departure from office.

Vicarious Emotions and Motivations

This dynamic (prioritizing the messiah's emotional state) finds its roots in childhood. As infants, we practice empathy by learning to read the emotional states of our parents. A healthy child learns to understand when mommy or daddy is angry, upset, happy or sad. Children then regulate their own emotional intensity based on that experienced by their parents. This is highly adaptive—a child who learns to be wary when his parents are wary, who learns to relax only when his parents feel relaxed, is more likely to survive. As they mature, many people learn to transfer this empathetic response to relationships with leaders at the organizational and societal levels. In popular culture, many individuals cease to participate as equals in the development and regulation of their emotional states, instead choosing to feel emotions vicariously through celebrity society. So rather than what they can affect through their own behaviors and roles, members of society consider the visions and states of reality occupied by celebrities. These could be sports or political figures, reality-TV personalities, acting stars or fictional characters.

Many people succeed in living their own emotional lives with full participation and also entertaining themselves by considering the emotional states of others. We can think of this aspect of emotional life as a spectrum. At one end associated with high levels of genership, people view their actions and present state of existence in terms of their own unique personal visions, having an intensity determined by and through their most intimate relationships. At the spectrum's other end, associated with high levels of leadership, people view their actions and present reality in terms of the leader's vision. At this other polarity, emotional intensity develops through a primary relationship with the leader in which individual identity is suppressed. The follower takes on the leader's perspective and lives vicariously through him. So the important consideration is one of degree, not whether but to what extent individual energy is determined through a person's own network rather than through a leadership cult of personality.

In this way, leaders operating within the messiah paradigm see themselves as the emotional regulators of their organizations, actively pushing followers to experience their emotional life rather than their own. This ethos is especially well illustrated in the feudal concept of chivalry (within Japanese culture, bushido). This entails a warrior code of conduct in which a knight or samurai pledges to defend and remain loyal to a lord and to sacrifice his life, if necessary, for the lord's benefit. The pledge entails the idea that the warrior's life achieves maximum meaning and value in reference to the lord's life. This idea is celebrated in the legends of knights who die valiantly fighting for their lords, as in the Song of Roland or the legend of the 300 Spartans who died with King Leonidas at the battle of Thermopylae. The nexus between the warrior and the lord is more profoundly illustrated by the practice of *oibara*, involving a ritual suicide following the death of one's master in Japanese feudal society.

Leaders play into these ancient cultural motifs when they manipulate the energy within their groups to achieve high levels of motivation; they foster and leverage emotional bonds with followers based on concepts of loyalty and fealty. Leaders may achieve this by intentionally distorting both vision and current reality, and also by creating emotional bonds involving extreme levels of empathy for the messiah experienced by team members. This may amount to a loss of ego boundary between the messiah and members. To achieve oneness is to live through the messiah and give up individual life at the psychological level, so that the messiah's emotional state is any member's obsessive focus. The messiah may also work to develop unity with a group so they believe that through the messiah's individual life their collective lives acquire definition and meaning. This often manifests as hero worship leading almost to apotheosis in which the followers cease to view their leader in realistic terms, ignoring obvious flaws in his behavior and character traits while attributing godlike perfection to the leader's being and actions.

You Are So Amazing

I once hired a director for a special project. After weeks of working closely together, she told me that I was the most amazing leader she had ever met. She was astounded by my leadership vision and ability to work with people, and in awe of the culture I had created within our organization. She expressed gratitude to be able to learn from me and honored to participate in the project. What was my response?

I told her that she would soon learn about my shortcomings and I hoped she would still feel good about the project when she came to grips with them. I explained my concern that she might be projecting onto me wishes and needs that I could not fulfill. I shared that I felt sure she was going to be disappointed in the future. I assured her that I felt good about her work and my own, but said that we should both keep grounded, recognizing that we are flawed. Through equal teamwork we could strengthen our efforts and compensate for our individual shortcomings. She replied that she knew I was just being humble. "Expect to be let down," said I.

Six months later, she came to me expressing dissatisfaction with her role and a list of complaints about the way our organization operated. "I really expected, given the level of your leadership ability, that you could fix these issues," she said. I reminded her of my warning regarding unfounded expectations. Several months later, she left the team and went through a long period of unemployment, trying to find an organization that "met her values."

As a leader in many organizations and programs throughout my life, I have experienced this pattern before. People become star-struck about the person in the leadership role, projecting onto him or her their fantasies and wishes for organizational life. They expect the leader to serve as combination magician/parent who will take care of their needs. When this fails, as it inevitably must, they become extremely disappointed, reject this person and go in search of others to provide rescue. The process is generally frustrating and unproductive. Psychological maturity is often about people seeing others accurately and not as they would wish them to be.

When a team member in my organization develops a clear vision about the shortcomings and strengths of everyone on the team, including me, *I know that we will succeed*. In our efforts to marshal complementary abilities, team members transcend their personal limitations. We maintain a grounded, realistic appreciation of one another based upon an accurate evaluation of our respective abilities. If we feel a sense of awe, it comes from the recognition that together we can—through struggle—overcome our individual flaws. Excellent teams magnify strengths and help members compensate for each other's weaknesses. We are not perfect and never will be. But working together, we can strive toward perfection in spite of this reality.

Those who consider themselves messiahs and heroes do not relate as equals to members of the organizations they inhabit. They enjoy a privileged status in which their visions and assessments of current reality dominate those made by other group members. This dominance often affords them heightened control over the group's resources, creating an aura of unparalleled power and influence. Accordingly, their emotional states also overshadow those of group members. Followers who insist on the worth and importance of their own emotional states as opposed to those of the messiah or heroes are perceived as traitors, rebels or competitors for the power enjoyed by the messiah and his inner circle. Self-assertion in such a culture is often met with the question, "Who do you think you are?" The unstated rule is that the individual emotional state of each group member does not matter. How the messiah or the heroes feel is key. Individual members are called upon to sacrifice themselves gladly.

Skilling Leads Enron Over the Cliff

The case of Enron remains a stark warning for boards of directors, managements, employees and stockholders to beware of offering too much concentrated power within a single individual, no matter the charisma and appeal, the promises and riches. When any organization's participants are pressed to believe that their personal visions and assessments are marginal or irrelevant, a man like CEO Jeff Skilling can make others feel almost glad for their sacrifice to the "larger good" despite persistent reservations. A term like "cult" would never survive in any company's annual report, but can well thrive in an obsessive man's dreams.

With the sharp skills of a master manipulator, Skilling

subtly and overtly encouraged those within his sphere to cull favor with him, the savior of a sleepy energy company that he was determined to turn into the world's most valuable corporation. Using peer pressure, ridicule and the ruthless hand of a vested leader, Skilling oversaw the systematic elimination of dissenting opinions while simultaneously consolidating his control. He also hired young employees willing to work up to 80 hours a week, actively encouraging them to sign onto his obsession. In the highly volatile energy sector, companies must consider multiple scenarios to remain competitive, yet Enron's culture dissuaded others from challenging its ordained leader, the man whose image—at least initially—became associated with large bonuses and secure retirements.

Skilling also came to see himself as utterly indispensible to the company's success, regardless of objective evidence to the contrary. This kind of singular self-regard must eventually implode; as the organization grows, it becomes increasingly difficult to maintain effective control with more employees, higher revenues, additional shareholders and relentless competitive pressures. Yet in a demonstration of the increasing fantasy that overtook Skilling's vision, the company's 2000 annual report spoke of imminent multitrillion-dollar market opportunities that were theirs for the taking.

In the absence of dissent, or at least constructive debate, the accumulated experiences, knowledge and client relationships of employees are subsumed. Yet agile corporations seeking to capitalize on fickle marketplaces must draw on the insight and feedback of those on the front lines, and less on the blatant self-promotion of a self-described visionary. Even though employees referred to Skilling internally as Darth Vader in light of his ruthless style, they nonetheless conformed and ultimately witnessed—along with the rest of the business and energy worlds—a vast implosion unlikely to happen again on that scale.

As a follow-up, Jeff Skilling remains in prison serving a quarter-century sentence (in contrast to Darth Vader, who ultimately redeemed himself by dying for his son, Luke).

—R.R.

Motivation via Genership

In contrast, when group members exhibit genership, thereby transcending the Messiah and Hero Fallacies, a radical transformation takes place in these emotional, motivational and relational dynamics. Three elements describe the transformation:

First, group members are no longer regulated by the vision of one person or small team struggling for messiah status. Instead, the group incubates and develops its vision dynamically, allowing it to evolve as members continue to interact with one another moving into the future. Every member is encouraged to offer amendments and refinements to the vision, which is not possessed by any one individual but rather floats within the group as a whole as they evaluate suggestions. In this context, what holds the group together is no longer allegiance to a particular person but rather sincere commitment to an evolving vision. Members may join or leave the group fluidly over time, when it may call forth new team members who have the required special skills, while at the same time releasing others whose skills are no longer critical to the work. The group self-organizes, focusing on the question of whose engagement is required for success. This contrasts with a more leader-centered approach in which the group defines—and often limits—a given task in terms of its capabilities. When members embrace effective genership, the vision continues to acquire increasing charge, active participation and *enthusiasm*, resulting in the group's displaying ever-larger investments of energy in moving toward the articulated vision.

Second, in the presence of effective genership, the assessment of current reality is no longer limited to one person or leadership team. Instead, the entire group enjoys the privilege of offering assessments about group progress and current status. The group embraces and values members for their ability to shed strategic light toward accomplishing its vision. Reality assessments are not viewed as challenges to leadership, but rather as helpful resources guiding the organization toward productivity and efficiency in realizing its ambitions. These make it possible for the group to govern its own emotions and manage its energy effectively. Because a more diverse and larger team is free to make independent reality assessments, rather than relying on a small group, such assessments are more precise and shed clearer light on creative strategies.

As a result of these two dynamics, a group practicing genership has the ability to marshal and manage energy more effectively. It increases overall motivation because its visions now carry a greater charge; its testing of present conditions becomes more precise. The process is similar to increasing the surface area of a sail (vision) while angling it more directly into the wind (reality assessment).

Third, the group's members are equal participants in its creative undertakings, rather than being relegated to the status of cells in the messiah's body or automatons to be directed by the messiah or heroes vying for messiah status. Because genership embodies the perspectives of multiple minds, the group is able to throttle motivational energy to serve its own best interests whether or not congruent with those of the messiah or a leadership subculture. A group that self-directs transcends manipulation; members live fully as individuals because their wills find expression in the group's creative undertakings. They do not lose their individual identities, otherwise subsumed by the messiah's ego. They do not live vicariously through him, but find their lives fully expressed within the group. The relationships in a genership culture form a network capable of sustaining the group's work even if particular members depart; each participant bears responsibility and enjoys fulfillment in connection with the group's creative work. In contrast, when a group labors under the Fallacies, the messiah's departure causes a state of crisis. Of course, such a crisis offers the potential to transition to a genership culture. All too often, however, hero wars erupt through the quest to anoint the new messiah and may continue indefinitely. The group's creative work cannot be sustained during this period unless it practices genership.

To further illustrate the difference between the leadership and genership, picture two contrasting athletic teams. One is built around two stars believed by the group to have abilities that significantly exceed those of other members, who come to believe that the team's success or failure depends on the performance of the stars. If they succeed, the team wins; if not, it loses. Team members understand their primary role as assisting the stars in doing what they do best. When the team wins, its achievement is to have helped the stars. The subsidiary players and the team's emotional life revolve around the stars. If they are highly motivated, the team will do well; if not, it will fare poorly. Popular culture abounds with stories that involve the idiosyncrasies of stars and their impact on team performance. If a sports, movie, business or political star is embroiled in personal problems—health-related, relationship-oriented or legal—the public expects to see performance of the organization (team, cast, corporation or political party) suffer.

In contrast, a team with a high level of genership functions differently: players expect to make strong, equal contributions. Each finds moments during which his individual talents are central to the team's success. If one is not playing to capacity, another will have the chance to step into the spotlight to play at the highest level. The team neither rises nor falls on the performance of one player or a small subset. Its performance stems from the overall ability to coordinate as a group. The individual narrative of a particular player does not cause the group to rise or fall.

League competitions have demonstrated that balanced teams made up of many players who contribute and coordinate equally are capable of competing with—and defeating—teams made up of a few superstars surrounded by players whose only job is to highlight the stars' strengths. In 2004, the Detroit Pistons faced the celebrated Los Angeles Lakers in the NBA finals. The Lakers' Kobe Bryant and Shaquille O'Neal were among the league's most dominant stars, combining to average 45 points per game and making the All-NBA First Team, unlike any of the Pistons' players. Nevertheless, employing balanced team play, the Pistons dominated the finals, winning the championship four games to one. The statistics demonstrate the power of shared teamwork. During the finals, the Pistons' tightly coordinated defense held the Lakers—who had averaged 98 points per game during the season—to less than 82. The Lakers' shooting stars could not overcome the Pistons' balanced scoring contributions. Bryant and O'Neil scored 60% of the Lakers' points during the series while none of their teammates scored more than 10 points during any game. In contrast, the Pistons' top two players scored only 47% of the team's overall points, with three others contributing more than 15 points during individual games.

Emotions and Relationships: Leadership vs. Genership

- Vicarious
  vs. Organic

- Leader-based vs.
  Group-based

- Manipulated
  vs. Authentic

- Identity-related
  vs. Vision-based

Building Relationships: Leadership vs. Genership

In the genership context, building relationships that generate highly motivated teams requires skills very different from those necessary within traditional leadership. Leaders under the spell of the Fallacies learn to manipulate the emotional state of their followers when they advance visions designed to elicit a strong emotional response, and when they manipulate their followers' impressions of current reality to maintain cycles of emotional tension and release. Such tactics can manifest both as creating false impressions of crisis (in which the group sees itself faltering in its progress toward the vision) and similarly fallacious ideas of victory (in which the group sees itself coming close to achieving the vision). Leaders entangled in the Fallacies also learn to develop empathetic responses among their followers, working to create intimacy by sharing personal details of their lives so that the followers may be enticed to see the world through the leaders' emotional lens. When a leader succeeds, followers cease to explore vision and current reality altogether, instead choosing to focus only on the emotional states of the messiah and heroes. This unquestioning focus is then regarded as the highest form of loyalty.

Genership's contrast is profound; individuals work to nurture and understand the independent emotional condition of other group members, ensuring that the state of each is personal and authentic rather than empathic to the leader's emotions. The practitioner of genership becomes adept at assisting others in exploring the dynamics producing their emotional condition, as well as the relation between their emotions and the group's shared efforts. This exploration involves teasing out both the vision and reality assessments that produce a personal emotional state. The inquiry is bilateral and equal; all members participate in sharing their feelings. Through this process, the group as a whole coalesces around common visions that generate maximum positive energy, which requires the development of excellent listening and dialogue skills among all group members. They develop empathy by learning to read and understand their respective emotional states, but do not allow any one member to dominate or direct the group's emotional energy. Nor do they sacrifice their personal emotional states; they avoid transference to the messiah's emotional narrative. It is the members' vision and progress that determine the group's emotion and motivation, rather than their being manipulated by a leader or leadership subgroup embroiled in the Fallacies.

Techniques for Exploring Emotion and Developing Motivation within Genership

Practitioners of genership explore emotions in a group by surfacing them and working with team members to understand their dynamics in terms of desire, fear and reality. Members thus gain insight about what their feelings mean for their creative energy. Those skilled in genership work to understand the specifics that give life to emotion and motivation. It is not enough to respond empathically; when group members explore the deeper context, they share, develop and refine the specific elements that produce it. They can then manage their own emotional and motivational resources rather than being manipulated by others.

Coaching Motivation

In all the years I have spent thinking about emotion and motivation, the richest experience I have had comes from sharing my son's participation in school basketball leagues. Youth who play ball are often extremely serious about their performance, dedicating many hours to practice and making significant psychological and emotional investments in the games. They love the sport, thinking of it as more than a game, caring deeply about how they play, whether they win and the nature of their team participation. They want to feel a sense of contribution while avoiding errors that bring down their teammates. I have been struck by two thoughts: First, my son and his friends take high-school sports much more seriously than I did. Second, he is learning lessons that will have tremendous relevance to success within adult organizational life. Teams in professional organizations that succeed are generally made up of people who have similar emotional investments and sincere concern for both performance and one another.

Among the most fascinating subjects in this arena involves managing emotional energy. Young teams sometimes give up when confronted with failure. The process unfolds as the team falls behind. Teams usually begin games animated with green emotions, filled with hope and longing to achieve. But as they meet resistance, hope can be transformed into anger and depression. Then, instead of focusing on the game, players start to disengage, becoming lost in their negative emotions; this progression produces additional failures and soon all is lost. What might have been a close game becomes a rout. Coaches often enable this painful vicious circle by piling anger and shame upon the players who have made mistakes. Instead of engaging, these players lick their wounds.

Yet teams do sometimes turn this process around, when players choose to let go of their depression and anger, instead focusing on playing in the moment. This refocusing often produces success, inspiring the team to rejoin the effort, filled again with green rather than red emotional energy; a dispirited team can come from behind. It is striking how players wear this emotional and motivational narrative so visibly, written all over their faces on the sidelines and in the field of play. It is particularly moving when their success also involves overcoming the negative feelings of their adult coaches, who unfortunately sometimes have less emotional resources than their players.[xii]

My son and I have had many conversations exploring these emotional dynamics, learning how to maintain positive feelings and high energy by staying in the present, focusing on each moment of the game rather than allowing negative emotions to become a distraction that reinforces failure. This requires players to recognize what produces their emotional dynamics at each moment. A player who misses a key foul shot sees that his anger and frustration is produced by failing to achieve his vision. Armed with this awareness, he can then choose to shake it off, focusing on the powerful positive excitement of turning the game around, and of building skills through emotional and motivational resilience. This in turn involves clarifying vision and desire, making choices that reflect what he is really trying to create. Is the vision merely to win, or to improve and gain capacity? What part does challenge play in the vision? What does overcoming limitations look like? When we clarify our desires, losing a game against a stronger and more skillful opponent can become a satisfying and exciting experience. Great creators learn to love the *challenge* as well as the success. Through practice, my son has developed powerful emotional resilience that will serve him for the rest of his life in many endeavors beyond high-school athletics. The profound insights from his development have enriched my work with teams building creative motivation.

Consider, for example, a business organization that develops strategies to confront a competitor. Some group members feel a sense of fear when they realize that the competitor will damage the group's economic prospects by gaining market share. A leader operating within the Fallacies may attempt to suppress this fear and create an empathic transference of confidence. This is like a father figure reassuring a child afraid of the dark: "Don't worry, I will protect you. Feel your father's confidence and relax. All is well." The leader's manipulation can proceed in many different directions. To motivate behavior, a leader may well attempt to strengthen a perceived threat. Imagine that father saying to his child, "Don't worry, the monsters never hurt children who behave."

Practitioners of genership take an entirely different approach, exploring the nature of fear as an equal group member: What is the specific state of being that the group wants to avoid? Equally important, genership calls for an assessment of reality. From what perspectives are the fears grounded and reasonable? What actions can be taken that will change reality? This is like the father who reasons with his child: "Let's explore specifically what you fear about the dark, to see if it's real. Let's look in the closet and under the bed. And if you fear intruders, let's see that our front door is locked."

For leaders and groups entangled in the Fallacies, emotions and motivation are a challenge to the leader, whose job is to manage and marshal the group's energy. The leader becomes the center of its attention and members learn to live through his or her emotions and motivations. When necessary, the leader manipulates members to heighten the group's overall energy level. Transcending these practices, genership calls for individual members to actively participate in the evolution of their shared visions and reality assessments. They do not live through the emotional prism of one leader or a small leadership group; instead, they live individual lives, and the group's creative energy evolves with increasing power through their combined aspirations and unflinching appraisals.

Chapter SIX
Conflict, Force and Violence, and Learning:
Using Conflict as a Wellspring for Innovation

Within a leadership culture, conflict entails the prospect of domination and control. In sharp contrast, genership embraces productive conflict as a pathway to new learning. What is conflict? What produces it?

Conflict in group work arises from two sources of difference: desires and perceptions. Understanding the nature of conflict between individuals and groups—along with its key connection to creativity—requires exploration of these two wellsprings.

Conflicting Desires

The most compelling features of human existence are those that fall within our span of influence. While we cannot at present manipulate many features of human reality (such as our need for water, food and oxygen, and the law of gravity), many are the subject of will and whim (whether to drink coffee or tea, to vote Republican or Democrat, what work to do, what to think about, what and who to love).

Over every matter subject to human influence, it is possible, and in many cases likely, that we will encounter people who wish to change the world in ways that diverge from our individual desires. Such conflicts make up a substantial portion of our everyday existence. Think about encounters with family, friends, colleagues, neighbors and fellow citizens. Life is full of people working against what we want. Conflicts in desire begin early in life with our unfulfilled wishes for attention, pleasure and satisfaction of our physical needs. As we move toward maturity, we experience similar interactions in school, community organizations, work and social settings. Particularly in Western culture, we learn to think of success as being able to resolve such differences by obtaining something or some experience close to what we desire. Recognition that the world often defeats our desires is what drives interest in leadership, negotiation and self-help.

Conflicting Perceptions

The other primary source of human conflict—differing perceptions of reality—bears little resemblance to differing desires. While conflicts in desire involve the full spectrum of *future* possibilities subject to our influence, conflicts about reality concern interpretations regarding the present and past: What is happening now and what led to this moment? Conflicts in perception also involve necessary futures: What will definitely happen in the future irrespective of human desire? Despite their divergent reference points (human potential versus reality), these two distinct classes of conflict—desire and perception—often become conflated in the minds of the combatants.

For example, one may perceive falsely that another person *shares* a desire, when in reality he wants something different. A consultant creating a marketing campaign for a client might incorrectly target a certain demographic when in fact his customer seeks a different audience. On the other hand, one may believe incorrectly that two people have *divergent* desires. An executive interested in competing for a promotion might falsely believe that a close colleague desires to win it when in reality he has no intention of applying. This kind of slippage is common within organizations: Perceptions can mask conflicts in desire or create their false appearance.

People who share desires may nevertheless have different perceptions of reality. Two people may want to travel to the same destination, but have different perspectives on what route will prove the most efficient. Differing perceptions of reality are usually grounded in each party's having diverging experiences or from calling forth inconsistent theories to bear upon observation and experience. Diverse ideas cause experiences to be filtered dissimilarly, resulting in the parties to a conflict reaching contradictory conclusions from a shared base. The presence of conflicting desires can also give rise to alternative interpretations, causing individuals to make incongruent judgments.

Like conflicting desires, different perceptions of reality begin early in life, continue through development and are a constant feature of experience. As children, our first encounters with competing perceptions of reality come from interactions with adults. We learn that the world may not be the way we perceive it with our senses. As children, we experience the earth as a flat plane. From adults we learn that it is round, not something that we can experience first-hand as children, but only through observations shared in drawings or pictures. Nevertheless, we learn to credit pictures over direct experience. Similarly, children may observe that the sun moves across the sky, but learn from adults that it is the earth and not the sun that moves, even though we do not perceive it as such. The process of education itself involves an ongoing encounter between conflicting perceptions of reality. When we learn, our incomplete or inaccurate perceptions of reality compete with new perceptions formed on the basis of additional experience.

Upon maturing, we learn that there are some conflicts in the perception of reality about which controversy lingers, which cannot be easily resolved by an appeal to experience. The function of higher education, especially within the liberal arts, is not so much to develop competence in any one discipline, but rather to gain mastery over the learning process itself; learners gain the insight that knowledge and beliefs are a function of perspective and theories. As contemporary philosopher and educator Mortimer Adler wrote:

> The liberal arts are traditionally intended to develop the faculties of the human mind, those powers of intelligence and imagination without which no intellectual work can be accomplished. Liberal

education is not tied to certain academic subjects, such as philosophy, history, literature, music, art and other so-called "humanities." In the liberal-arts tradition, scientific disciplines, such as mathematics and physics, are considered equally liberal, that is, equally able to develop the powers of the mind.

Within the realm of higher education, students develop awareness that educated thinkers—economists, philosophers, scientists, psychologists and theologians—have incommensurate views of reality. It is the diversity and conflict among their views, not necessarily their consensus, that produce deep learning and lead to human progress.

Primary Sources of Creative Conflict

Desires   Perceptions

Hamed Sabir, *Desert Leader* and *Virgin Dune*, 2006

Different Reference Points

These two major classes of conflict—desire and perception—appeal to different standards. Conflicting desires resolve through questions involving future-oriented, overarching visions regarding ultimate purposes. The often acrimonious political debate about America's healthcare system turns not so much on particular data sets or studies describing reality, but on background visions concerning a number of complex factors: the desired balance between the public and private sector functions in society, the level of inequality tolerated in the system as a whole, the extent of the systemic safety net envisioned, and the level of commitment to accept and sustain results produced through healthcare market activity at varying levels of regulation. Similarly, politicians resolving a difference about how to invest funds in the nation's infrastructure (e.g., building roads vs. creating public transportation systems) will not be able to study their way to agreement. Knowing the present cannot tell us what to strive for in the future. Resolutions entail inquiring more broadly about the ultimate visions for communities. Ideological truths often mask the long range-visions they serve, encoding choices within principles that sound like natural laws. An insistence on tax reductions grounded in free-market ideology masks the worldview it promotes: one in which inequality grows as private-sector organizations increase their power and influence over communities.

In contrast, conflicts regarding perceptions of reality resolve with reference to either personal experience or an appeal to trusted information systems that convey authority (a kind of knowledge, believed to be infallible, derived from other experience). So a couple sharing the desire to vacation in a warm climate may disagree about the average seasonal temperature at a resort they are considering. They can resolve this conflict by comparing experiences, either others' or their own, either personal or drawn from authority. Of course, if neither party has sufficient experience to resolve a claim, their best strategy may be to engage in further investigation.

We often confuse conflicts in desire with conflicts in perception of reality. We do this because our divergent visions create incommensurate perspectives; separate realities cannot be accurately perceived from within each competing vision. Confusion also arises when separate accounts of reality mask inconsistent visions. We talk past each other without exchanging meaning, advancing misunderstood truths to influence desires, and misunderstood desires to influence perceptions of truth. Communication and dialogue become distorted within a theater of such conflicts.

Conflict & Learning
embracing conflict as a resource for learning

Paul Everett, *Tug of War*, 2006

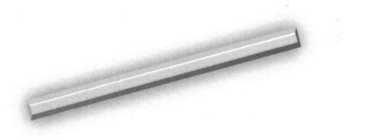

Conflict and Learning

Early in my career, I worked closely with about 15 leaders developing a new national nonprofit organization. The group experienced significant conflict in developing operating plans for the initiative. Members enjoyed close relationships with a large foundation that had provided resources for the startup work. Most members felt that the group's plan should be tailored to the interests of this foundation, hoping that it would provide the majority of the organization's support. The remaining members, a substantial minority, felt that the group's mission and activities should encompass areas beyond the foundation's interests, and that the team should develop a resource plan that did not depend on a single large funder. In observing dialogue between the two factions in the founding group, it became clear that they could not understand one another because their differing visions sensitized them to different information, and their divergent beliefs about reality reinforced desires for radically different outcomes.

The faction embracing a close relationship with the foundation envisioned a future in which the new organization would become almost an operating division of the larger foundation. This vision sensitized the group to all of the foundation's internal workings, including its long-range plan, the interests of its leadership and administrative staff, and internal politics. All of these considerations were necessary to build the kind of long-term, strong relationship with the foundation that the group's vision required. The majority felt that to ignore these considerations would be both impractical and foolish.

On the other hand, the minority faction seeking to create a more independent organization envisioned a future in which the foundation would no longer provide significant support. This vision sensitized the group to external factors and market conditions as they educated themselves about opportunities to build relationships with outside funders and clients. The minority faction also believed that ignoring external considerations was a recipe for failure.

Each side's view of what mattered in the operating environment reinforced its divergent vision of the organization's future. The faction focused on the foundation's interests became increasingly convinced about its plan's feasibility, given their intimate knowledge of the funder's objectives and decision-making processes. Meanwhile, the faction focused on external opportunities increasingly believed that dependence on the foundation was not feasible. This uneasiness resulted from a perceived lack of sufficient information about the funder's needs and doubt about effectively predicting how it would behave in future grant-making decisions. Because it was externally focused, the minority faction also did not share confidence in the strength of its relationship with key foundation decision-makers.

The dialogue between the two groups became increasingly strained, and several members of the minority faction eventually left the working group. At this point, the remaining members stopped advocating their different perspectives on the organization's future. "I guess we convinced them," said one of the majority's leaders, feeling that the task of resolving a fundamental conflict in the founding group had been completed. Several years later, the organization suffered a crisis when the foundation sharply reduced funding as a result of internal policy and leadership changes.

In this case, the organization lost an opportunity to craft a larger vision that would have embraced serving the interests of its major funder while building a more comprehensive mission capable of developing a more diverse funding base and additional program models for sustaining its mission. The root of this failure lay in the inability of team members to learn from conflict rather than simply having one side win, thereby silencing their opponents.

Under the umbrella of traditional leadership thinking, especially when the Fallacies have taken hold within a group, a key element of the leader's work is conflict resolution. What do leaders typically set out to do when they practice this crucial task?

In the leadership—as opposed to genership—domain, conflict resolution is understood as the practice of creating a shared set of goals and common understanding of reality. Most important in the practice is the peaceful feeling that arises when everyone is "on the same page" and feels as though they are "on the same team." In a quest to achieve consensus, many leaders are tempted to downplay differences and smooth over controversies. They fear that to let conflicts simmer may undermine their authority by forcing them to pick sides and then having to deal with sore feelings. To avoid losing control, the leader attempts to massage the warring factions to embrace a shared vision and perspective on reality. The resulting feeling of security that arises comes from believing that everyone has the same goals and desires, with a shared strategy for achieving them.

The leader in this setting (under the spell of the Fallacies) sees his or her objective as forging agreement among group members. In practice, the leader's work is often to persuade, cajole and reason with individual group members to gain their acceptance of a subset of all group goals and desires, as well as theories of reality or world views invented or at least promoted by the leader.

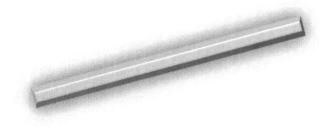

Negotiator in Chief

On February 25, 2010, after countless hours of divisive congressional and public debates including raucous town hall meetings across the nation, President Barack Obama invited congressional leaders to a publicly televised conversation on healthcare reform. In describing the reasons for the meeting, Obama said he wanted to "look at the Republican ideas that are out there," adding, "If we can go, step by step, through a series of these issues and arrive at some agreements, then, procedurally, there's no reason why we can't do it a lot faster [than] the process took last year." The televised session lasted more than seven hours. Throughout the event, the president framed the dialogue as a search for common ground. "We might surprise ourselves and find out that we agree more than we disagree," Mr. Obama said at the start. But he also conceded the difficulty of the dialogue: "It may turn out, on the other hand, there's just too big of a gulf." The summit proved to be a substantive debate that outlined the differing visions between the parties over how to reform the massive U.S. healthcare industry.

President Obama led the dialogue, energetically defending the Democrats' proposed healthcare bill while trying to focus on areas of agreement with Republicans and to address their concerns such as medical malpractice reform. The president framed himself as lead negotiator, articulating the issues and interests addressed in the Democratic legislation while debating Republican objections. In anticipation of the meeting and afterward, Republicans indicated suspicion about the president's intentions, suggesting that his goal was to convert them to agreement on his terms or paint them as inflexible on issues critical to the public. Obama asked the participants not to let the summit descend into "political theater," but with the television cameras rolling, Republicans declined to allow their ideas to be integrated into the Democratic proposals. In the end, the Democrats suggested that they would move ahead even without Republican support. When the Democrats' healthcare-reform bill passed on March 23, 2010, not a single Republican supported it.

In conducting the summit, President Obama worked hard to cast himself as leader of the policy conversation, showcasing his belief that leaders help forge consensus among warring combatants.

In this practice, the leader is the one who shows the way forward, isolating and changing the minds and hearts of those who do not share her goals, desires or understanding of the truth. Importantly, conflict is viewed as a barrier to progress and effective group functioning. A successful leader is one who creates a group passionately committed to her goals and worldview, so that maximum efforts are expended in succeeding and time is not wasted on pointless internal deliberations. Yet this leadership practice falls far short of achieving the benefits realized through genership: commitment to learn from the conflict and retain divergent viewpoints as energy sources for future learning. The danger of achieving consensus is that brilliant insights and innovations will be lost when those who disagree are silenced or depart from the team. A genership approach by contrast embraces conflict as a resource for continuous learning.

Terminating the Terminator

In June of 2008, after a widely publicized, nationwide search, the Philadelphia School Board of Education hired Arlene Ackerman, previously superintendent in Washington, DC and San Francisco. Here was a veteran of education and politics, an uncompromising and savvy educator who knew her way around and a black woman seen as someone who could bridge longstanding divides and close the achievement gap among the 155,000-student district, the country's eighth-largest.

Three years later the board fired her, and the courts and FBI became involved.

After awarding a $7.5 million no-bid, so-called emergency contract to a small minority-owned firm not qualified by the state to accept such work, Ackerman suspended five employees. These were not low-level servants, but included the Information Technology director and the senior vice presidents of procurement and capital programs. On the surface, to "inappropriately share confidential district information" would seem a valid-enough reason. Yet some members of her staff wanted nothing to do with such behavior and came forward publicly. The superintendent had earlier removed a state-approved contractor from work installing security cameras, saying that she did the right thing despite having to overrule her staff and leaving herself open to charges of breaking Pennsylvania contract rules and its Whistleblower Law.

Philadelphia's School Reform Commission, which oversees the school district, ended up buying out her contract for more than $900,000 after the controversy continued to fester. That only further fueled critics, many of whom referred to her as Queen Arlene given her imperious personality and high compensation. She made it transparently clear that those who disagreed with her goals and methods to obtain them would be fired, which represented the classic use of economic force to obtain consent; employees well realized that their livelihoods would be seriously jeopardized as a result of expressing disagreement, regardless of how they actually felt about the objectives presented.

Despite all the incriminating evidence against her, she lashed out at the "vicious, personal attacks." Here was a one-time messiah figure who appeared unwilling or unable to accept her misdeeds. In a speech to the district's principals, she attempted to reframe the question and paint herself as a victim:

> Is it a crime for this superintendent to do the superintendent's job of educating children but not playing politics? Is it a crime to stand up for children instead of stooping down into the political sandbox and selling our children for a politician's campaign victory? Is it a crime to believe that all of our district's resources should be allocated equitably, including contracts? Is it a crime? Is it a crime to expend additional resources on the schools that have failed students and communities for decades? I am guilty of wanting for other people's children what I wanted for my own. I am guilty of putting children, not politics first. Sentence me. I dare you. Or set me free.

She invoked the word "children" five times inside of a minute, without once addressing the actions that led her to that point. Hubris continues to prosper.

—*R.R.*

The Tools of Conflict Resolution Under the Leadership Fallacies

The most primitive tool of conflict resolution is the use of violence or threats. This strategy usually takes the form of a promise to inflict certain loss or harm to a person who fails to embrace a desire or understanding of the truth advocated by the leader, who then follows through to show group members that the threat is credible. The leader and group members who remain engaged after threats or violence often employ the messiah narrative to justify the punishments inflicted. The story goes that the leader is deemed to be a superhuman possessing the ability to perceive true goals and interpretations of reality. So conformance with the leader's will matters more than rational reflection and agreement on the part of group members.

Primitive Conflict Resolution:
Threats, Force and Violence

The Definition of Violence

In the conflict setting, violence is the use of force against a person or group either to gain consent or render it irrelevant. In extreme cases, violence involves the complete conversion of its target into an object. When a person is fully deprived of her subjectivity through violence, she is dead. The desires and understandings of the dead no longer factor as a resource or obstacle to the group's functioning. Consent in this context can mean agreement to work toward a goal or interpretation of reality, while the use of force entails any means of securing or eliminating the need for consent that bypasses the rational will or disregards the emotions of the person or group.

We need not look far to find compelling examples of the persistent role of violence in gaining consent in human culture. Even in so-called advanced societies, domestic violence remains prevalent. In the United States, one in four women will be victims of domestic violence during their lives; half of all fathers who abuse their wives also abuse their children. They use violence as a tool for gaining mastery over their victims. At a completely different but equally instructive level, international conflicts are often addressed through the use of force and violence. Taking the Bush administration's stated reasons at face value, the Iraq war involved an effort to dissuade that country from deploying weapons of mass destruction while ironically using force to compel the Iraqi people to move toward a true representative democracy.

Goodbye David Frum!

The American Enterprise Institute for Public Policy Research (AEI) is a conservative Washington think tank. With its stated mission "to defend the principles and improve the institutions of American freedom and democratic capitalism," AEI's scholars include the leading architects of the second Bush administration's public policy. Among the prominent government officials affiliated with AEI have been former U.S. ambassador to the U.N. John Bolton, an AEI senior fellow; former chairman of the National Endowment for the Humanities, Lynne Cheney, a longtime AEI senior fellow; and former House Speaker Newt Gingrich.

David Frum was a speechwriter for President George W. Bush. In a 2009 *Newsweek* column, he described his views:

I'm a conservative Republican, have been all my adult life. I volunteered for the Reagan campaign in 1980. I've attended every Republican convention since 1988. I was president of the Federalist Society chapter at my law school, worked on the editorial page of *The Wall Street Journal* and wrote speeches for President Bush—not the "Read My Lips" Bush, the "Axis of Evil" Bush. I served on the Giuliani campaign in 2008 and voted for John McCain in November. I supported the Iraq War and (although I feel kind of silly about it in retrospect) the impeachment of Bill Clinton. I could go on, but you get the idea. [xiii]

Frum became an AEI fellow in 2003. Despite his conservative credentials, after the 2009 election of Barack Obama, Frum became a vocal critic of the Republican Party, particularly its strategy on healthcare reform. In the days after the passage of the Democrats' healthcare legislation, Frum argued that the Republican refusal to negotiate and participate in reform had resulted in a bill that represented a huge ideological defeat. He went on to lay the blame at the feet of the conservative news media:

> I've been on a soapbox for months now about the harm that our overheated talk is doing to us. Yes it mobilizes supporters—but by mobilizing them with hysterical accusations and pseudo-information, overheated talk has made it impossible for representatives to represent and elected leaders to lead. The real leaders are on TV and radio, and they have very different imperatives from people in government. Talk radio thrives on confrontation and recrimination. When Rush Limbaugh said that he wanted President Obama to fail, he was intelligently explaining his own interests. What he omitted to say—but what is equally true—is that he also wants Republicans to fail. If Republicans succeed—if they govern successfully in office and negotiate attractive compromises out of office—Rush's listeners get less angry. And if they are less angry, they listen to the radio less, and hear fewer ads for Sleep Number beds.

So today's defeat for free-market economics and

Republican values is a huge win for the conservative entertainment industry. Their listeners and viewers will now be even more enraged, even more frustrated, even more disappointed in everybody except the responsibility-free talkers on television and radio. For them, it's mission accomplished. For the cause they purport to represent, it's Waterloo all right: ours.

Shortly after Frum went public with his criticisms, AEI fired him. He maintained that the axe fell as a result of pressure from AEI donors. AEI denied this account, suggesting that the dismissal resulted from a dispute related to the terms of his employment. Nevertheless, among both liberals and conservatives, Frum's departure was widely viewed as punishment for dissent from the Republican Party line. Bruce Bartlett, a former economic adviser to President Bush, had authored a book, *Imposter: How George W. Bush Bankrupted America and Betrayed the Reagan Legacy*. That book similarly led to his dismissal in 2005 as a senior fellow at a conservative Texas-based think tank called the National Center for Policy Analysis. Bartlett referred to Frum's departure from AEI as "the closing of the conservative mind." A guest on C-SPAN's "Washington Journal," Bartlett summed up the trend as he saw it:

[W]hat's really going on here is that adherence to conservative principles has been—is—out the window now. All that matters now is absolute subservient adherence to the Republican Party line of the day. And that's what got David into trouble. He was critical, not even of Republican principles, but of Republican tactics on the healthcare debate. And now, even that is considered, you know, you can't say that or you lose your job.

The treatment of Frum and Bartlett is nothing new. Leadership cultures view dissent as an operating problem. Force—economic if not physical—is viewed as a legitimate tool of persuasion; the goal is to forge (in both meanings of that word) consensus.

Around the globe, the use of force to secure agreement is highly prevalent in many societies and cultures, from the most primitive to the most advanced. Family and institutional violence afflicting women and children is well documented in developing Islamic cultures as well as within modern societies such as Singapore, in which caning is an official punishment for offenses including vandalism and rioting. Even in the most advanced organizations within Western society, while we pay lip service to the value of dialogue-driven consensus, conflicts often end in displays of power and authority or resort to court battles seeking involuntary compliance through injunctions and penalties backed up by police powers.

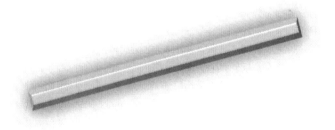

My Way or the Bench

I have learned a lot about leadership cultures through seeing my children play sports. I once watched from the bleachers as a recreational-league basketball coach chewed out a young teenager after a play, sending him to the bench. After the game, I asked my son what had happened. He explained that the coach did not allow players who were not highly skilled to shoot from beyond the three-point line. The player in question had broken the rule. The coach took him out for the rest of the game. After the incident, none of the players attempted a shot from beyond the three-point arc, except for one very experienced player. The team had gotten the message: Follow this rule or you won't play. "How will anyone learn to improve their three-point shooting in the heat of a real game?" I asked. "It doesn't matter," said my son. "What matters is to follow the coach's instructions."

Leadership cultures often promote agreement, consensus and discipline at the expense of other values. My son and I had a dialogue about what we might learn from this situation about leadership and creativity.

"What is the coach trying to accomplish?" I asked.
"He wants to win," answered my son.
"What do *you* want to accomplish?"
"I want to win too."
"But do you want to do anything else besides win?"
"I want to improve my game."
"Do you think the coach should want that too?"
"I guess so. It doesn't seem like he cares about that. He cares more about winning and not making mistakes."
"What would happen if you won every game but you didn't improve as player? Do you think it would still be worth playing?"
"No. I have to improve and also win."
"How do you improve?"
"By pushing myself to go beyond what I can do now."
"Should the coach encourage that?"
"Yes."
"Does he?"
"No."

By talking it through, my son was able to see that the coach was not always right and that what my son wanted as a player also mattered. He opened himself to the possibility that his vision as a player mattered as much as the coach's vision for the team. This line of dialogue caused him to move to a new team that balanced winning with player development.

Innumerable examples in the history of leadership involve using force to obtain consensus in groups. These could involve the infliction of corporal punishment or even death upon those who fail to agree or cooperate with the leader.

Old Way: Conflict Resolution Through Manipulation & Seduction

Ben Fredericson, *Mask*, 2009

One step removed from the use of force is manipulation through distortions in the perception of reality. Leadership cultures often condone the intentional manipulation of reality to induce group members to share a goal or embrace a belief. In political conflicts, leaders often exaggerate problems to induce group members to adopt worldviews. They may also intentionally mischaracterize the goals and desires of others to create or enhance the impression that conflicts exist. The leader and followers within a group may attempt to justify such behaviors through a messiah narrative. If the leader has the "true" vision and understanding of reality, then what matters is submission; any method of gaining it is valid, even those involving deception.

A step above violence, manipulation does represent an evolution in

211

conflict resolution from the most primitive strategy involving simple force. When a leader relies only on force to garner consent, members of the group are treated as if they were inanimate objects. Their individual creative spirits are irrelevant to progress. They are considered soulless parts of a machine. But psychological manipulation at least recognizes that each individual's creative spirit is a factor in the group's life, that the leader must harness or neutralize it. Nevertheless, manipulation sacrifices the group's creative energy by attempting to channel it through deceit and distortions.

Scott McClellan's book, *What Happened: Inside the Bush White House and Washington's Culture of Deception*, provides a detailed and chilling account of how leaders intentionally manipulate public opinion to achieve their visions. McClellan entered Bush's inner circle in 1999 when Karen Hughes, communications director for then-Governor of Texas George W. Bush, hired him as her deputy. McClellan served as Bush's traveling press secretary during the 2000 presidential campaign, joining the White House team as Deputy Press Secretary in 2001. In July of 2003, McClellan replaced Ari Fleischer as Press Secretary. Given his personal relationship with President Bush, and unique vantage point as an inside member—and eventual leader—of the president's communications team, McClellan was singularly equipped to understand the administration's efforts to influence public opinion. He offered this unflinching assessment:

> In the fall of 2002, Bush and his White House were engaging in a carefully orchestrated campaign to shape and manipulate sources of public approval to our advantage. We'd done much the same on other issues—tax cuts and education—to great success. But war with Iraq was different. Beyond the irreversible human costs and the substantial financial price, the decision to go to war and the way we went about selling it would ultimately lead to increased polarization and intensified partisan warfare. Our lack of candor and honesty in making the case for war would later provoke a partisan response from our opponents that, in its own way, further distorted and obscured a more nuanced reality. Another cycle of deception would cloud the public's ability to see larger, underlying important truths that are critical to understand in order to avoid the same problems in the future.

As only a White House insider could, McClellan described the development of the internal decision to pursue war with Iraq in the months immediately following the terrorist attacks of September 11, 2001. Key leaders within the administration had a broad spectrum of reasons for seeking war. The president shared the motivation of neoconservatives led by Paul Wolfowitz who dreamed that deposing Saddam Hussein could lead to the development of a democratic Middle East. More pragmatic officials such as Dick Cheney and Donald Rumsfeld wished to eliminate Saddam as a threat to regional and global peace, believing his ouster could promote greater economic security for the region and the United States, particularly in view of Iraq's enormous oil reserves. Nevertheless, the administration's ambitions to bring about global transformation had to be muted in making the case for war. The true reasons for the war did not fit well with the image Bush had projected. McClellan continued:

> The idea of transforming the Middle East coercively contradicted [Bush's] promised humility, and it would be very difficult for the president and his administration to sell to the citizens. It would provoke all kinds of debates that might not be easy to win…. Was it realistic to think about transforming a country like Iraq with an entrenched regime from tyranny into democracy primarily through military force? Were the peoples and civic institutions of Iraq fully ready to support self-rule? What kinds of sustained military presence and intervention would be required to maintain stability during a time of governmental or civil upheaval? What role would Islamic fundamentalism play in the newly constituted regime? What about the long-standing ethnic and religious tensions just below the surface in this tightly controlled country in the region? And how could we be sure that the new democratically elected government in Iraq would be pro-American and ready to live in peace with its neighbor (and American ally) Israel? The answers to these questions are not easily addressed, and require careful consideration and thoughtful planning.

But the administration downplayed its goal of regional transformation, choosing instead to focus on the threat of weapons of mass destruction allegedly controlled by Iraq, combined with allegations that the country was connected to terrorism and had played a role in the 9/11 attacks.

Rather than open this Pandora's box, the administration chose a different path—not employing out-and-out deception but shading the truth; downplaying the major reason for going to war and emphasizing a lesser motivation that could arguably be dealt with in other ways (such as intensified diplomatic pressure); trying to make the WMD threat and the Iraqi connection to terrorism appear just a little more certain, a little less questionable, than they were; quietly ignoring or disregarding some of the crucial caveats in the intelligence and minimizing evidence that pointed in the opposite direction; using innuendo and implication to encourage Americans to believe as fact some things that were unclear and possibly false (such as the idea that Saddam had an active nuclear weapons program) and other things that were overplayed or completely wrong (such as implying Saddam might have an operational relationship with al Qaeda).

In the lead-up to war, members of the president's inner circle delivered messages known to be speculative that were intentionally designed to turn public opinion in favor of the war. These included Vice President Dick Cheney, who referenced reports—later discredited—that 9/11 hijacker Mohamed Atta had met with Saddam before the attack, and Secretary of State Condoleezza Rice, who raised the specter of a nuclear explosion, reminding the public in a CNN interview "We don't want the smoking gun to be a mushroom cloud."

As we now know, in the war's aftermath, no weapons of mass destruction were located, and the stories about Saddam's connections to al-Qaeda, to the 9/11 attackers and to nuclear weapons proved to be false. In June 2008, the Senate Select Committee on Intelligence released the final part of its Phase II investigation into the intelligence assessments that led to the U.S. invasion and occupation of Iraq; this part of the investigation looked into statements of Bush administration members and compared those to what the intelligence community was telling the administration at the time. The report, endorsed by eight Democrats and two Republicans on the committee, concluded: "Statements and implications by the president and secretary of state suggesting that Iraq and al-Qaeda had a partnership, or that Iraq had provided al-Qaeda with weapons training, were not substantiated by the intelligence." The Iraq Survey Group was a fact-finding mission sent by the multinational force in Iraq after the 2003 invasion to find the alleged weapons of mass destruction that had been the ostensible reason for the invasion. In its final report issued in September 2004, the group found no support for the Bush administration's claims that Iraq was pursuing a nuclear weapons program.

The administration's manipulation of public opinion remains a vivid example of how leaders often resort to directing the beliefs of followers to achieve their leadership visions.

Beyond manipulation based on distortions or mischaracterizations, leadership often relies upon the use of incentives to gain consensus. Within this strategy, consent is purchased through the promise and delivery of rewards for compliance. Consider the leader of a business enterprise who rewards with money those who share his or her objectives and who profess allegiance to specific ideas; a political leader who promises power or influence to those who share his vision or ideology; and, on a more personal level, a father or mother who obtains a child's agreement to participate in a family project by promising a gift. In religions, the promise of a reward in the afterlife is sometimes proffered to induce loyalty to a certain set of desires, objectives and beliefs about the world.

Promises of love, affection, trust and friendship can themselves become rewards through which a leader forges consensus. The implied loss of the relationship and its attendant benefits is also sometimes used to maintain consensus. This technique for building agreement often manifests as a claim of love, respect or loyalty for the messiah or leadership group. Members are urged to consent because failing to do so is regarded as a breach of the relationship, while compliance becomes easily demonstrable evidence that the member is in good standing. Agreement and submission is a way of broadcasting the strength of one's relationship with the messiah or leadership subgroup. This technique—leveraging the social and emotional bonds between the leader and follower to acquire and stabilize consensus in the group as a whole—is visible in the full spectrum of organizational life, within families, teams, social and religious groups, businesses, and regional and national groups. As Abraham Lincoln said, "If you would win a man to your cause, first convince him that you are his sincere friend."

At the boundary between leadership and genership lies the delicate practice of persuasion in which the leader uses the force of his or her authority and influence to gain buy-in to ideas that belong to the messiah or leadership group. The metaphor of sharing wealth and making investments captures the messiah's hegemony in the transaction. His messiah's views about the future and present reality are compared and contrasted with others, together with the argument that his or her perspectives should be adopted to the exclusion of competitors'. This decision to agree or not is presented as a free choice to members, yet the decision is framed in either/or terms, so that members must choose to go along with the messiah or face exclusion. The decision to buy-in and become convinced in this regard is also often framed as a decision about personal identity and also about whether or not one will belong to the group in the future.

Underlying each of these primitive strategies employed in resolving conflict—force and threats, manipulation through distortions or incentives, relationship leverage and either/or competition among diverse viewpoints—lies a specific idea about the nature and purpose of the conflict-resolution process: to advance the messiah's or heroes' agenda. Others in the group can at best learn from the messiah and his legions. To learn is to perceive and embrace the messiah's wisdom. At worst, group members are expected to act on faith regarding what the messiah wants and believes to be true. They are taught that their intellects and souls are too puny to understand or contribute. What they must do is make way for the superhumans with the special powers required to lead the group to the promised lands. In this worldview, conflict is always an unnecessary and fruitless distraction from the messiah's plans.

Fallacy-Driven Conflict

A significant degree of conflict within groups and organizations derives from the Fallacies themselves, entailing these primary questions:

What does the messiah want or think?

Is the person who appears to be the messiah in fact the real one?

If the real messiah is in doubt, who are the heroes—those who will compete for the messiah role?

How should the group select the new messiah from among the heroes?

Who among them deserves attention and allegiance?

What is the past messiah's teaching and how does it bear upon the present and future?

These questions become focal points of conflicting desires and understandings that have a special capacity to waste time, energy and productive power within groups. They become meta-questions that distract from fundamental choices and challenges the members could otherwise confront about what kind of life to create and how best to proceed in the present. The life-and-death cycle of organizations is determined by those capable of staying focused on actual opportunities and threats while others wage war about who should decide these matters. A tribe is sustained by those who hunt, cook, look out for the children and watch for predators, while tribe members murder one another in a quest to lead the group. A business is sustained by those who stay focused on developing and selling products or services while board members and executives struggle for power. Real organizations draw power from their ability to withstand messianic conflicts through the activity of members (often uncelebrated) who are capable of creating value while the conflict burns.

The evolution from leadership toward genership entails a transformation in any organization's approach to the nature and role of conflict within group processes. The first and most fundamental step is to transcend Fallacy-driven conflict by focusing on the underlying opportunities and threats confronting the group, achieved by asking crucially different questions:

Leadership Questions (Old Way)	Genership Questions (New Way)
What does the messiah want or think?	What does each group member want and think?
Is the person who appears to be the messiah in fact the real one?	What can each member contribute to shape the group's aspirations, insights and actions?
If the real messiah is in doubt, who are the heroes who will compete for the messiah role?	How can the group engage each member's energies in shaping its vision and understanding of reality?
How should the group select the new messiah from among the heroes?	How can the group's vision evolve so that it offers something vital and fulfilling to each member?
Who among the heroes deserves attention and allegiance?	How can the group's understanding of reality and efficient strategic action evolve so that the chances of achieving the group's overall vision are maximized?
What is the teaching of the past messiah(s) and how does it bear upon the present and future?	What can the group learn from its past experiences that offers relevance to the present and future?

Differing Approaches to Conflict, Force and Violence

In the old paradigm under the spell of the Fallacies, conflict is something to be avoided. Force and violence are primitive tools to create consensus if the messiah cannot do so through manipulation or rational persuasion. Consensus achieved as a result of manipulation, fear or force, or by ejecting those who disagree with the group, is consensus nonetheless. Loyalty is paramount so the messiah can direct the group's actions as if they were members of one unified body. They experience a oneness with the messiah in which their individual identities are subsumed. The group understands this as conflict resolution.

Within genership by contrast, conflict is something to be embraced as essential to effective group process. At the same time, the group rejects force, violence and manipulation as tools for creating consensus. Group boundaries remain open so that those who disagree with its direction may leave if they choose to, but may well stay and continue to contribute. Genership creates a culture in which those who dissent from the group's direction nevertheless retain respect, dignity and focus as potential resources for learning and exploring alternative pathways in the future. The group rejects strategies that inhibit direct, free and individualized reflection. Genership recognizes that group members *compelled* to agreement cease to think independently and become useless to the group's ability to engage in CoThinking and CoVisioning. Consensus itself is generally questioned and transcended as a value within group processes. What matters is not whether the group agrees but whether its process allows progress in ways that enhance the lives and productivity of individual group members, who recognize that being in a state of conflict may actually empower it to forge ahead productively.

Genership depersonalizes conflict. When two or more individuals advance conflicting ideas for action, members understand the conflict as an opportunity for learning. Those participating remain open to the possibility that the group's perspectives will evolve in ways that transcend differences among members rather than force them into win-lose competitions in which only one perspective is advanced. In this context, no loss of status or sense of betrayal arises when ideas are modified or even abandoned as a result of dialogue and learning.

Consider two individuals inside a business with conflicting perspectives regarding a product design decision. Inside a leadership culture operating under the spell of the Fallacies, their dialogue would be distorted by underlying questions regarding the messiah's perspectives and, in the presence of a weak or failing leader, the heroes. Rather than honestly assess the decision's merits, individuals will speculate about what design the messiah will validate, or how his decision might be interpreted. The substantive question regarding the best design choice becomes twisted into a political inquiry about the will of the messiah or aspiring heroes. Instead of thinking about design, individuals attempt to project themselves into the minds of the messiah and heroes. Liberated from the Fallacies, however, two individuals with different perspectives can reflect exclusively upon the proposed design's merits. This often results in each party's observing strengths and weaknesses inherent in the design and then adapting their views in light of their dialogue. This opens pathways for real innovation and learning to occur.

All Those Who Disagree, Please Signify by Saying, "I resign."

Back to Iraq... In September 2002, during the lead-up to the war, Dr. Lawrence Lindsey (then serving as White House Economic Policy Advisor) speculated to *The Wall Street Journal* that the cost of the Bush administration's plan in 2002 of invasion and regime change in Iraq would amount to between one and two percent of GNP, or about $100-$200 billion.

Upon learning about Lindsey's remarks, Scott McClellan, then White House Deputy Press Secretary, informed the President. Bush reacted with anger and irritation, commenting that Lindsey's remarks were "unacceptable." What frustrated the president was not just that he disagreed with Lindsey's assessment, but he was off message, focusing on the cost of the war rather than the administration's main talking point: the serious threat posed by Saddam Hussein's regime. By December, Lindsey had been terminated.

To forge consensus, Bush's White House team chose to suppress serious dialogue concerning the cost of the war. Advocacy for the president's policy choices enjoyed a much higher priority than critical consideration of them. At the time, Mitch Daniels, Director of the Office of Management and Budget, discounted Lindsey's estimate as "very, very high" and stated that the costs would be $50-$60 billion. Defense Secretary Donald Rumsfeld concurred, calling Lindsey's estimate "baloney."

The cost of the Iraq war turned out to be more than 10 times higher, exceeding $800 billion dollars and continuing to mount. A genership culture promotes consideration of alternative, divergent perspectives to inform learning rather than emphasize consensus in support of a leadership vision.

Consider two individuals in a community debating the impact of a particular educational policy. Under the Fallacies, they would seek out the leader in his or her perceived role as having superior knowledge. The leader would then arbitrate the dispute, vindicating one or the other in the manner of a judge. The concept underlying this situation is that the leader has access to superior knowledge and experience as a result of his messianic status. In the context of genership, however, the individuals involved in this dialogue could seek to develop their own evidence or conduct an experiment to see what works in practice. Genership removes any sense of winning or losing in conjunction with the experiment. Members of the dialogue are simply attempting to learn through shared experimentation. All benefit from the results, even if over time not every prediction is verified. Learning through action educates all of the group's members.

Genership employs several specific techniques to ensure that learning emerges from conflict:

1. Directing into dialogue the destructive energy entailed in using force, threats and manipulation as tools to promote consensus.

Groups skillful at genership become adept at transforming primitive consensus-building strategies into meaningful dialogue that promotes learning. Picture a legislator who, to secure a colleague's vote, threatens to take away the party funding needed for reelection. A practitioner of genership would use the emotional tension in the ensuing conflict to deepen each legislator's understanding of the full spectrum of issues underlying the other's choices regarding the vote's subject matter. Instead of reacting with counter-threats, the move is to meet threats with invitations to exploratory dialogue.

In a different context, think about a parent who discovers one of his children experimenting with illegal drugs. The parent attempts to manipulate or coerce a change in the child's behavior by threatening to end his allowance or take away something he values until he demonstrates compliance. In contrast, practitioners of genership use the conflict to explore openly their differences. Such a dialogue entails exploring what the child hopes to gain in using drugs, what circumstances are motivating use and the child's strategies for managing his desires and current situation.

Within a work environment, a supervisor may confront an employee deviating from company policy regarding dress codes by wearing informal clothes. The supervisor informs the employee that if the behavior persists, he or she will be fired. The contrasting genership strategy is to create an opportunity for dialogue so that both can explore the visions and understandings of reality underlying the policy and the employee's efforts to deviate from it. During this dialogue, the possibility that the policy will be changed remains open. The supervisor is not defensive; instead, she chooses to evaluate the employee's reasons for divergence to determine whether there is anything to learn from the situation. Do employees who are more comfortable work longer and with greater productivity? What matters is not winning an argument but learning how best to advance the group's goals and visions.

2. Creating a culture that embraces divergent visioning and perspectives on current reality, while retaining and building strong relationships with those holding insurgent ideas and perspectives.

In a leadership culture ensnared in the Fallacies, members of an organization do not openly question the group's objectives, nor the assessments of reality promulgated by the messiah. Furthermore, members with views opposing him do so at their own risk and are driven out of the group or severely compromised in terms of their ability to engage effectively in group processes. Dissenters are marginalized.

By contrast, genership encourages critical voices and those who question the group's choices and focus, as long as they are not motivated by Fallacy-driven conflict (i.e., an effort to establish power as opposed to grappling with the actual threats, opportunities and strategies confronting the group).

Al Dunlap's Mean Business

Many corporate leaders rise to power by creating a top-down, militaristic power hierarchy, while actively seeking to minimize dissent and eliminate any kind of hindering circumstances. Team members who choose to stay—those allowed to remain—do not question authority; they blindly follow orders and operate within a centralized chain of command. Their culture of fear and domination is one in which employees actually work to insulate themselves from decision-making opportunities to avoid blame if something goes wrong. Members are punished for expressing opinions about corporate policy without permission, even within internal staff meetings. A messiah and his small team create policy in secret, while corporate transparency is relegated to the window blinds.

The case of Scott Paper remains a blunt and graphic warning of the Messiah Fallacy at work. With a moniker like Al "Chainsaw" Dunlap, could that CEO's motivations possibly be any clearer to the world? He hooked onto the 1990s wave of corporate raiders with a slash-and-burn philosophy that collected bales of praise from Wall Street and those within his tight leadership circle.

Dunlap attended West Point, the famed New York military academy, which he called the "best business school in the world." Although he graduated near the bottom of his class and came equipped with a brusque style, his obsession with getting ahead and generating huge wealth eventually led him to the top job at Scott Paper, the venerable company founded in 19th-century Philadelphia. His relentless focus on shareholders (a group to which he arrogantly belonged) at the expense of employees, communities and even customers provided a stark reminder of company priorities on a daily basis.

Dunlap called his book *Mean Business*, published a year after he sold the company to Kimberley Clark for $7.8 billion and booked $100 million for himself after 16 months of work. The book's title revealed a contemptible wordplay in the eyes of those whose lives he made miserable. He provoked fear even within his executive circle and few in the entire corporation summoned the courage to confront either him or his decisions. His skill at using coercion led to 60-hour and longer workweeks, mountainous sales goals and unforgiving productivity targets within an oppressive atmosphere.

As senior *BusinessWeek* writer John Byrne described in his book, *Chainsaw: The Notorious Career of Al Dunlap in the Era of Profit-at-Any-Price*, "In Dunlap's presence, knees trembled and stomachs churned. At his worst, he became viciously profane, even violent…. He would throw papers and furniture, bang his hands on the desk, and shout so ferociously that a manager's hair would be blown back by the stream of air that rushed from Dunlap's mouth. 'Hair spray day' became a code phrase among execs, signifying a potential tantrum."

Given his distaste for sustaining work relationships, Dunlap's exploitation and aggression simply ignored the needs of his employees. His insistence on being right, combined with a grandiose and manic sense of entitlement, led to all manner of anxiety and fear, combined with an utter lack of intrinsic loyalty.

As a footnote, Dunlap's next challenge led him to Sunbeam, where its board looked to him as a savior. His relentless evisceration of fat cut into muscle and bone, shareholder value evaporated and his one-time supporters left him as quickly as a thunderclap. He was eventually fired.

—R.R.

A genership-promoting culture encourages non-hierarchical and open communications. Members at the front lines of work are encouraged to voice their opinions. Members do not fear that engagement in deliberations and decision-making will damage their prospects in the organization. On the contrary, the genership culture challenges those who fail to contribute honestly and energetically to CoVisioning and CoThinking. Divergent ideas are nurtured and retained as potentially important for the future and as reservoirs for new approaches. Those who think differently are not seen as disloyal members or challengers to the organization's power structure. Within the organization, this openness destabilizes forces more interested in maintaining control than organizational learning. This ensures that the team does not become stagnant while falling subject to the hegemony of one leader or leadership group.

3. Working freely with ideas to discover their impact; allowing a group's visions to evolve over time.

Under the spell of the Fallacies, alternative visions are treated like competitors to the throne of power. Inevitably, the group sets up contests and battles; those who do not prevail are banished from the kingdom. The group's posture is either/or: Visions are not creatively recombined because they are believed to have an intrinsic unity attached to the messiah advocating for them. The group treats rejection of a vision as equivalent to the rejection of its advocate.

Genership moves in a different direction, exploring alternatives in an open and even playful manner, considering how group objectives can be changed to embrace competing elements, and assessing the overall impact if the group implements such changes. The group's vision remains open and dynamic, capable of evolving over time as elements are added and subtracted based on everyone's responses. The genership culture fosters an environment in which each member's creative spirit is fully engaged, generating a sense of energy and well-being. Members cease to think of themselves as automatons or soldiers directed by a commander-in-chief through a bureaucracy; instead, they see their work as a kind of collective art. Rather than experiencing burnout in conjunction with labor, they feel energized and renewed.

Within the Fallacies, a group deciding on a mission statement often witnesses several aspiring leaders advancing alternative visions, then selects one from among the competitors. Within genership, however, the work of crafting a mission statement is seen as a true dialogue among the members rather than a contest for organizational power. The competing forces would all contribute to the creative process. The benchmark for determining whether members share a vision is not the work of one leader or messiah to forge consensus but rather the freewheeling group process fostered by the members themselves.

4. Exploring diverse ideas about what is actually happening; playing with ideas promoted by differing perspectives to discover their impact; allowing a group's understanding of reality to evolve over time.

Under the Fallacies, conflicts are resolved by appeals to authority, and are seen as examples of ignorance, insubordination or insanity. Reality is understood as giving rise to only one unified truth. Varying interpretations represent degrees of error. The goal of dialogue is to discard error, working to come closer to the ultimate truth that will be the same for all observers. The word of the leader is the best proxy for this truth. If wrong, then he must be false. The solution is not to reconsider reality, but to find a new and better messiah.

Genership utterly transforms this system, seeking to understand reality through reflection, experience and action, recognizing that differing interpretations of truth and access to diverse views empower learning. Genership acknowledges that reality is a function of perspective and that diverse communities may yield a spectrum of creative possibilities. A community of scientists locked within Newtonian mechanics, for example, could not have created the technologies made possible by quantum mechanics. Newtonian physics is not wrong; it has not been discarded. But modern physics has created a picture of reality that diverges from the orderly clockwork underlying Newton's theories. New thinking has opened the way for development of untold trillions of dollars of technological innovation and development. Genership recognizes that when reality meets human intelligence, the outcome is freely determined. Many possible interpretations result and each may yield different creative possibilities.

Apollo 13: Genership to the Rescue
April 13, 1970
"Houston we've had a problem..."

These words mark the beginning of one of the most dramatic displays of genership in American history. Apollo 13 was to be the third manned landing on the moon, but the mission was lost when an oxygen tank exploded in the Apollo Service Module. Astronauts

James Lovell, Fred Haise and Jack Swigert, then more than halfway to the moon, were in terrible jeopardy. Exhibiting a tour-de-force of genership, NASA Flight Director Gene Krantz and his "Tiger" team of 15 engineers demonstrated extraordinary creativity and ingenuity in bringing the crew home alive.

As a result of the blast, the crew had lost two oxygen tanks and compromised two of the three fuel cells supplying the command module. The astronauts had no choice but to move to their lunar module, using it as sort of life raft for the trip back to Earth. But the lunar module was only designed to support two crew members for 45 hours, giving rise to a seemingly impossible challenge: stretch those resources to serve three crew members for almost 90 hours. The NASA engineers understood immediately that complete, unselfish cooperation of their entire team would be required to save the crew. Rather than generating solutions in a command mode and delegating implementation to his colleagues, Kranz deconstructed and delegated the effort, instructing his team members to "work the problem" in subgroups charged with reentry, spacecraft resources and using the lunar module as a lifeboat. Kranz's charge to his teams, related in his memoir, *Failure Is Not an Option*, displays many of genership's central themes:

> I want nothing held back, no margins, no reserves. If you don't have an answer, they need your best judgment and they need it now. Whatever happens we will not second-guess you. Everything goes in the pot…. [R]ely on your own judgment, update your data as you go along. If you are not the right person, step aside and send me someone who is.

Kranz described the extraordinary creative teamwork

that followed as "not concerned with voicing opinions freely [or] worrying about hurting anyone's feelings. Everyone became part of the solution." Addressing his fellow engineers during the crisis, Kranz said, "You must believe this crew is coming home. I don't give a damn about the odds and I don't give a damn that we've never done anything like this before. Flight control will never lose an American in space."

Working together on parallel assignments, the NASA engineers developed an amazing spectrum of innovations that could never have been generated over such a short time frame from within a top-down leadership culture. The engineering team's innovations included creating a method to charge the command module batteries using power from the lunar module, developing a variety of strategies for conserving water, and creating a device for removing carbon dioxide from the cabin using only materials that could be found in the spacecraft: plastic bags, cardboard, duct tape, plastic tubing and even a sock. To conserve power, electrical systems were turned off, causing the cabin temperature to plummet to 38 degrees and requiring extraordinarily rapid development of a special procedure for restoring power before reentry, after the command module's long, cold dormancy. This innovative work emerged from the creative conflict and argument generated among brilliant engineers working on each aspect of the challenged mission.

Thanks to the extraordinary creativity of NASA's engineering team, Apollo 13's crew splashed safely into the Pacific Ocean three and half days after the initial explosion. The team exhibited a vital capacity: not traditional leadership showing a command focus, but genership's effectiveness in creating an environment in which numerous minds could collaborate, and in which conflict generated rapid learning.

5. Creating shared experiences and experiments to allow group members to learn together, rather than having their visions and planning regulated by one leader or leadership team.

Under the Fallacies, the leader or leadership group employs experience to form knowledge, while group members (followers) access the results as received wisdom from the messiah. In this setting, what matters is obtaining the right authority, learning neither from direct experience nor from trial and error. The Fallacies give rise to a belief that situations facing the group are governed by rules of nature or other given laws, and what matters is understanding these transcendental truths. Group members are perceived as lacking the intellectual gifts to understand the laws governing their shared undertakings. What they must do, therefore, is follow the messiah's directions.

Genership's foundation provides the opportunity to shape the world through action and work; the presence of this opportunity suggests innovation and learning. Genership puts forth new ways and methods that can be refined through ongoing experience, and further, that only those directly employed in the endeavor can know about these inventions (accessible through reflection upon action). Received wisdom is open to be tested. Learning occurs through repeated trial, experimentation and correction. New patterns of experience constantly emerge.

A single architect may have the capacity to design a masterful building, but a team of architects will have exponentially more creative capacity, giving rise to a great metropolis. A single playwright may conceive of a dramatic plot, characters and dialogue, but an ensemble cast can bring it to life in ways beyond the writer's imagination. In the words of Alexander Graham Bell, "Great discoveries and improvements invariably involve the cooperation of many minds. I may be given credit for having blazed the trail, but when I look at the subsequent developments, I feel the credit is due to others rather than myself."

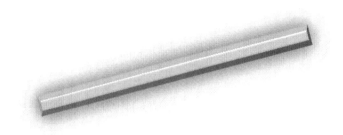

Genership Jazz

Major symphony orchestras are comprised of 80 to 100 musicians who have studied and practiced diligently since childhood, who love music passionately, who have strong ideas about how to present and perform the repertoire, who are gifted in technique and emotional expression. And yet to a person they must conform to the will of a conductor who may or may not be eager to accept the opinions of those under his tutelage. Orchestral musicians must swallow the salmon whether or not they like seafood.

Chamber ensembles such as string quartets, though much more intimate in nature, often live through active disagreements and spirited debates on their way to forging clear consensus for pieces in which every note is exposed to the listener. Despite the wide range of possible interpretations, classical music rests upon the printed note and the composer's sacrosanct intentions. As trumpeter Wynton Marsalis has said, "There was one thing Beethoven didn't do. When one of his string quartets was played, you can believe the second violin wasn't improvising."

Jazz ensembles, by contrast, thrive upon improvisation and take advantage of far more individual freedom, along the way deriving at-the-moment inspiration from fellow players. Performances go in directions impossible to predict from concert to concert, with creation, recreation and dialogue heightened through bursts of creativity in a lyrical testimony to the power of genership.

Accomplished jazz musicians must possess abundant technical skills and theoretical knowledge as a springboard for creativity, just as those within any organization of 2, 20, 200 or 2000 members should ideally demonstrate. As actor Christopher Walken has noted, "Improvising is wonderful. But, the thing is that you cannot improvise unless you know exactly what you're doing." Devoting themselves to true listening and not just token nodding, jazz players riff on one another and their chosen material in a process akin to inspired conversation. This spark separates genuine artists from mere craftsmen. Neither the musicians nor audience know just where that discourse will take them, which is part of the excitement and fluidity that jazz promotes. Risk and taking chances are not just within the province of reckless behavior, but can promote both memorable music and the next great invention.

Effective language skills offer key parallels, which begin with the assimilation of grammatical rules and increasing vocabulary, while inhibitions and self-consciousness gradually fade with further practice and knowledge. Without bona fide listening, however, conversations and meetings can easily degenerate into self-serving monologues from which it can be grueling to progress. Do participants bring something interesting to the table or are they inclined to rely upon clichés as fresh as long-dead lobster?

Whether masterful musicians or public speakers, amateur players or friends, students or family, those who communicate well convey interesting material and riff on what they hear. Endless facts or repeated scale patterns are little more than an invitation to the pillow.

—R.R.

CHAPTER SEVEN

SYSTEMS THINKING: *ENGAGING WIDESPREAD FORCES OF CHANGE IN WHAT WE CREATE*

Creativity always and necessarily involves change. To create is to transform the world so that it moves in the direction and takes on the form that our imagination wills. What we create rarely conforms perfectly to what we had envisioned, but it always differs from what was present before we engaged our creative faculties. A canvas becomes filled with color, a blank page engraved with words, an amorphous lump of clay shaped into a figure, raw materials transformed into a product, silence filled with sound, human energy orchestrated in patterns of achievement and service.

Effective genership requires its practitioners to serve as instruments—scientists and artists—of such transformation and to call forth the power within others to bring about change; they study the world to learn how it changes while strengthening their influence. As genership practitioners they develop knowledge about how to transform reality efficiently and comprehensively. But they are not content merely to observe and document discovered processes. Creators bring vision to bear upon the world, calling forth changes that were not predestined but result from choices among infinite possibilities; they are artists who hone the skill of orchestrating transformative processes to achieve desired results.

Transformation and change require not only physical tools but ideas. The preceding chapters on CoVisioning and CoThinking explore the concept that the tools we use to understand the world around us affect our understanding of it. In the case of physical instruments, this impact is clearly evident. When we look at the moon through a telescope, we see a different moon than that seen with naked eyes. Similarly, a sensitive microphone records sounds that we cannot hear using only our ears.

When we employ ideas as tools of observation, they affect what we see in equally profound ways, if more difficult to describe. Primitive man looked at the sun rising and setting and concluded that it circles a flat Earth. Later, humans who studied the appearance and movements of stars and planets concluded that the Earth was round, itself spinning and circling the sun. It was not just that our ancestors had new observations; they understood them through a new prism of ideas.

Since the late 1960s,[xiv] society collected a body of insights under the banner currently known as *systems thinking,* which employs very specific strategies to understand the world around us. Humans have been practicing elements of systems thinking for as long as they have been thinking about the world. For this reason, systems thinking is both very old and very new: to understand the world around us in terms of change is an ancient practice, but explicitly identifying it as a coherent and key approach is relatively novel.

Thinking About the Solar System

Early cosmology demonstrates the power of systems thinking. In primitive man's everyday experience, the Earth appeared to be the observable universe's flat center. The Greeks were the first to suggest a spherical

Earth. At about 340 BC, Aristotle argued for the Earth's roundness based on several careful observations of changes. First, that the sails of a ship coming over the horizon appear first and only later its hull. Second, that the Earth cast its spherical shadow on the moon to produce a lunar eclipse. Third, that the North Star shifts higher in the northern firmament than in the southern. But Aristotle rejected contemporary claims that the sun, rather than the Earth, occupied the center of the universe.

Around AD 150, following Aristotle, Ptolemy advanced a complete cosmological model. In his geocentric vision, the Earth remained stationary while the sun and other celestial bodies circled it. A difficulty in the geocentric view arose because it struggled to explain why several of the planets show "retrograde motion"—they appear to reverse direction when observed against a backdrop of distant stars. Ptolemy attempted to manage this phenomenon by developing the concept of epicycles (smaller circles revolving around an orbital path). While highly complex, they allowed for reliable predictions about planetary movements within the celestial system. Later adopted by the Christian Church, Ptolemy's system remained the dominant cosmology for more than a millennium.

In 1514 Copernicus then advanced a heliocentric system, in which the sun is at the center of the universe while Earth and all the other planets revolve around it. Copernicus theorized that planets farther from the sun take longer to complete a revolution, and also that the sun's apparent movement across the sky results from the Earth's rotating around its north-to-south axis. Copernicus' sun-centric view explained retrograde motion without the need for Ptolemy's complex epicycles. Man's view of the universe was about to undergo a transformation.

The invention of the telescope allowed for more detailed observation of changes in the sky. Galileo (1564-1642) employed it to discover Jupiter's moons. Ptolemy's theory held that all celestial bodies orbited Earth. Galileo's observations of moons orbiting Jupiter demonstrated that another pattern was possible. Through this and other observations such as phases of the planet Venus, Galileo developed additional evidence consistent with a heliocentric system.

A contemporary of Galileo, Danish nobleman Tycho Brahe (1546-1601) dedicated himself to making painstaking observations of planetary positions. Brahe's records are considered to be 10 times more accurate than the best previous observations. To document movement in the heavens, Brahe built vast instruments including a variety of ingenious clocks and timekeepers. Based on his findings, he developed an extraordinarily accurate celestial model (in terms of perceived planetary movements) even though assuming that the Earth was at rest, the sun circled it and the planets orbited the sun. Johannes Kepler (1571-1630) worked as Brahe's assistant. Kepler desired to prove a connection between Platonic geometry and cosmology. He realized that Brahe's painstaking observations could provide the detail necessary to confirm his ideas and, upon Brahe's death, Kepler stole his data, analyzing it for almost a decade. Kepler's systems analysis ultimately caused him to develop three laws of planetary motion consistent with Brahe's data if not his model:

1. The planets move in elliptical orbits with the sun at one of two foci.

2. In their orbits around the sun, the planets sweep out equal areas in equal times.

3. The squares of the times to complete one orbit are proportional to the cubes of the planet's average

distances from the sun.

Using Kepler's concepts, Newton was able to develop the universal law of gravitation. The work of these men—Copernicus, Galileo, Brahe, Kepler and eventually Newton—brought about the transition from the geocentric to the heliocentric model of the universe that we use today. These scientists, who created new worldviews to explain the changes they painstakingly observed taking place in the heavens, demonstrated the power of systems thinking, a fundamental capacity in humanity's effort to understand, and thereby master, nature.

At the center of systems thinking is a focus on how the world changes, rather than what remains constant. If one awoke every morning and always saw a cat sitting in exactly the same place at just the same time, its unchanging presence would remain the focus, perhaps prompting the conclusion that "there is always a cat outside my door in the morning." Systems thinking, however, approaches the world from a different perspective. Instead of asking the question, "What remains the same?" it becomes "What changes?" So rather than simply noticing the cat in the morning, one might check to see where the cat is at other times of the day, only to discover that it comes and goes. Systems thinkers pay attention to changes in the world; they concentrate on understanding its features that remain stable in context of those that change.

Many features of the world do not change; we come to think of them as facts: a birthdate, the original name on a birth certificate, that we had a mother and father, that we were born on Earth, that the sun rises in the East and sets in the West, that our average body temperature is 98.6 degrees Fahrenheit, that the Earth has one moon, that the capital of the United States in January 2008 was Washington, D.C., that the speed of light is 186,000 miles per second for all observers, that water freezes at 32 degrees and so on. We consider such observations to be facts because we do not observe them change. The critical point to understand is that the world presents to us a large number of observations that do not change as far as we can tell.

On the other hand, much about the world is constantly changing. Systems thinkers use the term "variable" to describe a quantity or quality that can change and upon which we want to focus attention: body weight, location in space, air temperature, age, car speed during a road trip, the moisture in the air, and the total amount of money earned and spent during a lifetime.

It is much easier to observe what is not changing than what changes. Why? What does not change remains present and available for observation. Constant laws of the universe may be reconfirmed at any moment. The patterns of sunrise and sunset, the moon's phases and planetary motions are stable and predictable. Focus on a feature of existence such as our age, however, and we see immediately that it is more difficult to capture. The second a baby becomes a year old, she becomes older than a year. Age increases constantly. Parents well know that it is more difficult to remember the ages of their children than their names. Why? Because those change while their names remain constant.

The mind is not adept at observing very slow changes. Plants turn toward the sun so slowly that their motion is difficult to perceive. Grass grows too slowly to observe from minute to minute, but over days and weeks, its growth is obvious. In autumn, the leaves turn color from green to red and gold. Color changes from minute to minute are invisible. Many of the most important changes in our environment happen this way, and so the process is unnoticed while it takes place. A glacier's retreat at the rate six inches per day will be imperceptible from week to week; yet over 30 years (a microsecond of geologic time) it will retreat more than a mile, totally transforming the landscape in starkly visible ways.

Slow, incremental changes may well surprise us more than large, sudden shifts: You grew up in a very safe community. Slowly crime and violence increase in frequency. Property values begin to decline, which starts a cycle of diminishing taxes, public infrastructure and services such as policing. As a beautiful neighborhood becomes rough and troubled, many may fail to notice the incremental changes as they unfold.

The discipline of systems thinking trains creators to focus attention on what may appear to be unchanging but is actually dynamic. As creators learn to do this consistently, something surprising happens. They begin to notice that almost *everything* is changing *all the time*. They become sensitive to even the smaller and slower changes in our experience.

Many of the creative challenges we experience are deeply affected by changes that we did not adequately anticipate: changes in our health, the economy (including in our work) and key relationships that matter to us in our families, offices and communities. Learning to observe change strengthens us significantly as we work to anticipate those we wish to avoid and those we desire.

The Foolishness of Crowds

Complex systems often elude common sense, producing behaviors that backfire, leading to unintended results. Perhaps you have had this experience... You are driving in two lanes of traffic moving in the same direction. The lane that you are *not* driving in seems to be moving faster than yours. You switch lanes only to discover that the lane you left behind is now the one moving faster. Why does this happen? Of course, because you fail to appreciate the system of drivers who are creating the traffic lanes. As one lane moves faster than another, more and more drivers will attempt to join it, causing it to slow down until the *other* lane is now the one moving faster.

I once planned to see a very popular movie opening at

my neighborhood theater. Anticipating a crowd, I decided to arrive extra early to get a seat. My plan backfired since many intelligent moviegoers attempted the same strategy. A large crowd arrived especially early and nevertheless struggled to find good seats.

Similarly, systems can defeat us in trying to beat the crowd to a good investment opportunity. Unless we are insiders with knowledge not shared by the general public, by the time we understand that an investment offers a high likelihood of gain, many others will also have this insight and the price will already be high, eliminating much of the hoped-for gain. Hence investment guru Warren Buffet's advice, "Be fearful when others are greedy, and be greedy when others are fearful."

It is not impossible to master complex systems, yet doing so requires *uncommon* sense. Mastery requires deep insight into the dynamics of a particular system along with some measure of good fortune; highly complex systems often become chaotic. When we master systems, rather than acquiring complete control, we learn to improve the likelihood of achieving a desired outcome by exposing ourselves to more optimal opportunities and risks.

A central skill of systems thinking—and therefore, of genership—involves learning to identify and evaluate changes. When we spend time reflecting on changes, we notice that our mind evaluates them as qualities or quantities that increase or decrease over time. Every variable shares this feature of increase or decrease. If we were to analyze the changes to our bodies over the course of a month, for example, we would begin to think about weight, energy level, alertness, comfort, hunger and other qualities that we perceive as increasing or decreasing. If we were looking at changes to an organization, we might think about staff levels, income, assets, receivables, number of customers, liabilities and a host of other aspects related to the organization that can increase or decrease.

Can there ever be an experience not understood as variable? It is possible to think about qualities or other features of our world not as variables but as steady states. Anything that we do not perceive as having the potential to change, or that cannot increase or decrease, is by definition not a variable. One example is standard measurement. A foot in length does not change; it is always exactly 12 inches. A pound does not change; it is always 16 ounces. The original name on our birth certificate does not change. The fact of our existence, once we are born, does not change. Reliable, unchangeable patterns of experience may be perceived as constants. Einstein maintained that the speed of light is constant for all observers, no matter their frame of reference. The meaning of numbers does not change: One is one and two is two.

Masters of systems thinking come to understand that whether or not something changes is a function not of some intrinsic property but of its relationship with the mind that observes it. For most purposes, we understand the length of one rotation of the Earth to occur at a constant speed of 24 hours. Physicists understand, however, that the exact time lapse for one rotation is closer to 23 hours and 56 minutes per day. Moreover, physicists have calculated that the Earth's rotation is slowing at the rate of .005 seconds per year, meaning that billions of years ago the Earth's day was significantly shorter, while billions of years in the future, it will be longer. So with the application of thought and analysis, something that appeared to be stable can be understood as variable.

This is true even of mental concepts and categories: Even though we might agree that 12 inches equals one foot, we can also understand the idea, using Einstein's concept of general relativity, that as lengths approach motion at the speed of light, they become contracted in the direction of motion (this is known in physics as the Lorenz contraction). So we can imagine that a foot-long arrow moving near the speed of light is much shorter than 12 inches measured on a ruler sitting at rest. In this sense, we can understand that the length of objects can depend upon our perceptual framework.

Practitioners of genership learn that systems thinking is a powerful tool for changing what appears to be stable or unchangeable; something that we formerly thought about as fact may now be understood as variable. We might think of our lifelong gender as a fact; we are born either male or female and will remain so. Modern medical science, however, using surgery and hormone therapy, can change aspects of a person's gender, so that today it might make sense to understand certain aspects of gender as changeable rather than fixed. We may have understood our raw intelligence as a fact, imagining that we are born with a fixed, stable IQ, yet intelligence may vary as we acquire education and knowledge, exercise our minds and focus our perceptions through practice. Intelligence may be understood as a quality that varies over time.

Systems thinking grows out of our increasing capacity to identify, observe and even to create variables; it entails our ability to perceive, develop and exploit the dynamic nature of the world around us to support our creative activities.

Systems: Cascading Changes

Writers have felled small forests of paper explaining what a system is in the context of systems thinking. A system arises when an observer notices that one variable influences another. This also illuminates what is not a system: when variables share no influence. True systems thinkers pay attention to relationships among variables and also to their absence. The insight that there is no system at work in a given situation can be of enormous value. Our perceptions and mental models of the context in which we perceive variables may influence our understanding about whether one influences another.

A businessman might draw the conclusion that there is no relationship between the amount of coffee he drinks and the cost of his telephone bill. On the other hand, if drinking coffee makes him very talkative, he might notice correlation. The presence or absence of connections among variables depends upon both personal observation and also the mental models applied in thinking through the relationships.

Systems are in the eye of the beholder. Many variables in our experience do not appear to have any systemic influence on one another. The amount of money in our individual bank accounts does not appear to influence the price of goods in the supermarket. Our height does not impact intelligence. The strength of our wishes for sunny weather does not change the amount of rainfall. By contrast, we perceive many variables as being connected in important but difficult-to-observe ways. The amount of our education usually influences our total income earned. The amount of our expenses influences the amount of our savings. The quality of our diets directly influences the extent of our energy and illnesses. The amount of stress we endure influences the quality of our health and personal relationships. Our level of exercise influences our cardiovascular fitness.

Systems thinking provides a clear tool for understanding how two variables can be related: They can move in the same (reinforcing) or the opposite direction (described interchangeably as negating, opposing or balancing). As we add a network of variables, such simple relationships can become extremely complex. To master this discipline requires that we think clearly about simple systems as building blocks. A helpful analogy is learning to write and read sentences. The student who learns the architecture of basic sentences can then master long and complex ones.

Strategic Considerations: What Is Systems Thinking Good For?

Systems thinking is most productive when we use it strategically in pursuit of clearly defined visions and discrete goals. It provides powerful strategic insight in helping us to understand and analyze our objectives in light of what we can change. Then we are able to explore how to influence the world, employing the power of systems to achieve our goals and visions. Thinking about systems for their own sake is not useful, but in connection with concrete aspirations empowers creativity. The examples below intentionally describe fundamental relationships so that we can then employ the analytical tools they provide on much more complex situations.

A person envisions running a mile in less than five minutes. He might simply begin an exercise routine and hope someday to reach his objective. Using systems thinking, however, he would begin to identify specific variables that will impact running performance, including body weight, body fat to lean-muscle mass, his body's ability to absorb oxygen, the level of development of muscle fibers in his legs, the efficiency of his stride and the productivity of his training routines. With systems thinking, he can develop a much more sophisticated strategy through which he works on changing goal oriented variables. He can also work to make those changes reinforce one another. Certain kinds of exercise will help him lose weight and also gain the kind of cardiovascular conditioning required to achieve his vision. The less body weight he has, the less energy required to achieve his goal. The more his weight is composed of muscle, the more calories he burns and the more fat he loses. By orchestrating the movement of related variables, he can move toward his goal with increasing efficiency.

A woman desires to improve her health. Without systems thinking, she might engage in common-sense strategies such as visiting her doctor to see whether anything is wrong with her, or exercising and trying to watch what she eats. Using a systems approach, however, she begins to look at health from a quite different perspective, thinking through the variables that impact her overall health status, such as cardiovascular stamina, quality of foods eaten, sufficiency of rest, immune-system strength, psychological stress, and exposure to viral and bacterial infections. The systems approach to health will provide insights into the variables that limit or disrupt her health status. Even if she eats well and exercises regularly, she may discover that being under significant psychological pressure and exposure to communicable illnesses limit overall health, causing her to suffer despite proactive efforts in the areas of diet and exercise.

A man works to achieve financial self-sufficiency. Common sense dictates hard work, thrift and wise investment as essential strategies. Thinking about systems, though, will provide much more sophisticated strategies. The man might begin to look at variables such as investment risk, personal earnings growth and savings per year. He may discover that his current income level cannot attain his goals no matter how hard he works nor how much he saves. This would likely lead him to employ different strategies to achieve his financial goals, such as changing the nature of his employment, the structure of his business or the level of risk he tolerates in investments.

These illustrations reveal a crucial truth encountered through systems thinking: Common sense is often not enough to achieve our goals. If that were the only factor required, people would succeed in most endeavors. We know that the opposite is true: Many creative efforts fail. Success requires *uncommon* sense, the kind of understanding derived from deeply considering all of the variables affecting our vision, then forming a strategy that harnesses the power of systems to help us achieve our desires. The world is constantly changing, and thus typically provides opportunities to advance our goals. Systems thinking allows us to be aware of such changes and to harness them immediately. Systems-conscious creators are able to achieve their ambitions more efficiently and consistently. A man in a rowboat can only go where rowing takes him—not very far. A woman who knows how to sail can harness the power of the winds, enough to travel around the Earth. An astronaut in a space ship—harnessing sophisticated electrical systems and rocket, solar and nuclear energy—can leave the planet entirely.

Systems Thinking

- Change
  vs. stasis

- Variables

- Links

- Loops

- Feedback

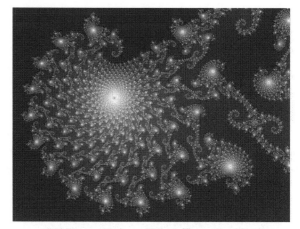

Wolfgang Beyer, *Mandelbrot Set*, 2006

Positive (Reinforcing) Relationships

Think of two climbers connected by a rope. One climbs to a higher level, then pulls up the second; he in turn ascends and pulls up the first. In this way, they move higher and higher up the mountain. Variables that move in the same direction are connected by such a rope: When one goes up, the other follows and vice versa. When a climber falls, he drags down his partner; as he falls farther, the first tumbles lower as well. Reinforcing variables move in tandem. Expressed in systems notation, when the feeling of hunger changes, the amount of eating activity generally increases or decreases:

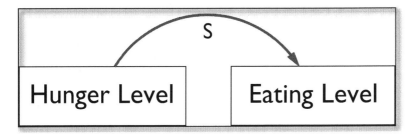

This type of diagram is called causal-loop (the "S" notation on the arrow shows that the variables move in the same direction) because it helps orient a systems thinker to the causal connections among a set of variables, and assists in understanding the best strategy for influencing one or more of them.

Other examples of variables that most people would observe as moving in the same direction include eating and gaining weight, income and spending, organizing and level of order, studying and level of knowledge, and practicing and level of skill. Whether there is a link observed between one variable and another, and the link's direction, depends on the individual observer; there are no universally correct answers in systems thinking. For a particular observer and situation, the link and direction may well appear to be different. A terrible piano player might discover that there is no relationship between the amount of time spent practicing and the level of skill attained. Systems thinking represents a way of expressing concepts about the world, and like any way of thinking, it can be accurate or inaccurate compared to what is actually happening in a specific circumstance. Systems thinking is a language employed to make certain aspects of the world—the interrelatedness of changes—more accessible to us.

Since the practice of genership entails collaborative creativity, systems thinking is essential to learn and share the connections between changes. Groups involved in creative work may disagree, or may be engaged discovering how changes within their span of control impact other changes currently beyond reach. Systems thinking allows these deliberations to become more precise.

Negative (Balancing) Relationships

What about variables that move in opposite directions? Take the connection between eating and hunger levels. When eating increases, hunger declines. The connection between hunger and eating levels move in the same direction, but the connection between eating and hunger (the "feedback") moves in the opposite direction. When we are hungry, we eat. Using systems notations, when we eat, we become less hungry:

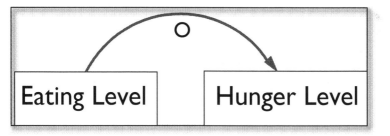

As in the previous picture, the boxes represent variables, the arrow the connection between them, the "O" movement in the opposite direction. Other variables that we tend to perceive as moving in opposite directions include the amount of sleep and degree of tiredness (when we sleep more, we are less tired); spending and saving (the more we spend, the less we save); bank balance and depositing (when our bank balance declines, we deposit funds to restore the balance). This opposing relationship between variables is like a seesaw: pushing one down makes the other rise; lifting one makes the other decline.

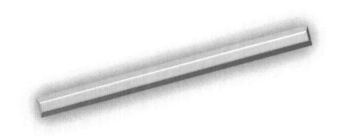

Becoming a Systems Sleuth

While these simple examples allow for clear understanding of basic concepts, in real cases the practice of systems thinking involves rigorous analytical work. When we attempt to influence complex situations, we must manage a host of interrelated variables. Systems thinking gives us the ability to isolate and investigate the factors influencing variables of particular interest to our creative aspirations.

Early in my organizational-development experience, I worked with a small nonprofit facing an unexpected budget shortfall. The board was attempting to understand why it was suffering reduced contributions when it appeared that no critical changes had occurred in its environment over a 24-month period. There had been no staffing changes and no unusual conditions in the market for its work. Indeed, the funding environment had been slowly improving. Nevertheless, the organization's income was declining.

Working with the board, my team identified a staffing decision the board had made three years earlier to cancel the contract of a key development consultant, who had succeeded in laying a foundation of multiyear relationships that remained in place for two years after the consultant ceased work. But because little had been done to sustain these relationships, critical grants had not been renewed. The organization had been coasting for two years on earlier work. As a result, it now faced a shortfall resulting from a decision made three years earlier. Because the organization had been able to thrive for two years after the consultant's departure, no one on the board understood or even remembered the dynamic that had caused the shortfall. Board members worked to construct several explanations for the lack of funds premised upon details of the organization's recent work quality. Yet the reality was more stark: The organization had simply failed to understand that its primary funding relationships were withering. It was not that the organization had failed to perform; it had failed to communicate its performance to key funding audiences.

The work of systems thinking often involves drilling down and carefully examining a critical cluster of variables impacting outcomes, the way a heart specialist searches for the cause of hypertension. This requires detailed knowledge of system functions and careful assessment of changes and possibilities among variables and structure.

The power of systems thinking lies in its basic simplicity: Identify variables, determine whether they influence one another and explore the resulting direction (positive/same vs. negative/opposite direction).

The challenge of systems thinking arises when mapping and exploring complex relationships among groups of interacting variables causing movements in the same or opposite directions. There is strong potential for feedback: When one variable sets off a chain reaction that then returns to influence the variable itself. Feedback happens when variables form a loop and begin to influence each other in one or more cycles. In real systems, there is no starting variable; they exist simultaneously.

Consider this basic balancing system: I grow hungry, I eat, my hunger diminishes, I stop eating.

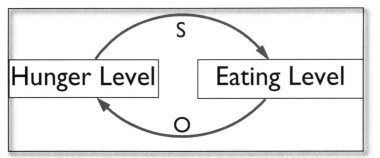

Now consider this basic reinforcing system: I invest my money at a certain interest rate, it grows; as I have more invested, it increases even more.

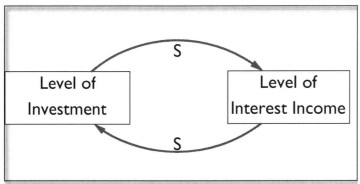

These figures form two archetypal system patterns. In the hunger example, through feedback, variables trigger a chain reaction that stabilizes the system (balancing). In the investment example, the variables trigger a chain reaction that causes growth (reinforcing). Much of systems thinking concerns exploring these signal patterns of interaction among more complex sets of variables.

Challenges of Systems Thinking

- Language

- Observer
  Isolation

- Delay

Karl-Ludwig G. Poggemann,
Looking Down Stairwell, **2008**

Why Is Systems Thinking Difficult?

Systems complexity can quickly cause analysis to become overwhelming, suggesting unending chains of balancing and reinforcing patterns within our environment. Our maps can quickly become so large and complex as to be useless. When we first encounter systems thinking, we may believe that by performing this analysis on all aspects of the world we inhabit, we will increase the overall mastery of our environment. This is impossible, however, due to the extraordinary intricacy and interrelatedness of real-world variables. If we were to attempt to understand all systems, we would descend into analysis paralysis, an unending effort to comprehend complexity that ultimately interferes with taking creative actions.

Observing change is challenging. The typical tool of analysis that we employ to manage and understand complex change employs spoken and written words. Yet traditional language can obscure variables and systems. How?

The first problem arises from the use of word labels to mask intricate underlying systems; they often provide a feeling of security that enables us to understand or manage a situation even if we have no real insight into the system's behavior. Labels give us the feeling that we can freeze something while thinking about it, that it will stand still for analysis. Labels also give the false impression that there is unity and coherence in a situation where the reality might be only a poorly understood set of volatile variables.

Take the word "government." Listen to people talking about public policy and you will find them use that word constantly. But what exactly is the referent of this word? It has many different branches (executive, legislative, administrative and judicial) and levels (federal, state and local). When people speak about the government it is often ambiguous to what element they refer. In another sense, people sometimes use "government" to talk about idealized institutions—their vision of what the government should be. But they also use the word to mean the actual people currently occupying positions of power. Contrast the word's use in these two statements:

The government depends upon a series of checks and balances.

The government intends to raise your taxes.

This word label is an indefinite term that can be used as a placeholder in thought to mask enormous complexity and uncertainty within the underlying systems it purports to describe.

The use of language to obscure systems, whether intentional or not, extends to the ideas that underlie words themselves. The mind often chooses to enclose complexity in a conceptual box that creates the illusion of unity and persistence over something dynamic and evolving. A powerful example of this tendency can be found in the idea of one's personal identity. We tend to think of our being and consciousness as something that is stable through time. The self, in other words, that we saw last week, last month or several years ago, seems to have a correspondence that we presently observe. When we take the lid off this concept however, and look within the system that composes the self, we find a dynamic set of variables. Consider that the body is composed of water and protein; indeed, water comprises more than half, yet that water and protein is not currently the same as what it previously contained. The process of living itself depends upon the consumption and expulsion of water, protein and fuel (carbohydrates); the physical stability of the body itself is largely an illusion. Our bodies are systems of change—patterns of energy rather than physical structures. Reflect on the reality that our individual conscious processes are produced by electrochemical reactions inside our brains, which themselves are fluctuating as ongoing patterns of energy relationships arising from electricity carried between neurons. These vary from moment to moment. So what are we, really, at the systems level? Our sense of self is actually a dynamic pattern of electricity inside an ever-changing pattern of water and protein molecules. The stability—indeed, the very object nature—of the self is largely an illusion. It remains a complex whirlwind of ongoing changes, not at all static. When we come to grips with this, we may see our very existence in radically different terms, better understanding the observation that we are a spirit as much or more than a body. We may also well treat our bodies to less fat, sugar and abuse!

These thought experiments suggest that language masks complexity and obscures intricate, highly dynamic systems. Language can provide us with illusions and allusions, and allows us to behave and think as though evolving situations were static or regular. This makes it difficult for us to perceive dynamic systems so that we can work effectively as creators with variables.

The tools of analysis for understanding complexity within language are quite clumsy. When confronted with elaborate systems, our natural instinct is to discuss them with others using words. A team attempting to address a complex situation will usually begin by holding a meeting. What happens then? People attempt to describe complex situations in sentences.

Two problems emerge. First, teams are driven to seek facts rather than variables. Why? Facts are easier to spot; they do not change within an intricate situation. Second, teams work to describe multifaceted relationships using the linear logic of noun-verb-noun constructs. To illustrate, try to verbalize a simple system such as filling a cup with water:

I begin to pour water into the cup. As the water fills it, I notice the level in the cup rising toward the rim and I slow the action of pouring. As the water level reaches that which I desire, I shut down the pouring action completely.

The simple system of filling a cup with liquid takes humans many attempts to master, as anyone having watched young children learn can attest. Notice that the language description of the system presents the process as a series of defined steps, each one following the other. In reality, these things happen in a continuous flow involving critical feedback links among the volume of liquid poured, the distance between the desired and actual level in the cup, and the estimate of time required to fill it. In systems notation, we capture the relationship like this:

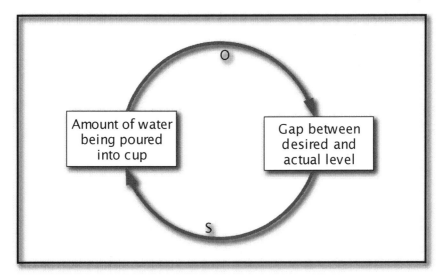

To describe more complex systems using words becomes almost impossible. We need to observe them in action or to study pictures and diagrams of their behavior. Unfortunately, in most cases involving the strategic assessment of complexity, we fall back on verbal descriptions that fail to capture the system's living dynamics and instead work to reduce it to a linear series of steps. The result is the failure to appreciate the feedback mechanisms that give life to the system. As opposed to learning by experience, anyone who attempts to learn how to fill a cup solely by following a series of written instructions would eventually have to clean up quite a bit of spilled liquid!

Another impediment to understanding systems is a failure to see ourselves as part of those we are studying. We have the ability to write observers out of descriptions; indeed, in professional writing, we are encouraged to take on an objective voice associated with omniscience or at least with authoritative knowledge. But in reality, there is no knowledge without real observers who are flawed and embedded within what they are working to describe. The objective observer is a pretense, a mythological construct. In the real world, we are like the blind men interacting with the elephant from different directions. One grasps the trunk and finds the elephant to be like a snake; one holding a tusk imagines the elephant is like a stone; one touching an ear thinks the animal is like a great jungle plant. The experimenter is part of the experiment. Because it focuses our attention on changes and points in reality for which we can influence behavior, systems thinking overcomes these tendencies in language to isolate the observer.

Systems Thinking and Junk Science

During the 1980s and '90s, class-action lawsuits claimed that Dow Corning's silicone breast implants caused a broad spectrum of health problems including breast cancer, a range of autoimmune diseases and various neurological problems. Numerous lawsuits throughout this period culminated in a 1998 multibillion-dollar class-action settlement that relegated Dow to bankruptcy protection for nine years.

Nevertheless, after this settlement, a number of large, independent reviews of the scientific literature, including U.S. Institute of Medicine studies, found that silicone breast implants do not cause breast cancers or any identifiable systemic disease. How could this happen?

The culprit was a phenomenon known as junk science in which plaintiffs who had breast implants and who were also sick intuited a causal relationship between the two events. This connection was then supported in court testimony by expert witnesses who testified that they believed implants caused illnesses despite the lack of rigorous scientific studies proving it. The experts induced other plaintiffs to observe similar connections, causing the number of complaints and claims to grow exponentially, although the connections between use of implants and disease are now believed to have been entirely coincidental.

The experience with silicone implants was unlike that observed in the connection between smoking and lung cancer, in which careful scientific studies ratified rather than rebutted the claimed causal link.

In highlighting the ways in which observer bias may skew system observations, systems thinking calls upon creators to understand how the engagement with systems on the part of users and observers influences behavior and interpretations.

A pollster asks a voter early in a campaign cycle whether she believes a certain political leader has been effective. While most voters have inclinations, they often do not have a settled opinion before being questioned. Once asked, the voter forms an opinion. These early results are then broadcast and influence the opinions of others; pollsters subtly shape the views of voters, even though they may claim to simply measure views formed independent of the polling process. Similarly, when a consultant polls employees to ask them about their company's weaknesses, she describes a range of possible symptoms. Having surveyed many possibilities by the end of the interview process, employees now believe that their company has weaknesses in a variety of areas. The consultant then presents these findings, leading management to believe that the employees independently verified certain weaknesses in the company's operations. In reality, the consultant planted them in employees' minds. Objectivity becomes an illusion.

Another feature of language that makes it extremely difficult to understand systems is disassociation of related events. The mind, especially when it employs the thinking tools of traditional language, creates connections between events that co-locate or coincide. In systems, however, two causally related variables may become removed from one another, exerting effects that become recognizable only after long delays. Intuition often misses such links. It is easy to write the sentence, "Exposure to carcinogens causes cancer," yet to observe this influence in reality requires years of painstaking observation and study. The link is not immediately obvious or intuitive with real certainty. After exposure to unsafe levels of benzene, for example, cancer may take several decades to develop, despite what we now know is a clear link.

The construct of delay and separation between causal connections manifests not only in physical systems, but also in social and psychological contexts. The link between education and economic success, for example, may take many years to become evident. In the short term, a programmer without formal education but with practical coding skill in a highly specialized computer language may earn higher wages than a college graduate. Over the long term, however, the college graduate—whose education allows her to travel over a range of social systems and organizations—may slowly gain ground while the specialized worker finds himself unable to adapt in a highly dynamic labor market. When a person who lacks higher education becomes disconnected from the workforce, he understands his predicament in terms of labor demand. He will likely blame unemployment on a downturn in the economy or layoffs as a result of mismanagement. When this worker becomes years beyond the traditional time frame for higher education, it may be difficult for him to see the connection between early investments in education and lifetime adaptability to the labor market.

Two Kinds of Action: Leverage and Design

The true power of systems thinking stems from its ability to enhance creative power: the ability to manifest desired results. A *leverage* intervention employs the existing causal influences within a network of variables. A *design* intervention relies on newly constructed influences. Increasing the heat of water in a tub by turning the hot water faucet describes a leverage intervention. Building a fire beneath the tub describes a design intervention.

Leverage Interventions

A leverage point is any place within a system where interaction affects the system's behavior. Think about a car; with respect to motion, an automatic has six leverage points:

Ignition point (button or key)
Brake
Accelerator
Gears
Emergency brake
Steering wheel

These are points at which the user can interact with car's system and radically influence its motion. Small changes are magnified through the car's system. Slight pressure on the accelerator can cause speed to increase rapidly. Pressure on the brake causes the collapse of momentum, slowing the car to a crawl within seconds. A turn of the steering wheel can cause a complete reversal of direction. Because most people are familiar with the operation of a car, they find this system to be nothing extraordinary. But on the scale of invention, the car is a miraculous system, allowing humans to travel exponentially faster and farther than they can by walking or running.

Another illustration of leverage is the use of an Internet search engine. In the seconds it takes a user to type a search term into a computer and click a mouse button, computer technology harnesses links to information resources spanning the entire globe within milliseconds, a process that would take years of time if lacking such resources. Of course, typing words into a text document and clicking on them produces nothing. To perform an Internet search, the user must engage with the system's leverage point: a web browser's search field on a functioning Internet-linked computer.

The study of systems promises to reveal such leverage points—places in the system where small inputs produce substantial desired outputs. To actively engage leverage points is to become a master creator.

Design actions differ substantially from leverage. When using the former, we do not work within existing systems; instead, we design a system to produce the desired result. It is the difference between stepping on the accelerator vs. building a new kind of car, or between using Google vs. designing a new method to search the Internet. Creators often resort to design actions because existing systems do not offer satisfactory leverage points to fulfill their desires.

Thinking Outside the Box—Literally!

I was recently involved with a construction project for a charter school that required building a special corridor to secure safe passage for students from the building in the event of a fire.

During the final inspection of the corridor, local code officials discovered a very large electrical box (more than six feet high and five feet wide) within the new passageway that they deemed a potential hazard. They asked the building owner to move the electrical box, a task that would have cost over $100,000 and delayed the project by months. The problem was that the box itself was embedded within one of the corridor walls, tightly integrated into the electrical system and building infrastructure. Moving the box would have required demolition of part of the corridor as well as rewiring a significant portion of the building's electrical system.

Our team spent several hours looking at the situation. The time delays and increased costs resulting from a decision to move the box were extreme enough to threaten the entire project. Would we have to raise additional funds and delay the entire start date for the school? We needed a creative solution. Staring at the building plans, our team finally proposed a design intervention. Instead of moving the box, why not move the corridor and enclose the box within a fire-rated closet? This was our version of bringing the mountain to Mohammed! The solution cost $3,000 instead of $100,000 and took one day instead of months. This is an example of systems thinking at the level of design, rather than moving variables within the existing system.

A vivid case of the use of leverage and design actions in combination involves Barack Obama's presidential campaign. In seeking office, his team engaged effectively with numerous existing systems including traditional media channels, gave speeches across the country and sought contributions from standard political campaign sources. This part of the campaign required intensive knowledge and experience with existing systems, and the ability to master leverage points within them (media cycles and strategic delivery of speeches). Obama's speech at the 2000 Democratic Convention essentially launched him into the national political limelight.

Obama's successful campaign also entailed a large quotient of system-design actions. His campaign built an unprecedented Web-based social media application that allowed his constituents to self-organize and also resulted in an unprecedented ability to raise small contributions from millions of voters. His team raised more than $500 million online in small contributions, an amount equaling the entire online contributions of Senator Kerry and President Bush combined in 2004. This was not the result of using existing leverage points; it resulted from design genius in forming an entirely new system of campaign finance.

Leadership, Genership and Systems Thinking

Understanding systems thinking to engage in both design and leverage actions is essential to creativity. Systems knowledge and experience form the bedrock of effective strategy in any creative project. Failure can often be attributed to the lack of sufficient systems understanding.

Leadership—as opposed to genership—can be profoundly disabling to the development of systems knowledge and experience, arising from the Fallacies and leadership group dynamics that give rise to hierarchical command structures, top-down approaches to communications, obsession with power and the development of bureaucracies. Living systems demonstrate extraordinary complexity and rapid change. They do not stand still awaiting observation and study. It is likely that they will have evolved during the period when analysis is being performed, rendering study nearly irrelevant. Because leadership tends to consolidate analysis and strategic planning in one person or within a small leadership team, it performs poorly at systems analysis, which requires continuous data gathering, open dialogue and ongoing experimentation. Leaders can be reluctant to embrace strategies that come from outside the organization or that emanate from members who lack status, because they fear losing credit for success and upsetting internal power structures.

In contrast, genership excels at systems thinking because it decentralizes analysis and planning, allowing those on the front lines of creative effort to participate in framing and assessing organizational strategies. Teams of co-creators establish a culture that eagerly learns from conflict while promoting open dialogue to accelerate and maximize learning. Such teams are able to experiment with leverage points and system-design changes to see how diverse strategies affect progress toward the common vision. Teams practicing genership are open to learning no matter the source. They care more about success than status or preserving internal organizational power.

Tale of Two Thinkers

In the early '90s I consulted with two small nonprofit organizations engaged in community-development work. One had a strong traditional leader who worked very hard in a focused and disciplined way, governed by what she perceived to be best practices in the field. To this leader, such an approach required diligently doing all of the tasks that she could see within other successful organizations. Her work was filled with checklists, governance processes and committee meetings. This organization had some successes, but more than a decade later, it was essentially the same organization as it had been, and even declined somewhat as a result of shrinking philanthropic resources and increased competition.

At another small organization, I had the opportunity to work with a quirky, nontraditional leader who ignored most rules and procedures set forth in best-practices guides. She didn't have a high tolerance for process, meetings and checklists, but instead focused on transforming the organization's fundamental business strategy. She wanted to create an earned revenue model for a community-based organization rather than increasing its ability to engage in traditional philanthropy. She had an unusual creative vision and the ability to create a novel system that did not exist for competitors. A decade later it is thriving and enjoys a capital base approximately 15 times larger than the one with a more traditional leader at the helm.

The ability to construct and master systems separates organizations that achieve their visions from those that don't. Consider the dramatic rise and fall of Digital Equipment Corporation (DEC), a manufacturer of mainframe computers and an innovator in the development of minicomputers. In the late '80s DEC grew to $14 billion in sales, employing over 130,000 people worldwide. But the company failed to grapple successfully with the emergence of the personal computer. DEC possessed microprocessor technology, but its business model relied on selling computers for tens of thousands of dollars. With its technology imprisoned by this high-cost business model, it could not compete and eventually was acquired by Compaq. What killed DEC was not a lack of technological innovation per se, but rather the inability to navigate the external system changes affecting its business.

In contrast, Microsoft successfully harnessed external systems to promote explosive growth during the same time that DEC was in decline. By working with a large community of application developers, Microsoft was able to dramatically expand the number of customer applications for Windows. This created a massive reinforcing system in which customers who bought Windows applications drove sales of PCs that used Microsoft's operating system, thereby further expanding the opportunities for Windows software developers in a reinforcing spiral. In addition, Microsoft licensed the use of its operating system to multiple hardware vendors, allowing for many businesses to share in the benefits of the scaling demand for Windows PCs, thus further increasing the opportunities for application developers. This system allowed Microsoft to become predominant among personal-computer users, relegating its competitor Apple to 5% of the overall market. Nevertheless, Apple learned the lesson of systems thinking in the development of its iTunes ecosystem and its successful partnership with third-party developers for apps on its iPod line and smartphone platform, iPhone. As a result, Apple redefined and was able to dominate the smartphone industry.

These examples illustrate the fundamental point: Systems thinkers become empowered to succeed in their creations while those lacking such consciousness falter and often fail.

CHAPTER EIGHT
CREATIVITY: *THE SOUL OF GENERSHIP*

The core differences between leadership and genership unfold within the creative process. In leadership, personality takes precedence over what is created. Leadership tends to co-opt the creative process, making it subservient to the leader's power and legacy. As a result, in organizations with a dominant leadership culture, we celebrate the leader as a person rather than what has been created, seeing the results of the creative process through the prism of individual identity. We grasp what has been created by understanding the leader as an individual, thus creative meaning becomes equivalent to biography, imputing the qualities of the created to the creator. Many mistakes result, not the least of which is to think and behave as if creating something of value is the same as being a good person or group, and vice versa.

This transference also implies the false belief that to create something valuable *requires* an individual or team to be good as a foundation for their creativity. The danger in this line of thinking is to believe that focus on improving the self necessarily translates into effectiveness. Avoiding this mistake liberates creators from a perpetual process of self-help.

The risk stems from the egoism produced by the Fallacies. Messiahs and heroes inevitably come to believe that their organizations are mere extensions of personhood. If the organization and its work are avatars of the leader, then working to improve the leader is the same as working on the organization's vision. In this way, both are understood to share an almost mystical connection. If one succeeds, so must the other, a circumstance often given false credibility by the massive paychecks and bonuses involved.

This narcissism drives the operation of the Fallacies in a circle. Believing in the power of an individual with supreme personal qualities, the group seeks a messianic figure to lead, heaping its expectations upon that person believed to have super powers, waiting for him to produce miracles. The supposedly perfect leader eventually fails in this miraculous task or is exposed as having some tragic flaw that renders the messianic role untenable (i.e., how could an imperfect person possibly produce miraculous performance?). After the people drive out or sacrifice the messiah, heroes competing to take his place are themselves compared to previous messianic figures by employing leadership nostalgia. The messianic leaders of the past are viewed through a distorted historical lens that writes their flaws out of the record and puts them on an imaginary pedestal. One of the heroes is then selected with the expectation that she has the messianic perfection required to lead. When the messiah reveals weaknesses, the cycle begins anew.

But experience and reflection regarding the work of great creators shows that deeply flawed individuals and teams can produce masterworks. Messianic status is not required to be an effective creator. Indeed, observed with clarity, almost all creative genius is deeply flawed. If only perfect individuals or teams could create, nothing would be created. The problem in our culture—one driven by the Fallacies—is that we associate perfection with people who are strong creators. We expect them to be like gods because their creations are godlike, a clear category mistake. The praise due to the Almighty is that he allows mortals—despite gross and persistent imperfections—to have access to his creative abilities. Imperfect people can and do produce works of art, entertainment, business and social justice that tend toward perfection.

Because leadership mistakenly associates creativity with personality, to lead a group differs from engaging it creatively through genership. In many ways, the act of leading compromises—even drains—a group's creative energy. The leader moves away from the group to command personal attention, and recruits others to follow based on recognition of personality (rather than creative vision). The inchoate purpose of leadership is to move the group, which differs substantially from engaging its creative energies or stimulating it to fully participate.

From this tension between the leader and group, leadership (operating within that pure paradigm, as opposed to one that includes elements of genership) is always premised on the power relations between those who lead and those who follow. Leadership demands attention so that the group's activities may be orchestrated, albeit through voluntary actions. Leadership may even entail working to suppress the individual creativity of group members so they can follow effectively. There is often a contest of wills; that which dominates is the one that leads. To prevail in this context is to force an agenda, to suppress diversity of opinion and thought. We can find in the work of someone like Tom DeLay, a Republican majority leader in the House of Representatives (2003-05), known as "The Hammer," an illustration of this style of leadership. DeLay enforced party discipline on close votes by threatening members with political attacks in primaries. The message was clear: Agreement with leadership matters more than personal opinion.

Because leadership entails this power contest between the leader and followers, it inevitably sets in motion Fallacy-driven conflict; wherever there is a leader, there will invariably be one or more followers who dispute the leader's claim of authority. They may resist only subconsciously or privately, but over time, this conflict over power within the group may threaten to disrupt its creative agenda. This sets in motion a narrative in the group's life that will result in one of two outcomes:

1) the leader's successful defense of authority (messiah status);
2) the leader's demise and the search for a new messiah through hero combat

As early as 2010, the public narrative on President Barack Obama's first term shifted. Prior to his election and during the first year of his presidency, the public remained focused on the wisdom of his policies, debating the economic stimulus as well as financial and healthcare reform. In the lead-up to the 2010 midterm elections, the conversation shifted from policy to identity. The question on the public's mind evolved into an inquiry about leadership: Is Obama the true messiah? Republicans derided him as a fraud (even questioning his citizenship), while disaffected Democrats complained that he had failed to deliver on the plethora of promises made during his 2008 campaign. A subtle but critical transformation took place: The national dialogue about progress became derailed while the country (once again) debated the leadership question in search of a more perfect leader rather than a more perfect nation. The expectations thrust upon Obama—that he could (within a hyper-partisan environment) reverse a near economic collapse while ending global conflict and solving major structural policy problems (achieving, for example, entitlement, financial and healthcare reform)— were beyond all reason.

When real innovation and bold creative processes are required, leadership alone becomes insufficient. While many have tried to reframe enlightened leadership as a practice that includes the skills entailed in stimulating group creativity, the preceding chapters have shown that the required skill set is sufficiently distinct to merit genership's entirely new approach:

CoVisioning
CoThinking
Building creative passion
Harnessing conflict in support of learning
Systems thinking

How do these practices combine in an effective creative process?

Creating as a System of Skills

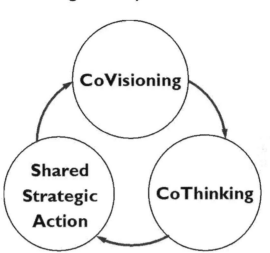

1. CoVisioning: Dreaming and Achieving Together

This practice involves working with others to articulate and develop a clear picture of a desired future. It entails stimulating freedom and creative playfulness, enhancing experimentation and engaging in practices of invention including reframing, construction and recombination, as well as iteration and variation. This skill includes finding and engaging those in the group with the energy and inclination to innovate on a particular project of group work, entailing recognition that the ability of group members to innovate will vary substantially across different tasks and challenges. In a creative culture that transcends the leadership construct, innovation is wide open, not controlled or burdened by any one leader or leadership group. The only relevant question is this: Who in the group has the energy and interest to bring imagination to bear upon some particular aspect of a shared future without having to become the leader? In a clear demonstration of genership, CoVisioning entails harnessing conflict as a resource to heighten learning and creativity.

2. CoThinking: Assessing Reality in Light of Desire

A genership practitioner engages group members in dialogue about reality in light of desire. This involves seeing the world as a creator rather than observer, and recognizing that reality can evolve in response to a purposeful interaction with the mind. In the hands of one skilled in genership, the contemplation of reality becomes an exercise in observing how the world changes and can be altered to yield to the group's shared desires. CoThinking involves a careful analysis about how the world in its present state is incongruent with the group's desires. Through CoThinking, the group must also work through competing perceptions about its desires. Group members may disagree about interpretations of both desire and reality, as well as what they should create and where they stand in terms of progress and strategic action. This process entails harnessing the energy created from conflicts in both desire and understanding reality, leading to improved strategic action and learning.

3. *Shared Strategic Action*

The third component of creativity is shared strategic action as part of a dynamic system. The group is always acting or failing to act in ways that lead either away from or toward its desired future. People who develop genership skills are able to engage group members in consciously shaping their actions. Those skilled in genership are also able to employ systems-thinking tools to assess and alter their strategies to increase leverage—the level of progress achieved for the effort expended. Systems thinkers embrace the momentum already present in the world to bring their visions into existence.

Putting It All Together

Genership closely weaves these major practices, allowing a group to shift among the activities of shared visioning, assessing current reality and undertaking strategic actions, repeating the cycles as the group makes progress. The interaction among these practices produces two additional features of the creative process: development of structural tension and recognition of structural conflict.

Structural tension and *conflict* are ideas developed initially by Robert Fritz in his groundbreaking work on creativity, *The Path of Least*

Resistance (1989). Structural tension is the energy that arises from the difference between what an individual or group wants to create and what it has at the present moment. So a mountain climber wanting to reach the summit feels tension when standing in basecamp; this provides the energy that drives her ascent. In contrast, structural conflict arises when the primary tension between what is to be created and what presently exists faces an additional, competing psychological element, such as a contrary belief or desire. A climber who wants to reach the summit but who also needs to leave basecamp to care for a sick family member will experience structural conflict. As he approaches the summit, the conflict he feels will increase. Mastering these two dynamics—structural tension and conflict—are critical to the creative process within individuals and groups.

Creative Energy & Structural Tension

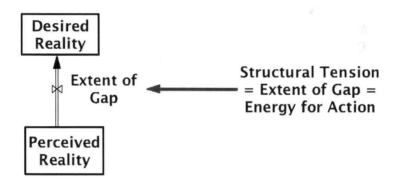

Structural Tension

We can understand structural tension in terms of energy and momentum. These arise when group members observe tension between their desires and current reality. Creativity does not happen without such tension; it is *structural* arising from this gap. This produces energy that can be invested in work, thereby generating momentum to create what is desired. The group experiences the process of closing that gap, thereby overcoming the conflict as a pleasurable release of tension.

Examples Involving Individuals:

1. Mark yearns to change his body weight after observing that he is currently 20 pounds overweight. Every morning upon waking he steps on the scale to record the difference between his desired and actual weight. This recognition creates energy for action. Throughout each day, he experiences the tension caused by his desire, which compels him to diet and exercise. Slowly he loses weight; upon reaching his goal, he experiences the pleasure of the reduced tension between his desire and current reality. Finally one morning he awakes and discovers that he has achieved his desired weight. Now his reality is congruent with desire and he experiences release. Rather than conflicting, his desire now describes reality.

2. Ann wants to become skilled at playing the piano. Each day she tests herself by practicing, playing compositions of increasing difficulty. She regularly notices the disparity between her current and desired skill level. This difference creates the energy that impels her to improve through painstaking practice. Over time, her skill level increases and she feels the pleasure of the reduced tension between her desire and present reality regarding her skills as a musician.

3. Dan desires to achieve a quality relationship with a companion in terms of intimacy and love. During their encounters, he notices the ways in which their relationship diverges from his desires, a contrast that creates energy for action. He works to foster experiences that increase intimacy and affection. Over time, the character of their relationship becomes more congruent with his desires. Dan experiences his ability to manifest the quality of relationship that he desires as a pleasurable reduction of tension.

Examples Involving Groups:

1. Members of a high-school basketball team are eager to win their league's championship. Playing each game during the season, they score and defend points in competition with the opposing team. If they are even, behind or sense that their opponent may yet prevail, they

experience the tension between their desire and reality (measured as the probability that their team will not win the game and thus fail in their quest to win the championship). This tension manifests as energy to play harder. As they pull ahead or gain on their competitors, they experience the pleasure of reduced tension. The energy may oscillate during the game, increasing as the risk that they will lose grows, dissipating as they move closer to their goal. As they win each game, team members experience the pleasure inherent in the release of creative tension; they notch another win and move closer to their goal of winning the league championship.

2. A small software company desires to achieve a certain profit goal within a fiscal quarter, seeking to build a company that grows more profitable over time. The team knows that failure to achieve its goals may cause key executives to leave the company, causing the firm to face even greater challenges in the future. As they work to develop and market their services and products, energy arises from the gap between their desired profit margin and what they achieve from actual sales. As they approach achievement of their profitability goals, they experience the pleasure of reduced tension. If their progress falls behind during the cycle, they will experience increasing creative struggle while encountering realities they wished to avoid.

3. Members of a political campaign desire to win an election. As they work to develop their messages and meet with voters, they receive feedback in the form of polling data and endorsements, observing the disparity between their desires and the current reality of their level of public support. They experience the pleasure of reduced tension as the feedback suggests that they are gaining ground and have an increased likelihood of success. They experience increased tension and energy when the feedback suggests that they are losing ground or that the likelihood of success is diminishing.

Each of the examples above involves situations in which the individual or group experiences success during the creative process. Of course, it is possible to experience failure or perpetually delayed success as well. Despite noticing and observing the contrast between desire and current reality, an individual or group could nevertheless fail to move closer to its desired objective. In such cases, we are unable to employ the energy to succeed that arises from the conflict. True genership finds a way to transcend these moments so that the creative process remains energized and effective, rather than paralyzed.

Understanding and Transcending Creative Paralysis

There are five distinct causes for failure or stalling in creative initiatives. Transcending them liberates the creative process, but first requires that we understand how these challenges undermine creativity. Genership provides practical strategies for overcoming them.

Challenges to the Creative Process

• Dissipating desires

• Failing to observe current reality

• Competing desires (conscious & unconscious)

• Conflicting understandings of reality

• Committing to failed ideas or strategies

Timetrax23, *Going Out of Business*, 2006

It is critical to note that our efforts to understand and provide examples of these challenges do not imply that they are necessary, essential or productive in creative work. On the contrary, an effective creative process meets these challenges and transcends them. But many creators and their teams will find themselves beset by these kinds of issues at some point during a lifetime of creative work. We cannot build an effective creative process without a deep understanding—grounded by examples—of how the following challenges impede creativity:

1. Dissipating Desire
2. Failure to Observe Current Reality

3. Competing Desires: Conscious or Beneath Awareness
4. Conflicting Understandings of Current Reality
5. Committing to Ideas or Strategies that Do Not Yield Progress

Dissipating Desire

While often exhilarating, creativity can be painful and exhausting. Anyone who has worked hard to create something recognizes that endurance can fail. Pleasure comes from success, by bringing what we desire into existence. This happens when reality is changed according to our desire. But reduced tension can also happen by relaxing our objectives, even though this response may undermine creativity.

Michael is a runner engaged in a competitive race, pushing the limits of his abilities. His legs ache, his lungs burn and his heart seems to beat out of his chest. As he pushes himself up a steep hill, he suddenly pulls to a stop and begins to walk. For the moment, Michael has abandoned his desire to run, for the next few minutes feeling the pleasure of releasing the terrific tension he has placed upon himself.

Linda is an aspiring novelist working on a particular scene in her latest work. She wants the scene to produce a certain emotional response and works diligently, but after days and weeks, the scene fails to come together for a reason she cannot quite understand. Finally, she takes the pages in hand, throws them away and goes for a walk, telling herself to abandon that scene. She feels the fleeting pleasure of giving up the tension arising from her own creative struggle.

Relaxing desire in this way usually does not work to reduce tension over the long-term; the runner driven to run and the writer impelled to write will very likely experience a powerful return of their fundamental creative desires. Yet the temptation to release creative desire is palpable. Many lose their ability to create because they meet the pain and tension by relaxing their desires. For many creators, the retreat to alcohol or drugs functions as a respite from creative tension. Under the spell of chemicals, the mind releases its creative demands. Intoxication offers momentary release from ambition.

Another manifestation of relaxing desire arises from *modifying* our goals to release tension. Using the examples above, Michael may say to himself, "My goal is now to walk up the hill instead of running." Or Linda may say, "It's acceptable if this particular scene does not evoke a strong, specific emotion in my reader." These concessions reduce creative energy by lowering expectations so the process imposes less tension on the creator. Clearly, genership does not advocate relaxing desires as a way to manage creative tension.

In lowering collective expectations, groups as well as individuals are able to relax desire. This can produce a sense of well-being similar to achieving an ambitious goal. A small business weathering an economic downturn might view breaking even, rather than profit, as a significant success. A sports team in a highly competitive league might view playoff participation, rather than championship, as a sufficient accomplishment. That lowering expectations produces pleasure has been validated in cross-cultural studies of European societies. For more than 30 years, two-thirds of Danes have reported being very satisfied with their lives, in contrast to Italy, Greece and Portugal, in which less than 25% express such satisfaction levels. Researchers believe the key to the differences lies in expectations. Danes consistently express very low expectations for the coming year, while nations that rate low in satisfaction persist in reporting high expectations.

There is a critical difference between relaxing a desire and choosing to focus upon one to the exclusion of another. Society may judge whether particular desires are good or evil, but individuals and teams tend to experience desires simply as realities within their current psychological landscape. Nevertheless, passions change and evolve over time. Every individual and team has the power to choose particular desires to invest creative energy in pursuing or manifesting. This issue is always at the heart of the CoVisioning process. What we choose to invest our creative energies in achieving defines who we become to ourselves and others.

A successful runner is not a failed swimmer. A successful painter is not a failed writer. But it is possible for runners, swimmers, painters or writers to experience creative failure because they relax their desires, lowering expectations of what they can achieve to gain the fleeting pleasure of momentary relief from creative struggle. The difference comes in giving up a desire to achieve the pleasure of diminished tension, as opposed to selecting where to invest creative energies and welcoming the tension that the focused creative process entails. It is true that the pursuit of a creative dream may entail the abandonment of others. But we only experience true creative tension around those desires in which we invest creative energy.

Failure to Observe Current Reality

Denying reality or rationalizing it can severely undermine the creative process; a creator can gain temporary respite from the tension between desire and progress.

Jamie labors over a short story about a love affair gone wrong, based on painful personal details of her life. Feeling vulnerable, she lacks the courage to show the work to anyone. She puts it away, promising herself that she will return to it again someday. But lacking feedback about what she has written, Jamie is not able to focus on whether the work fulfills her creative vision. In this way, she avoids confronting the tension between her aspirations for the work and its reality.

Steve is a middle-aged man struggling to balance work, family and personal health demands. He knows he is overweight and begins to diet. But he is reluctant to step on the scale because this will reveal specifically how much weight he has gained and how much work he has to do to achieve his goals for personal health. Lacking such specific knowledge, he avoids the creative tension that comes with confronting reality about the state of his health. He tells himself a lie that reduces his tension: "Everything is fine; I am making progress."

Cheating Reality

The 2001 federal education law known as "No Child Left

Behind" required schools to engage in mandatory annual testing of student progress. This effort to hold schools accountable for student performance has caused enormous tension within local public educational systems. For the first time, the failure of students and schools in the mission of educational progress became starkly visible across America. Coming to grips with this failure spurred many school boards to take remedial action. The law also caused widespread debate about how educational goals for schools are defined and measured, and whether comprehensive learning could be successfully evaluated using standardized tests. There was also widespread concern about the practice of "teaching to the test," in which students' scores might improve at the expense of sacrificing other valid educational objectives.

Certain schools in Atlanta, Georgia, responded poorly to federal pressure. A 2011 investigation revealed that teachers and administrators had falsified test data, correcting thousands of student responses to improve the apparent performance record for their schools. Investigators reported that 178 teachers and principals working at 44 schools were involved. The educators, including 38 principals, were either directly involved in erasing wrong answers on a key standardized test or they knew—or should have known.

Policymakers have identified other school systems that have responded similarly to the creative challenge of improving schools by masking the truth about their lack of achievement. This illustrates the use of denial and fraud to relax creative tension. Schools deluded about their actual performance were deprived of necessary creative energy required to undertake more aggressive reforms.

Harriet, a single mother, struggles to pay her bills and knows that spending is over budget. When her credit card statement arrives, she leaves it unopened, instead choosing to mail a check for an amount sufficient to cover the minimum payment. By failing to check on her total debt, she avoids the increasing tension that comes with her vision to become debt free.

Bryce is a politician running to serve as a state representative. He senses that he is falling behind as the election approaches. During the last weeks of campaigning he ignores the polls, allowing his team to believe that they are making progress despite contrary evidence, thus avoiding the tension inherent in learning where they actually stand with the voters.

Randy is an aspiring basketball player. Late at night he stands alone in a neighborhood gym practicing foul shots. Before each shot, he imagines crafting the perfect arc from the foul line, popping the net with a satisfying swish. He misses more than he makes, experiencing the tension between his desire to shoot consistently and the current reality that he is missing 70% of his shots. To reduce his creative tension, he turns the ball closely in his hands and concludes, "There is something wrong with my basketball." Then he looks closely at the rim he is shooting at. "I think the rim is not at the right height," he mutters. These rationalizations set him on the course to obtain another basketball and a new place to shoot, rather than to alter his shot to make it more accurate and consistent. During this time of exchanging basketballs and courts, he enjoys fleeting release from the pressure to create. "Everything will be different when I get a better ball and proper rim," he tells himself.

Failing to observe reality robs an individual or team of the opportunity to harness creative energy. It may produce false pleasure that comes from an erroneous belief that the gap between desire and reality is closing. When reality intervenes, the tension can be so painful as to cause a relaxation of desire. Individuals or groups persisting in a state of denial may simply give up their desires when confronted with this gap, representing a complete collapse of the creative process.

Jim falls in love with a close friend. He loves her so passionately that he turns a blind eye to the reality that she loves someone else. Because he does not comprehend the divergence between his desire and the underlying reality of their relationship, he lacks the creative energy required to take steps to build the relationship he desires with her. When he finally confronts the reality of her love for another, the pain and tension are overwhelming, so he relaxes his desire for her. "That was not the right partner for me," he acknowledges, even though his initial desire for her was substantial. He may never really understand whether his choice to *dissipate* the creative energy, instead of *managing* it, caused the failure of his relationship.

Failing to Confront Reality

In 2001 Blockbuster was America's dominant source for movie rentals, with a mighty market capitalization exceeding $5 billion. Blockbuster's primary business model involved its national chain of movie-rental stores. Meanwhile, Netflix was advancing a new business model premised on mailing DVDs to customers using an Internet interface. Netflix had a lower cost structure and offered convenience that would eventually topple the Blockbuster empire. Nevertheless, the Netflix IPO in May 2002 barely succeeded; its share price fell from $15 at the time of the IPO to $4.85 in October.

As Netflix emerged onto the competitive landscape, Blockbuster chose to ignore its competitor's alternative model, proceeding with business as usual and making only a few minor alterations to its strategies. Blockbuster first announced that it would let customers return videos whenever they liked, with no penalty for lateness. This failed to improve business as customer defections continued and revenues dropped. As Blockbuster lost revenues, its high capital costs caused profits to collapse, forcing the company to close store locations. This scenario led to further competitor gains. In 2007, Netflix launched a download version of its service and, soon after, iTunes began distributing movies to its portable devices and Apple TVs.

Because Blockbuster wanted to see itself as a movie and game rental provider rather than an entertainment distributor, it ignored market innovations. Blockbuster imagined that customers primarily valued the convenience and experience of the physical retail outlet. But the Internet provided recommendations and the ability to rent with a few mouse clicks at a significantly lower price.

When Blockbuster finally realized that Netflix and iTunes were advancing seriously competitive business models, it attempted to create automated kiosks in grocery stores and other locations to increase convenience, as well as to implement an on-demand service that would stream movies to portable devices. But the moment had passed; Blockbuster was hamstrung with high capital costs. Bankruptcy followed, and in 2011 Dish Network acquired the company's assets for a mere $230 million. The downfall came because of failure to confront reality. As late as 2008, Blockbuster CEO Jim Keyes remained in denial: "I've been frankly confused by this fascination that everybody has with Netflix... Netflix doesn't really have or do anything that we can't or don't already do ourselves."

The failure to observe reality drains creative energy precisely because it thwarts actions designed to close the gap. An individual or team thus becomes incapable of formulating strategy and taking action, because there is a lack of coherent, accurate information to serve as the basis for progress.

Competing Desires: Conscious or Beneath Awareness

The third major fault in the creative process occurs when the creator experiences conflicting desires, which may be conscious or not. To create requires focused energy. A major fault in any creative process occurs when energy becomes channeled in competing directions. When desires conflict, creative energy is either dissipated or turns against itself like a swimmer kicking one way with his feet while paddling in the opposite direction with his arms. The examples below illustrate pathologies in the creative process, demonstrating creativity gone awry. Genership offers strategies for reinstating a healthy creative process, allowing us to transcend these challenges and realize a robust creative process within our lives and work.

Challenges: Competing Desires

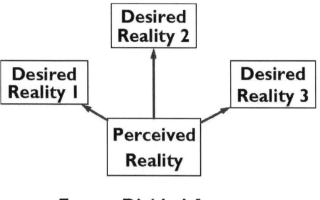

Energy Divided Among
Competing Desires

Conscious Competing Desires

The creative process within an individual or team often fails because of the presence of conscious conflicting desires, representing urges to move in either divergent or self-defeating directions. John is a football player who desires to play both as a quarterback and receiver. In developing skills, he becomes torn between time invested as a quarterback working on his ability to read the defense, scramble and throw, and time as a receiver working to sprint, break free of coverage and catch passes. As he excels in one area, he will take time required for development from another area.

Susan desires to excel at personally meeting her daughter's every need and simultaneously attaining the highest level of professional success. These desires require investment in competing activities that move in separate and divergent directions. Susan's professional success calls for complete dedication to advancement and development in her workplace, while parenting excellence requires investing time and energy with her daughter. Such competing desires rarely can be fulfilled at the same time.

Another kind of conscious conflict in desire causes failure when it moves in self-defeating—as opposed to divergent—directions. Success in achieving one desire directly undermines progress in a competing impulse. Picture someone who wants to obtain optimal physical health while eating whatever and whenever he wants. His fitness goals make it impossible to satisfy every craving for food. Similarly, eating whatever and whenever will likely limit physical health and a sense of well-being, unless innate desires are perfectly calibrated to optimal health (an experience enjoyed by few human beings). An individual's natural cravings for fatty foods or sweets (having evolved over millennia of development in food-scarce environments) lead to eating more than would be necessary for optimal health, which entails some personal denial regarding pleasurable foods.

To further illustrate this concept of self-defeating desires, consider once again the case of Bernard Madoff. By all accounts, he did not start out intending to create a fraudulent scheme; it unfolded when, early in the life of his firm, Madoff did not earn the returns he had expected for his clients. At this point he was confronted with contradictory (and self-defeating) desires: his wish to appear successful and the desire to be honest and law-abiding. Honesty (admitting the losses) would undermine his apparent success while masking the losses would undermine his honesty. The years that followed demanded ever greater dishonesty to keep up appearances; Madoff's lies eventually destroyed the very desire (apparent success) that it was designed to maintain, resulting in worldwide humiliation and loss of freedom for the rest of his life.

Greed vs. Integrity at Research in Motion

The business pages are littered with stories that reveal conflicting desires. An entrepreneur with a single-minded drive to succeed and amass vast wealth may well be nagged by the desire to achieve a maximum state of transparency and ethical behavior, yet he may discover that an across-the-board commitment to ethics and integrity reduces his ability to earn maximum profits. That intrinsic conflict has brought down more than a few business icons, even those who accumulated more money than could liberally be spent in a dozen lifetimes. The example of Research in Motion, a once highflying technology company with beloved products and enamored stockholders, offers a stark example of competing—and to be sure, unnecessary and self-defeating—desires.

Research in Motion helped to put Canada's Ontario on the map as a business center, mentioned in press releases and on product brochures worldwide. Its co-CEOs at the time, Mike Lazaridis and James Balsillie, CFO Dennis Kavelman and VP of Finance, Angelo Loberto, illegally granted millions of immediately profitable stock options to themselves and other employees, by backdating them for eight years. This led to huge "bonuses" that were never disclosed and that would have provoked a blowtorch of complaints and regulatory scrutiny.

The insiders who occupied the soft leather seats within Research in Motion's executive suite accounted for and priced their option grants with fabricated dates designed to give them exercisable options at prices well below where the stock then traded. This practice worked as long as it did not only because of a steadily rising stock price, but with the complicity of those very officers vested with the power and responsibility to prevent such sham transactions. Their actions directly violated the company's option plan as well as the Toronto Stock Exchange's clear rules.

These executives became highly adept at hiding their

deception not only from regulators, but from their independent auditor and outside counsel. They deliberately chose the dates of the stock's low points during each quarter and made it look like those were the dates of the option grants. Yet in a further demonstration of focused deception, they cleverly stayed away from the stock's absolute low point to avoid detection. Kavelman even wrote in an email, concocting a crème brûlée of hubris and faux integrity filled with saturated facts, "FYI, it is a major breach of protocol to be discussing (and documenting via email) using option pricing other than that allowable by the Ontario Securities Commission and the SEC in the US." (He even explicitly denied during the company's 2006 shareholder meeting any kind of backdating scheme!)

The consequences took time to strike, but they inevitably came in the form of public disgrace, permanent injunctions and, in the case of Kavelman and Loberto, a consent order prohibiting them from serving as directors or officers at any SEC-regulated company. The wrongdoers also paid penalties ranging from $150,000 to $500,000 and gave back all monies garnered from their backdated options, plus interest. In addition to these SEC-ordered penalties, the Ontario Securities Commission squeezed another $77 million from Research in Motion and its complicit officers.

Shame and illegal-profit disgorgement may well act as a deterrent, but are bruised wrists really enough?

—*R.R.*

Joan desires to improve her health by losing weight, but she also wants immediate results. To accelerate achieving her goal, she takes appetite suppressants and begins to smoke instead of eating. She becomes physically dependent upon the stimulants, thereby damaging her health. In this case, the desire for immediate gratification undermines health, whereas the desire for weight loss pursues health. One desire nullifies the other even though they appear to have synergy over the short term.

When conscious desires conflict by moving in self-defeating or divergent directions, creativity often fails. This creative paralysis stemming from conflicts in desire can also proceed below the level of consciousness.

Competing Desires Beneath Awareness

Desires beneath awareness may be subconscious or unconscious. The difference is subtle but material. The word *subconscious* refers to desires that we know about and can call to mind, but that we may nevertheless choose to suppress as a coping mechanism. A dieter may have a strong desire to eat rich desserts. He is capable of speaking about this desire; he knows it is real. Yet he can successfully suppress it so that he does not think about it for substantial periods. By contrast, unconscious desires are deeper and not immediately accessible. They may require significant introspection to surface. A person who has been sexually abused as a child may have completely repressed memories so that her status as a victim cannot be brought into consciousness without deep reflection, meditation or analysis. The effect of this repression may be an unconscious desire to avoid intimacy.

Levels of Desire/Vision

- Conscious

- Subconscious

- Unconscious

David Goehring, *The Sun and the Moon*, 2010

Desires operating either subconsciously and unconsciously can create a powerful drag on the creative process within individuals and teams when they interfere with other, conscious desires at the heart of creative effort. Like invisible black holes in outer space, these underlying desires can exert a powerful gravitational pull on our energies. Creators may psychologically submerge desires that do not conform to their social context; for example, those that are out of sync with values acquired from parents, moral authority figures, friends, role models, business contacts or legal regulators.

A married woman who suppresses attraction to someone other than her spouse may acknowledge being drawn away from her marriage. She may admit her feelings but choose to ignore them. This same woman experiencing repression would be able honestly to deny even the existence of the attraction. She might experience her feelings only through apparently unintentional episodes such as dreaming about the person she desires or arranging her schedule to allow for increasing contacts, without really understanding her own behavior.

A pervasive and simple example of this dynamic involving the unconscious involves the quest for immediate, selfish pleasure. The process of socialization within families, schools, organizations and communities teaches us both to suppress and repress our fundamental selfish desire to seek personal pleasure. We learn to deny this in the pursuit of creative work pleasing and meaningful to us and to the larger community.

Thirteen-year-old Colin tries to learn algebra and strongly desires to master the material. At the same time, he wants to listen to music that pleases his senses, or to watch an intriguing Internet video. He wants to take a ride on his bike because he enjoys the sensation of coasting downhill in the open wind. Whenever he sits down to pursue mastery of algebra, he feels the pull of these other desires—his interests in immediate pleasure. Nevertheless, he may fail to see how this distraction drains him of energy to master algebra. After all, what does enjoying a bike ride, or listening to music have to do with mathematics? At the common-sense level, nothing. But with regard to energy, everything.

Todd wants to improve his physical fitness. His pervasive desire for immediate gratification conflicts with his creative plans. As he tries to exercise or diet, his unconscious desires for pleasurable rest and food drain his energy. As he prepares for exercise, his body longs to relax in the armchair with a bowl of ice cream. The energy required for good health must compete with his underlying desire for instant gratification.

The drain of our creative energies may result from one or more conflicting desires operating beneath awareness. We often deny these desires because we know that they are frowned upon by others. We internalize these critical voices and ignore or try to banish them from consciousness. Because they remain below the level of awareness, we lose the ability to address them; they remain a drag upon our creative process.

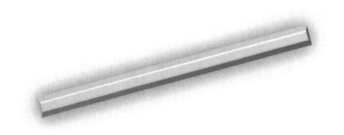

Our Creative *Ki-Ai*

Over thousands of years, many Asian cultures have developed concepts describing the energy flow within life, referred to as qi (also *ki, chi* or *ch'i*)—an active spirit animating any living thing. The literal translation of qi is "air" or "breath." Philosophers imagine qi as a life force or cosmic energy in which local manifestations always share a deep connection to the whole throughout the universe as a kind of animating spirit flowing through all living things. People are filled with it; when they die, *qi* transcends their physical bodies.

Within Asian martial arts, the *ki-ai* refers to a short exhalation before or during a strike or technique. This release of breath expresses an inner energy concentration unleashed in a single explosive focus of will. Through the *ki-ai*, practitioners do not direct qi energy but rather allow it to pass through their physical being when executing a technique. *Ki-ai* arises from the concept of qi, meaning mind, breath or spirit, and *ai*, a stem of the verb *awasu*, meaning "to unite," literally becoming "united spirit." This allows for the practitioner to leverage the force in the universe, beyond that available within the local body. In this sense, *ki-ai* celebrates the connection of local to universal action. We are part of the universe, a manifestation of it; what we do is something that the universe does. We have the ability to allow universal force to pass through us.

Using these ideas to help us understand and describe

creative energy, we can think of an effective process manifesting a powerful *ki-ai*, a concentration of mind and spirit directed coherently into action. On the other hand, in the presence of conflicting desires, creative energy becomes self-defeating or fractured, like a martial-arts practitioner who either strikes himself or pulls his punches. Transcending such distortions requires us to gain awareness of how our creative energies have become bent or splintered. Once aware, we can perfect our technique, unleashing a pure flow of creative energy and thereby experience breakthroughs, like punching through a strong board by concentrating energy on a single point.

In his youth, Gary pursues hobbies like hunting, fishing and hiking in the wilderness, deeply enjoying being outside in natural surroundings. As he grows up, his parents and siblings tell Gary that his love of the outdoors is impractical and would not allow him to achieve his financial goals. In his conscious mind he agrees with this advice and devotes himself to the practice of law, spending hours in buildings surrounded by books, computers and paper. He suppresses his desire for the wilderness, telling himself that his longing is impractical and childish. Eventually, he loses awareness of this fundamental desire, remembering it only as a childhood interest. Yet this pull deep within Gary's spirit drains his creative energy for the practice of law. He feels listless and bored at work but does not understand why precisely. He cannot comprehend why he has no energy for this work because the competing desire lingers below consciousness. All he knows is that he feels most alive when walking in the park on a Sunday afternoon or vacationing in the mountains. Subconscious conflicting desires like those at work within Gary often form the root of creative enervation. They operate like vines slowly strangling a tree, choking off air and sunlight from the competing creative desires.

Many of them involve negative beliefs about the future. The dominant motif running through these desires concerns the creative process itself.

A common unconscious negative belief holds that we cannot influence our future at all. Within that chokehold, we see the future as a form of unchangeable reality. It is as if we were handcuffed to a roller coaster with immense inertia and now impelled to follow its track. At first it may be difficult to understand why anyone would maintain such a belief contrary to the pervasive human experience of being able to influence and improve one's circumstances. When we look deeply into the sources of this belief that the future is preordained, we encounter a psychological anchor: a deep longing to accept reality and to be accepted as we are, along with the release of tension that comes from letting go of struggle.

This too is a primal desire: to avoid putting forth creative effort. For if it is true that the future has been written for us, then we have no choices to make and can relax, ceasing to feel burdened by the possibility that we can change or influence our circumstances. These desires and beliefs beneath consciousness create the possibility of an ultimate release of tension associated with death itself. We are who we are and whatever will happen to us will happen. So be it. It is no longer our responsibility or opportunity. If this is so, we can sigh, sit back and watch our lives unfold without us, like watching an exciting sporting event being played by someone else. To allow oneself to be ruled by a sense of powerlessness offers the prospect of a complete, if fleeting, pleasurable release of creative tension.

This often deep-seated desire is captured in the words of Ajahn Chah, an influential Buddhist teacher and a founder of two major monasteries in the Thai Forest tradition, one that attempts to adhere to the strictest ascetic practices:

> Do not try to become anything.
> Do not make yourself into anything.
> Do not be a meditator.
> Do not become enlightened.
> When you sit, let it be.
> When you walk, let it be.
> Grasp at nothing.
> Resist nothing.

Of course, our human hearts are filled with wanting, striving and desiring. This is the source of all creative tension and achievement. When we let go, we often experience a pleasurable release of that tension. There is irony and paradox in the observation that the desire to be *without desire* is itself (surprise!) *yet another desire*. So the Buddhist in deep meditation struggling to let go is shot through with yet another creative vision: to achieve the state of "letting go." The creative orientation is inescapable. To create is part of being alive and so we always carry some level of creative tension, even if only the counter-vision to let go of all such aspirations in pursuit of ultimate peacefulness. But the existence of this primal desire to let go yields profound insight into distortions in our creative process. When operating beneath awareness, it diverts energy from creation. When we wish both to grasp and to release at the same moment, our energy to grasp is splintered by the urge to "let go." If we want simultaneously to "become" and to "let it be," our energy to become will be divided. If we wish to resist and give up, our resistance will be drained of energy.

Genership offers a compelling strategy to transcend this conflict. It begins by recognizing and surfacing this profound countervailing wish: to accept everything and be accepted "as is."

Celebrating the Urge to Give Up

Many songwriters and poets have celebrated the deep-seated inner desire to let go of our aspirations. In 2004 Gavin DeGraw's song, "I Don't Want to Be," made it to the top of the U.S. pop charts. It is a rollicking tribute to the fundamental human desire to be accepted (and to accept oneself) "as is," without trying to stretch or achieve beyond what comes easily and naturally. DeGraw's refrain captures the raw emotional longing to let go:

> I don't wanna be anything other than what I've been
> tryin' to be lately,
> All I have to do is think of me and have peace of
> mind,
> I'm tired of looking 'round rooms wondering what I
> gotta do,
> Or who I'm supposed to be,
> I don't wanna be anything other than me.

A similarly powerful emotion is conjured in the Beatles' international hit, "Let it Be," ranked 20th on *Rolling Stone*'s 500 greatest songs of all time. Its simple words recount "times of trouble" and a visitation by "mother Mary... speaking the words of wisdom, 'Let it be.'" In an interview about the song's meaning, Paul McCartney explained it as having been inspired by a dream about his mother, who had died when he was just 14 years old, delivering this reassuring message. "It was really like she had visited me at this very difficult point in my life and gave me this message: Be gentle, don't fight things, just try and go with the flow and it will all work out."

Many individuals and organizations build upon this longing for resignation and disengagement expressed in abandonment of the creative process. This is not an isolated trend. The National Institute of Mental Health reports that more than 18 million people (six percent of the U.S. population) suffer from major depression each year. A key risk factor for depression is life stress, which generally involves situations in which deep-seated creative desires are frustrated (such as the desire to be healthy, economically self-sufficient and loved). More than 100 million Americans over age 12 admit to having used illegal drugs. More than 15 million experience alcohol dependence. While this reliance has many causes, not all of which involve creative frustration, these behaviors suggest a strong need to escape creative tension—to extinguish desire and loosen one's grip on reality to allow for the relaxation associated with the move to "let it be." Under sedation, users cease to ask the question, "Who do I want to be?" and instead ask, "Who am I?" In this regard, their current reality is often transformed into their final reality, as they strive to give up all creative aspirations for the future. Yet pain and suffering follow because the human need to create is profound and equal in measure. So those who seek retreat from aspiration and awareness inevitably experience terrific conflict with the desires and truths from which they seek respite. This dynamic creates a cycle of self-destructive behaviors designed to blunt (and thereby offer relief from) creative urges.

Under the spell of an unconscious desire to let go, a certain subconscious fatalism can also take hold. This psychological motif associates maturity with resignation to reality even though it may differ substantially from one's creative desires. In the words of the famous stoic, Epictetus, "Do not seek to bring things to pass in accordance with your wishes, but wish for them as they are, and you will find them." After this psychological move (one that usually takes place below our visceral awareness), any creative desire even considered immediately finds itself in direct conflict with an unconscious desire to do nothing, premised on the belief that nothing can or will change in the future. Individuals and organizations resigned to stagnancy inside this mind frame will actually work to undermine progress toward a creative vision to demonstrate their belief that nothing can change, so they can maintain a posture that does not require the expenditure of creative energy.

Jerry has often dreamed of becoming a professional pop singer. An audition for "American Idol" is coming to town, but when the day comes he feels hollow rather than excited and decides not to go, thinking to himself, "I will never be selected; this is a waste of time." In his mind, this appears to be nothing but a practical assessment of reality. What drives it, however, is his belief that he will never be a professional pop singer, grounded in his desire to avoid the creative tension entailed in trying. It is much less stressful to accept this perceived reality that his dream will never come true. Participating in such an audition requires an enormous amount of creative energy and stress. Even if Jerry makes it to the audition, he may be listless, his energy sapped by his belief that success is impossible—all to avoid creative tension. While thousands will travel to the audition, many thousands will not, no matter their level of talent. And many there will not put forward their best efforts because they are sapped of energy by their conflicting wish to give up.

Negative beliefs operating below the level of consciousness can affect groups as well as individuals. Barry is the coach of an amateur soccer team. After losing several games, he forms a belief that his players cannot win, which provides relief from the creative tension entailed in striving to win. "We are going to lose," says Barry to himself driving to the field each weekend. He then pushes this belief down into his subconscious, telling himself that to dwell on such thoughts cannot be good for him or his team. Nevertheless, Barry's belief satisfies his subconscious desire to relax, to cease to strive. In such a circumstance, Barry and his team members may even provide inchoate clues to one another that they feel certain about losing every single game. "We've really got a chance today," Barry tells his players. In his own mind, however, he mutters to himself, "Sure thing, buddy." His players smile grimly at one another while defeat approaches, signaling an innate fatalism. Publicly, the underlying belief that success is impossible goes unstated and unacknowledged; it operates as a subconscious or unconscious facet of group psychology. This desire to avoid the creative tension entailed in really attempting to win, premised upon the belief that winning is just not possible, creates a self-fulfilling prophecy. Mentally assured of failure, team members not only cease to try, but actually relax at precisely the moment they gain any advantage, to ensure that they are not threatened with mounting the struggle entailed in attempting to compete. The team is drained of creative energy in every contest; as a result, it cannot win.

Walk into any bookstore and you will see aisles of books dedicated to helping people accomplish their goals. The works usually have emphatic titles like *Do It Today!* or *Get Started Now!* or *Stop Procrastinating!* Such useless advice generally involves breaking large into smaller tasks combined with exhortations about the importance of becoming an effective and successful person. But for one drained of creative energy, these strategies and cheerleading efforts are futile. Anyone with truly high energy and passion for a creative task would laugh at the idea of reading a book to give them the passion required to do it. We do not need user manuals to create the energy to do what we love. In the words of Nike, people driven to create "just do it!" In contrast, the advice offered by genership is uncommon. If you lack creative energy for a task, it is likely because there is something diverting your energy. You need to explore and understand that; your life as a creator then has the potential to change.

Genership provides a pathway to transcend conflicting desires that disable creativity. The first and most critical step is to use reflection and observation to courageously surface and comprehend every conflicting desire that steals energy from the creative process. When brought into conscious awareness, they can be transcended. The moment at which the creator acknowledges the power of such conflicting desires is the beginning of liberation from them.

Conflicting Understandings of Current Reality

Conflicting interpretations of the truth from an individual or team dissipate creative energy when they lead to divergent or self-defeating strategies for constructive action.

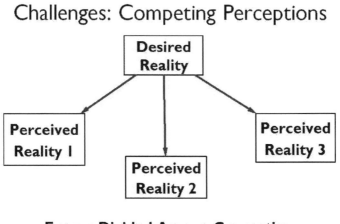

Challenges: Competing Perceptions

Energy Divided Among Competing Perceptions of Reality

Peter and John are members of an amateur group climbing a mountain, nearing the summit. As they approach, a dense snow begins to fall, decreasing visibility. They continue to climb in the blizzard, losing sense of their exact location. Taking a break, the group huddles inside a tent planning its next day's activities. They take out their maps, but because of the reduced visibility, they cannot determine exactly where they are on the mountain. Peter believes they are at one location, while John's observations suggest elsewhere. As they speculate about their position, subgroups form and take sides with Peter or John. Plans about the timing and trajectory of their path to the summit become stalled. Since its members cannot agree on where they are, the group can achieve no consensus about the most effective route to employ.

Jill and Sheila are members of a marketing team planning the launch of a new Web service providing small-business accounting services. Their analysis on how to conduct the launch turns in part on the timing of a competitor's offering. Reviewing the market intelligence, Jill believes that the competing service is more than a year away from launch, suggesting an initial marketing period without a strong challenger. Reviewing the same information, Sheila believes that the rival company will be ready to move in the next quarter, suggesting the need to address the adversary's strengths and weaknesses immediately. Jill and Sheila do not agree about the nature of the competition's plans. Subgroups in the marketing team form around their divergent plans for the product launch. The effort stalls as the group attempts to grapple with divergent accounts of reality.

Carlos is a middle-aged man writing a memoir about his parents' difficult divorce, which occurred when he was a toddler. His vision is to write a definitive and clear version of what happened. His parents are both deceased, so he speaks with his elder siblings as well as aunts and uncles, each of whom provide different accounts that offer multiple alternative paths for understanding what happened. While reviewing his notes of many interviews and conversations, he notices that they are in tension and do not relate a coherent picture. Depending on which views he credits and which he judges as wrong or distorted in some way, Carlos' narrative may take many different forms. His creative effort stalls as he struggles to choose among the accounts and develops a strategy for managing the tensions among them.

Jane is the mother of a three-month-old baby boy with a 102-degree fever. She is unsure whether the fever is being caused by a virus that several family members have had recently or whether her baby has an infection that should be treated with antibiotics. A virus is probably not a matter of significant concern, but an infection should be investigated and treated with medicine. She could wait a day to see if the fever passes. If there is an infection, however, waiting could make it worse. On the other hand, Jane knows that going to the doctor's office may expose her baby to other children with contagious illnesses. If Jane could know with certainty, her decision would be easy. But as her mind shifts from one interpretation to the other, her impulse to go to the doctor strengthens and fades like a flashing siren light. As many parents know, this quandary is not always cured, even with a call or trip to the pediatrician. Educated guessing is part of practicing medicine and parenting.

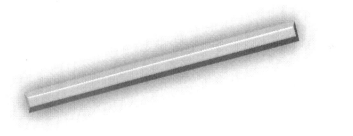

Inflation vs. Deflation

During 2010 and 2011, economists vigorously debated whether the U.S. economy was heading for inflation or deflation. In economic theory, inflation is a sustained general *devaluation of the currency* resulting from an increase in the money supply. Deflation is the opposite: a sustained general *increase in the value of the currency* resulting from the collapse of spending related to a decrease in the money supply. Following the great recession of 2009, economists faced a powerful conundrum: their models suggested that both trends were emergent.

Many actions of the federal government and Federal

Reserve were understood as radically increasing the U.S. money supply. These took the form of deficit and stimulus spending, transfers of questionable financial assets from banks to the Federal Reserve in exchange for cash, bailouts of troubled industries and quantitative easing in which the Federal Reserve repurchased billions of dollars worth of government securities with the intention to manipulate the value of U.S. currency and stave off deflation.

Economic theories suggested that these actions would cause rampant inflation. The price of gold and silver soared, and many interpreted rising oil and food prices as objective evidence that inflation had taken hold.

On the other hand, many economists observed strong evidence of deflation as well, including generally falling wages, housing prices and record-low bond yields. In a paper released in July of 2010, James Bullard, the St. Louis Federal Reserve President, warned that the nation could be facing a long-term deflation similar to the Japanese experience during the 1990s. More than 20 years after achieving its high of nearly 39,000 in 1989, the Nikkei languished below 10,000, remaining weak in the wake of earthquakes, tsunamis and nuclear accidents that destabilized a Japanese economy sluggish for decades.

Inflation and deflation require radically different investment strategies. In a period of inflation, the value of cash erodes. To counter this trend, investors look for investments that appreciate at least at the rate of inflation, such as Treasury Inflation-Protected Securities (TIPS), commodities or carefully selected real estate parcels. During inflation, it is acceptable to maintain debt with fixed interest rates, since interest payments become less expensive in real terms as cash devalues. In a period of deflation, however, the reverse is true. Cash is king; other investments decline. Debt becomes more expensive going forward as the real cost of fixed interest payments increases during deflation. Thus investors have a strong incentive to repay debts heading into deflation.

Investors confronted with the prospect of both inflation and deflation find themselves tangled in knots, like someone planning for a trip both to the Sahara desert and Antarctica. What is needed to survive in one climate is useless in the other. The inflation vs. deflation quandary powerfully illustrates how conflicting understandings of current reality can impede strategic creative action, draining energy from creativity to the extent that the strategy employed comes into conflict with shifts in perceived reality.

In each of the above cases, disparate understandings of reality cause creative energy to be divided and dispersed until one understanding is selected or forged anew from among them. The reason for this is straightforward. When we invest creative energy in shaping the future from the raw content of the present, the only medium for this work is current reality itself. Creators must always start where they are, using what they have. Yet there may be doubts and uncertainties about the nature of these resources. When we bring to bear inconsistent understandings of our current situation (i.e., "this seems to be an infection" vs. "this seems to be a virus"), we take action in divergent and possibly opposing ways (i.e., "we can wait" vs. "we should get treatment now"). This causes the creative process to falter as energy divides across competing strategies and actions.

Committing to Ideas or Strategies that Do Not Yield Progress

Insanity, as the saying goes, is doing the same thing over and over and expecting different results. We can extend this concept, observing that thinking the same thoughts tends to lead to the same results. The creative process falters when we continue to rely on the same ideas and practices that have produced frustration or failure. The world places a high value on maintaining effort without fully recognizing that persistence alone does not produce progress; it must be coupled with variations in thinking and strategy. Creative breakthroughs flow from the sometimes small—and often unintentional—changes that result from a range of creative efforts repeated over time.

Challenges: Commitment to Failed Ideas or Strategies

insanity: expecting difference from consistency

the importance of persistent variation

Franz Stuck, *Sisyphus*, 1920

Flash of Persistence

The light bulb, the airplane wing and Moore's Law all share something profound: a painstaking commitment to try, try and try again. Contrary to popular belief, Thomas Edison did not invent the design of the light bulb. His success came from tirelessly testing literally thousands of different materials as light-bulb filaments. Innovation resulted from experimenting with the composition of the filament as well as the vacuum housing it. A key breakthrough came when Edison's team began to think about the role of electrical resistance in getting a filament to glow without burning out. Using the concept, they began to focus on high-resistance materials, leading to the development of filaments that could glow for more than 1000 hours. Creative success came from developing and implementing many different ideas pointed at the same target, and persisting until one hit the bullseye.

Similarly, in their development of the first self-propelled airplane, the Wright brothers tested more than 200 wing and airfoil designs, recording the effects of each variation on airflow and pressure as it passed over the wings. They used the data developed to persist in making alterations until they could construct an aircraft that could take off and stay airborne. Their invention succeeded only because they continued to vary their strategies throughout the course of their developmental process.

In computer technology, Moore's Law famously states that the number of transistors able to be placed on an integrated circuit will double every two years. The viability of this trend, which has proven true over the past few decades, depends on continuous innovation and development of new techniques for working with microcomputer chips, such as using optical lithography to create microcircuits.

Creativity embraces continuous changes in thinking as well as changes in practice. A flash of genius is generally born of extraordinary persistence in variation. When thinking and practice become rigid, creativity falters.

Uncovering and Comprehending Sticking Points in the Creative Process

A person skilled in genership displays two disciplines: first, building a healthy creative process, and second, surfacing barriers such as those described above that arise within individual and group awareness. Like a gifted engineer, a genership practitioner observes the flow of creative energy, determining whether the structures giving rise to the flow maximize, impede or dilute it. A healthy creative process exhibits simple and powerful tension between a unified, if complex, desire and clear picture of reality. Barriers arise when this structure suffers from one of the difficulties outlined above: dissipating desire, conscious or unconscious conflicting desires, failure to observe reality, conflicting understandings of the truth, or commitment to failed ideas or strategies.

Such barriers within the creative process can only be transcended by a healthy approach to creativity that strengthens the individual and group focus on fundamental creative processes: CoVisioning, CoThinking and Shared Strategic Action. This is a critical insight; a person skilled at genership recognizes that any effort focusing on eliminating barriers to creativity as a primary strategy only succeeds in becoming a distraction, leading to additional frustration and failure. The sole way to overcome creative difficulties is to focus fundamentally upon creating.

You Can't Fix It!

When we create, we transcend problems and difficulties emerging within the creative process.

In the many years I-LEAD has worked with individuals and organizations to improve their creativity, one of the most challenging ideas we confront involves addressing barriers within the creative process. Students are usually able to perceive clearly that creativity arises from the tension between vision and reality. They are also able to understand the above ways in which the creative process can become entangled. But when we say that one cannot fix such problems, students often become puzzled. The conversation goes something like this, with the student beginning:

"So you are saying that if I have two contrary desires, then my creative energies will be split in two different directions?"

"Yes."

"Well, that's easy to fix."

"Really?"

"Yes. I'll just pick one desire and reject the other one. Problem solved."

"Not so fast."

"What?"

"You can't do that."

"Why?"

"Because you are going to discover something very strange. When you try to pick one of your desires, you are going to wish you had picked the other one. And that desire to have picked the other one is going to split your creative energy going forward."

"I don't understand. Why can't I just pick one?"

"Because if you could 'just pick one,' then one of your desires would not be real. The problem is that you have two *real* competing desires. When you say 'I'll just pick one,' you might as well be saying 'I am going to pretend that one of my desires doesn't exist.' Your *real* passions are not going to let you off the hook so easily. What's going to happen is that you are going to experience that neglected desire as a wish that you had made the other choice."

"That's confusing."

"Yes it is. If it wasn't, you would not experience the confusion of having two conflicting desires."

"I don't get it."

"I want you to spend some time thinking about it."

A similar conversation follows the insight that dissipating desire undermines creativity. Again, continuing with the student:

"So I am not able to create because I lack passion for what I want to create."

"That's possible."

"I can fix that."

"How will you fix it?"

"I'll become more passionate."

"How?"

"I'll get myself psyched up for what I want to create, make myself want it passionately. I've heard you can do that with mantras and affirmations. I'll just tell myself that I am passionate morning, noon and night... until I finally have passion."

"That probably won't work."

"Why?"

"It's curious, but here's what will happen. You will discover that you lack passion for generating passion."

"What do you mean?"

"When, you say, 'I'll become more passionate,' it's really just a way of being in denial about your lack of passion. It's like saying, 'I wish it wasn't true that I lack passion.' But it *is* true, and you see it's true, or else you wouldn't feel the need to change it. You can't will yourself to have passion. *Willing yourself to have passion is the opposite of having it.*"

"I don't understand."

"Have you ever been in love?"

"Yes."

"Did you have to talk yourself into being love, or did you just feel full of energy?"

"I just felt full of energy. I just couldn't stop thinking about and wanting to be with that person."

"Great. That's what it's like to have real passion. If you have to talk yourself into it, then you don't have it. If you have to go to school or take a program to learn how to be in love, then you probably aren't in love."

"But I don't know what to do then... What do I do to fix my lack of passion?"

"I want you to think about it. Sometimes we can't solve problems and that's OK. Sometimes problems just need to be understood, not solved."

"I don't get it yet."

"Have patience. The key question I want you to think about is different: What *do* you feel passionate about?"

Issues within the creative process cannot be addressed as if they were wires in a machine that had become disconnected. The creative process can be understood, after which the creator may try again. When this effort succeeds, the creator will *transcend* rather than necessarily solve the problems in the process. This outcome will be a byproduct rather than a focal point of the creative work. We do not create as a way to solve our creative problems; we simply create. When we do, they are often overcome.

Distortions in the creative process are not like a malfunctioning machine that can be tinkered with and then will start operating again. They are not mechanisms to be re-engineered but rather important messages that creators send to themselves about their inspirations and the world around them, communicating something profound about the creative spirit itself.

When we sense dissipating desire, the question is not how to ignite passion for our creative efforts but which will inspire passion. Jane is a teacher who has lost her love of teaching. When she enters her biology classroom, she feels bored and listless. To try to fix that problem, it seems rational to believe that she must find her lost passion for biology.

But the reality is that Jane's spirit may want her to do something other than teaching, or to teach something other than biology. To develop one's passion is not about engineering a fix for its lack, but inventing the creative vision that will ignite it fluidly and authentically.

Similarly, when we feel tangled in the pull of inconsistent desires, the solution is not to sever some of them and choose. Each of our desires communicates something profound to us about what we really want to create. When we deeply understand our inconsistent desires, we may—for the first time—be able to make them coherent. John passionately wants to write screenplays and also be a good father. If they conflict, the solution is not a matter of choosing one desire and letting go of another. This would simply be to deny one of John's real passions. Upon considered reflection, and with the insight that comes from exploring his desires, John may decide to write a screenplay inspired by his relationship with his children. Failing to understand reality, or being caught in a conflict between competing accounts, seriously undermines the creative process. But this is not a challenge like failing to install the ideal software, which one can cure through simple remedial action. Failing to confront reality is a message from the soul about a lack of serious commitment to what one is trying to create. We can build a powerful creative process when we gather courage to confront the truth about such challenges. This involves coming to terms with desires or perceptions that may be incoherent. We can then begin again, building a clear vision and a meaningful perception of reality.

Simon expresses a desire to take on a political leadership role in his community. He dreams of being the mayor, addressing City Council, and attending block parties and fancy fundraisers with his entourage. Yet Simon knows little about policy and has no patience to learn the daily management of city systems. His lack of understanding the daily reality of politics and policy is not simply a problem in his creative process; it is a message from his soul that he is not committed to taking on a political leadership role in his community. The questions for Simon are these: What is he prepared to be serious about? What desire would matter enough to impel him to spend the time required to fully grasp reality?

Roseanne is an investment adviser helping a client consider an investment in a social media Internet startup. She is confronted with competing accounts of business reality, one suggesting that the startup will experience rapid growth in a new market, another that it will confront significant competition from companies using similar technologies easily transferable to the new market. One account suggests that the investment is sound; the other that it is dangerous and should be avoided. Roseanne should not approach this incoherence as a mere challenge in the creative process. She should not just pick one reality to move forward without conflict; rather, these conflicting realities suggest real uncertainties in the world that need to be addressed as part of Roseanne's strategy to help her client invest successfully. Incoherent and disparate accounts of reality provide opportunities not necessarily for choices but for deepening understanding through innovation.

The commitment to failed ideas or strategies seriously undermines successful creativity. But a team that confronts such failure cannot simply abandon the problematic causes. Joseph is the leader of a minority political party in a small town. The party has not successfully elected a candidate to local government in more than 30 years. Joseph makes an annual speech to the members of his minority political committee stressing the same ideas that have failed to gain traction in election after election. He professes frustration and disappointment, but his commitment to failed ideas suggests that he and his fellows are not sincerely interested in achieving their stated goals. His recognition of failure, and even his abandonment of ideas that do not work, will not result in success. This creative failure has a diagnosis but not yet a cure. Nothing will cure Joseph except getting serious about winning a campaign and then developing a message that wins.

Transcending Structural Conflict

Structural conflict must be surfaced.

Structural conflict cannot be fixed.

We transcend structural conflict through a healthy creative process.

H. Koppdelaney, *Euphoria*, 2011

It is critical to observe impediments to creativity so that we can be aware of our barriers, but they can only be overcome by strengthening the individual's and group's creative process through a direct focus on what is created. Beyond this, to address barriers achieves nothing and is a distraction from creating. When the creative process is strengthened, barriers fall. Many unskilled in genership respond to this insight by suggesting that this involves mere semantics. The reply is that this distinction entails much more; semantic differences remain solely at the level of language, but the broader differences involve changes in thought, which drive new results in practice. Creating is not the same as solving problems. When one effectively creates, problems will be solved; the reverse is not always true.

How does one skilled in genership strengthen a group's creative process?

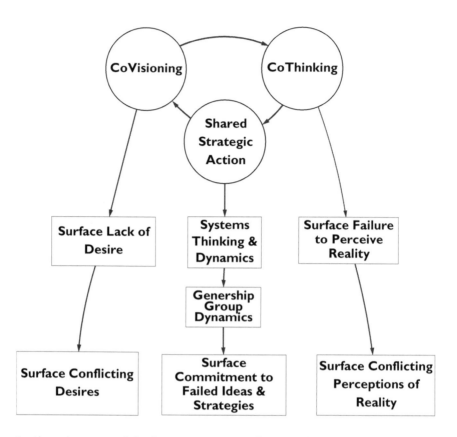

In the above model, the practitioner of genership moves through a creative cycle embracing CoVisoning, CoThinking and Shared Strategic Action. The activity of surfacing impediments to creativity increases the energy and momentum for action. The focus remains on the creative process; impediments are transcended rather than becoming opportunities for distraction from the group's work. The process is not linear, but continues to iterate; the group's vision, analysis and activities can evolve as the work continues. The creative process is not like a recipe or algorithm that yields guaranteed results through a mechanical execution of pre-defined tasks. Nevertheless, consciously increasing our practice of the core disciplines—CoVisioning, CoThinking and Shared Strategic Action—will directly cause our personal and communal creative powers to strengthen.

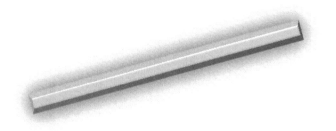

Genership at IBM

The strength and health of creative processes is the number-one reason that organizations survive and thrive over long periods. The breakdown of these processes is the primary cause of financial loss and failure. The history of IBM vividly illustrates the cyclical process of visioning, assessing reality, taking strategic action and then reimagining and reinventing the organizational vision based on performance and experience. IBM's roots go back to the 1880s when the company's predecessors invented products and services to assist businesses with employee timekeeping, recording and accounting processes. During the 1920s, IBM's first president, Thomas Watson, introduced its famous slogan: "Think!" This inspiration applied not only to leadership but to every employee, no matter their station in the company. The "Think!" campaign became synonymous with the company's overall culture, one that valued the intellectual awareness and engagement of every single member.

During the Depression, unlike other companies that scaled back operations, IBM invested by adding personnel and building up inventory. As a result, when the opportunity surfaced, IBM had the necessary capacity to supply the federal government with the systems used to track Social Security benefits. This gigantic contract led to other federal work that steadily expanded through World War II, creating the foundation for what would later become IBM's key role in the development of computer science and systems for the military.

In the postwar period, IBM's vision continued to evolve as it became the leader in the emerging fields of electronics and artificial intelligence, leaving behind the world of scales, clocks, tabulators and other devices focused merely on recording rather than also processing information. IBM continued development of a corporate culture that stimulated employee creativity and engagement, inventing the open-door policy that encouraged low-level employees to speak their minds to upper-level management. By the 1970s, IBM had become so dominant in the established computer industry that it became the target of antitrust litigation.

IBM's innovative work continued unabated, giving rise in the last decades of the 20th century to the personal-computer era and the birth of a new generation of corporate giants, including Intel and Microsoft, which began as IBM partners, and also competitors such as Apple that would change the business landscape. As the market shifted from mainframe and micro to personal computers, robust competition from myriad hardware and software companies caused IBM to suffer huge losses, forcing it to evolve once again. In the 1990s, the company completely reorganized, selling off commodity businesses with low profit margins, recommitting to areas where IBM had competitive advantages such as specialized chip engineering and manufacture, and building global consulting services that offered businesses integrated technology and management solutions. In addition, IBM developed a software strategy targeting organizational rather than individual consumers, investing heavily in development of middleware that connected corporate operating systems to end-user applications. The transformation succeeded; where others failed to evolve and became extinct, IBM survived and thrives.

IBM's story over the past century powerfully illustrates numerous core genership concepts, particularly the cyclical, iterative processes that inform creative work. The public has sometimes wrongly imputed IBM's success to the work of a small handful of visionary leaders. Not so. IBM's leaders have always understood that their primary value was to engage employee creativity throughout the organization. IBM's success grows out of a multidimensional dialogue within its countless creative teams, oscillating among vision, reality assessment and strategic action. Performance and experience transforms vision over time, and renewed vision in turn repositions assessment and strategy. IBM's team members recognize that tomorrow the company will look nothing like it does today, except that it will retain the cultural commitment to creativity captured in its legendary imperative: Think!

CHAPTER NINE
GENERSHIP GROUP DYNAMICS:
WE ARE WHO WE HAVE BEEN WAITING FOR

One of the most important insights derived from the study of groups is that they influence individual behavior in ways that are often beneath the awareness of individual group members. In the leadership paradigm, a leader can be deeply influenced and even controlled by dynamics within the group that members do not intentionally plan or coordinate. This is true not only of the leader but of each group member. An individual can easily be swept up in the perceptions and emotions of those around them.

Evolutionary anthropologists have theorized that the size of the human brain, particularly the growth of the neocortex responsible for the higher functions of thought, is an adaptive response to challenges presented by complex social environments. That group processes should be both conscious and unconscious does not surprise us. In nature, we are surrounded by animals that exhibit complex and dynamic social behaviors without planning or practice. Think of geese flying in V-formation, dogs hunting in packs, schools of fish migrating across oceans. Humans are not different in this regard; evolution over millennia has hardwired us for certain kinds of group behaviors.

Our basic propensities for conscious and unconscious group behavior form the foundation for a challenging overlay of group dynamics associated with evolving societal and organizational cultures. Body language involving eye contact and personal space has meaning in every culture, but the significance varies from place to place. Our brains are naturally attuned to eye contact and personal proximity. In the United States, staring at someone you do not know is considered to be aggressive. In India, however, staring at someone you do not know is commonplace and not considered rude. On the other hand, in the U.S. it is not considered rude for subordinates to make prolonged eye contact with their supervisors; for an Indian, doing so is perceived as aggressive and inappropriate. Similarly, the concept of personal space is vastly more expansive in North America than in India or China, where individuals may feel free to peer directly over the shoulder of a person they do not know to see what they are reading.

Such social conventions evolve over time and circumstance, changing according to the dynamic interactions among people, organizations and societies. Perceiving, processing and responding to these changes require individuals and teams to undertake sophisticated analyses and coordinate subtle changes to their behaviors in order to influence and adapt to their social environments.

Attending to group dynamics, both conscious and unconscious, is an essential function of both leadership and genership. The practice of genership, however, takes a fundamentally different approach to certain critical elements of group dynamics. Organizations exhibit a combination of approaches that fall along a spectrum from pure leadership at one end to pure genership at the other, greatly impacted by the quality of group dynamics.

Authority and Permission

In a leadership culture, the concept of authority plays a critical role in group functioning. The primary question concerning group members is, "Who is responsible?" Once answered, group members adopt a passive posture and wait for instructions. They do not undertake actions related to the group's purpose without explicit assurance from the command structure that they are permitted to act. The default rule is that members may not take action without direct permission. The group's primary function is to process instructions from above. The group also functions to call attention to members who may threaten the leader's authority by acting without permission. Members also maintain a private dialogue regarding whether the leader is fulfilling the group's needs. They may choose to communicate elements of this dialogue to the leader for the purpose of increasing their own power within the command structure. When the Fallacies have taken hold, this dialogue foments the development of competitors to challenge the person playing the messiah role.

In contrast, within a genership culture, the primary question concerning group members is founded on generosity and shared objectives: "How can I contribute?" Members undertake experimental actions and then seek feedback from their immediate peers to understand whether their actions are contributing, undermining or irrelevant to the group's work. The default rule is that members are permitted to take any action unless there is an explicit injunction forbidding it embraced by the group as a whole. In this way the group self-regulates. Its function is to perform a task owned by the group as a whole and not by any one leader or leadership group. Members reinforce actions that help the group make progress and discourage actions that inhibit it. The group's internal communications concern whether or not it is able to fulfill its tasks. Participants share in assessing their respective roles and responsibilities, and may experiment with adjustments without seeking permission from a leader. Group members unselfishly celebrate—and thus reinforce—each member's contributions when perceived as promoting success.

Power

In a leadership culture, the group attends to questions involving the distribution of power and privilege. The primary question concerning power: "How can I acquire it?" The members compete in a win-or-lose fashion for relative shares of capacity to take action through command of the group's resources, including its property, funds and capabilities. They also evaluate potential courses of action in terms of their impact on the alignment of power within the group. Political considerations are paramount, occupying substantial portions of group processes. Members observe intragroup relations through a competitive lens.

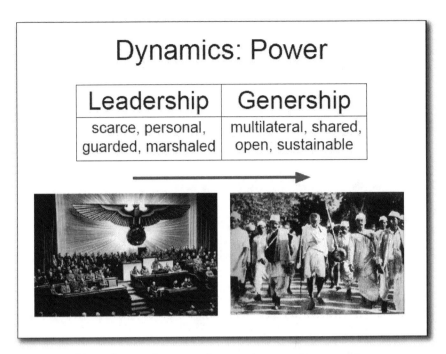

Dynamics: Power

Leadership	Genership
scarce, personal, guarded, marshaled	multilateral, shared, open, sustainable

In a genership culture, the group's conscious and unconscious concern about power revolves around its task. The primary question: "How will we harness energy to complete the task?" The group functions without concern for the internal power allocations within the team or organization. Members may understand the need to obtain sufficient resources to sustain their own efforts, but they see power through the prism of the group's task rather than as an end in itself. Within genership, members observe intragroup relations through collaboration and play.

Hierarchy and Bureaucracy

The focus on authority and power within a leadership culture causes the creation of hierarchical command structures (as opposed to flat structures or networks) in which authority radiates from a central post through intermediaries who form complex rules and procedures, giving rise to bureaucracies. Their purpose is to stabilize internal power allocations, ensuring centralized coordination with a leader or leadership team. These structures also work to garner credit for the organization's accomplishments to the leader while insulating him from blame for setbacks or failures. Hierarchies and bureaucracies work to combat the risk of failure from unauthorized actions on the part of subordinates. Many reporting requirements and procedures dissuade risk-taking and innovative actions.

In the genership culture, by contrast, there is a strong effort to limit the scope of hierarchies and to reduce bureaucracy so that the team can focus all of its efforts to accomplish the tasks at hand. Decision-making structures are flexible and dynamic, shifting as conditions in the field of action evolve. Experiments are conducted continuously until successful strategies develop. During this process, there is little focus on who gets credit and scant concern about failure. Setbacks—understood as essential to the learning process—are the focus of group dialogue to distill knowledge relevant to the development of new strategies. Power distributions occupy the group consciousness only to the extent that they are relevant to marshaling energy.

Communication

In a leadership culture, communications within the group flow from the center and top-down to subordinates. The relevant inquiry is, "Do the subordinates understand the message?" Messaging is paramount. Everyone in the organization needs to understand and repeat information themes, and in general be "on message." The task of members is not to think, evaluate and innovate but simply to understand and execute. In the leadership context, feedback is analyzed not for the purpose of thinking about the group's vision or current reality, but rather to ensure that no one is deviating from the message (and thus perceived as a threat or unstable element within the power structure). The leadership culture monitors communications among subordinates to ensure loyalty and efficiency in the execution of instructions.

In a genership culture, communications circulate in multidirectional networks relevant to the nature of the group's task. The group works to transcend political dimensions of communications, seeing beyond any such elements to grapple directly with its work. Inquiry regarding communications involves how the message relates to the task: "Does this provide relevant information that enhances my understanding of the task, of current reality or of the strategic action required at this moment?" Group members expect and encourage one another to comment meaningfully regarding their roles and activities. There is no sense of suspicion or concern about power loss arising from critical commentary. The group embraces such commentary as enhancing the power and resources available for progress toward its goals.

Position, Role, Influence and Relationships

In a leadership culture, position and role tend to become static. One of the key functions of leadership is to assign important roles to subordinates. The group judges the leader on whether these assignments are successful and understands that a perceived messiah shows wisdom in making successful assignments. The need to make adjustments as work progresses is viewed as a sign of weakness or failure in the leader. Roles are defined in terms of access to power, and assessed in terms of how much power they wield. In a leadership culture, positions are measured by budget authority and number of direct reports. This is a shorthand way of determining the extent of authority and wielded influence.

In a leadership culture, the group understands that position and role are a function of political relationships and networks in which trust and loyalty are critical qualities. This culture respects deal-making in which groups of leaders agree to promote one another in an effort to increase their total shared power. Relationships become the currency within the culture through which roles are allocated and teams developed. Trust and loyalty have equal and sometimes greater value measured against competence and effectiveness, particularly when the leadership culture places a strong value on power stability, management and enhancement. Success is gaining increasing power; achieving the group's goals is a byproduct of that success. A generous view of this perspective is that a leader who does not satisfy his group members' goals cannot stay in power. The leader seeks power to serve the group; to remain in power is the reward for perceived effective service.

As an organization moves from a pure leadership framework to one that incorporates genership, position and role become increasingly fluid in service of the task at hand. The group transcends political calculations, choosing instead to focus on the creative demands of the current situation and allocate roles to those group members exhibiting competence and efficiency. These allocations are not negotiated in political deals measuring traits of trust and loyalty to the leader but rather are geared toward the work that the group must accomplish. Trust and loyalty are measured with members as a whole and with regard to the group's vision. Relationships are not observed through dealmaking arrangements that preserve power, but arise from shared creative struggle. Members still must exist within a power relationship in which resources may not be allocated equally. Genership, however, isolates these calculations from the creative process, liberating it from the constraints of politics. As the culture becomes more expressive of genership than leadership, political calculations dissipate.

Credit and Blame

Leaders seek to garner credit and avoid blame, while group processes work to regulate these objectives. Groups operating within the leadership paradigm assign credit to the leader for the good that happens during his or her tenure. The leader and leadership team work to isolate themselves from blame for failures, but the group constantly works to assess responsibility. The default position is that the leader gets both the credit and blame, no matter the underlying reality of the circumstances confronting the group. Leaders work hard to manipulate these fundamental group dynamics to preserve their power. This often involves developing team members who can take the blame for the leader's errors. Leadership cultures are sometimes reluctant to incubate the development of new capacities within group members for fear of destabilizing existing power structures. Team members must be trusted to pass credit to the leader while absorbing blame. Failure to do so may be perceived as an effort to question the leader and compete for his role.

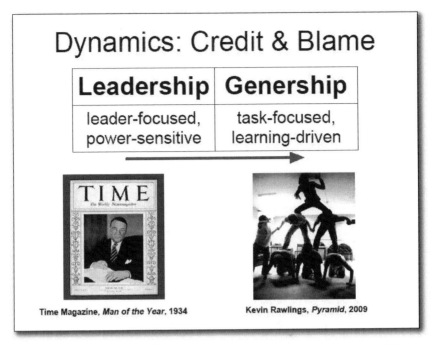

Dynamics: Credit & Blame

Leadership	Genership
leader-focused, power-sensitive	task-focused, learning-driven

Time Magazine, *Man of the Year*, 1934   Kevin Rawlings, *Pyramid*, 2009

In a genership context, however, group members employ credit and blame primarily to assess whether role assignments are productive and efficient. Credit reinforces assignments that lead to success; blame works to modify roles so that the group may experiment and innovate in the face of changing circumstances. Team members fluidly work to help each other discover or even invent successful roles. A member may leave a team if he cannot be productive over a substantial timespan. Genership depersonalizes role assessments and assignments; it seeks to understand each member's best contribution and encourages the development of knowledge, skills and capacities that prepare for new challenges and improvements.

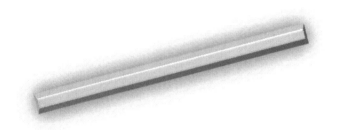

A Genership Team in Action

During the summer of 2011, I facilitated a team launching a charter school. The group included a mix of volunteers and paid staff working on a broad array of tasks including enrollment, instructors, facilities and procurement of furniture, equipment and books. As usual with such projects, the initiative had a tight budget and schedule. As a result, our teams had to be creative and resourceful to accomplish clear goals. As we approached the deadline, there was some significant conflict over the role of a paid staff member who seemed to be participating in many tasks without successfully following through on any one. Several members urged me to remove her from the team. Instead, I encouraged them to have patience and help guide this person toward a productive role. Ten days before the school was scheduled to open, the team member who had been struggling to make a contribution creatively sourced an in-kind gift to the startup efforts worth approximately $50,000. The once-lost team member ended up as one of our most valuable players.

Another highly qualified team member who had been extremely valuable during the startup phase as a volunteer chose to resign from a subsequent paid job once the school got underway. She explained to the team that she had tremendous respect for our work and did not feel that her talents were a good fit for the project's implementation phase.

In a team operating with a high level of genership, members help one another contribute and also decide when there is no longer a good fit. What guides these decisions are the team's vision and its assessment of the talents necessary for progress. The team evolves without the need for heavy-handed interventions from a leader or leadership subgroup.

Conflict

Within the leadership context as explored in the chapter on conflict, opposing visions and perspectives on reality are problems that need to be overcome. Leaders perceive that one of their most fundamental tasks is to develop a shared vision within the group, together with consensus about reality. When there is agreement, the leader's command and influence achieve maximum stability. In leadership, disagreement contains the seeds of political instability, including the possibility of a new messiah arising within the group. Its power struggle, however latent, always threatens to become the dominant narrative, overriding what the group is working to create.

Groups practicing genership, however, embrace conflicting visions and perspectives as providing the impetus for learning and action. Because the focus in genership shifts from power and personality considerations toward the group's creative work, there is genuinely little concern about how disagreements will impact individual status. Members remain vigilant against efforts to seize power for its own sake, unrelated to the tasks at hand. Groups embracing genership work to insulate themselves from power struggles that surround the creative process, shielding the work from political influences that subvert innovation and progress.

Membership Consciousness

In the leadership culture, members understand their identity as leaders or followers. Followers are expected to listen, be loyal and work diligently to implement the leader's agenda. They tend not to question, show initiative or worry about matters beyond their immediate tasks. They are expected to express faith, trust and confidence in the leader's agenda. Questions or criticism directed to the leader or leadership team are understood as threatening to topple the existing power structure. Followers may earn a coveted role in leadership through the demonstration of loyalty.

In the genership culture, though, group members recognize that they will take charge of a situation when the opportunity for progress demands their vision, analysis and specific skill set. Members who possess the competence required at a particular moment will take, but then recede to subordinate roles when the moment calls for new skills and capacities. Because members are focused on specific tasks rather than on power and status, these transitions are efficient and minimize conflict.

Emotional Dynamics

In leadership the critical questions occupying the group's imagination concern the leader's desires, experience and legacy, and center around whether he succeeds or fails. When the leader's agenda falters, the group falls into a state of emotional crisis as it questions its own judgment about the leader's messiah status and its own loyalty. This is typically resolved through a dramatic change in which either a new leader is selected or the leader transcends his challenges, resulting in members' renewal of faith and loyalty.

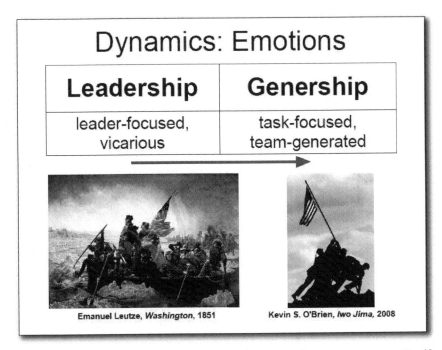

Dynamics: Emotions

Leadership	Genership
leader-focused, vicarious	task-focused, team-generated

Emanuel Leutze, *Washington*, 1851   Kevin S. O'Brien, *Iwo Jima*, 2008

Within genership, the group's emotional energy does not concern itself with the fortunes of one leader or leadership group, but rather with the group's creative task and overall productivity. The narrative that captures this energy concerns its progress toward a creative result, focusing intensively on how group members meet the creative challenges they share as a team.

Illustrating Group Dynamics in Leadership vs. Genership

Leadership and genership group dynamics produce radically different behaviors. We constantly see major corporations steeped in a leadership culture. They spend significant assets searching for a messianic leader who has the presumed extraordinary gifts required to lead the company into the future. Once identified, the leader will assume total control over the corporation's employees and resources, dismissing those who do not share his vision and show loyalty to him as an individual. He will likely be compensated with a sum that represents grossly disproportionate multiples of the pay afforded to entry-level employees. He will have the largest office in the organization's headquarters, looking something like a royal chamber. He will have many people circling and attending to his every need and whim. He is the center of organizational power; nothing happens without his blessing. He controls all aspects of organizational life like a kind of god. When the organization confronts a crisis, he will huddle in a secret chamber with a small team of his most loyal advisers working on a brilliant solution. Members of the organization will dutifully await it, working simply to understand and faithfully implement the leader's instructions.

Numerous modern CEOs have illustrated this kind of culture. In 2000, psychoanalyst and business consultant Mark Maccoby wrote an insightful description of such leaders in his *Harvard Business Review* article, "Narcissistic Leaders: The Incredible Pros, the Inevitable Cons." He described the culture of "superstar" business leaders who spent enormous amounts of time working with publicists, giving speeches, selling books, and generally promoting their personalities as central to the work and success of their companies. Maccoby noted that narcissism entails significant risks such as failing to listen, being overly sensitive to criticism, lacking empathy and failing to mentor.

Commenting on Larry Ellison, CEO of Oracle, an executive interviewed by Maccoby said, "The difference between God and Larry is God does not believe he's Larry." In the same vein, Oracle Board member Donald Lucas once said in a *Forbes* interview, "This is a team, and Larry is the only captain. If someone wants to pop up and announce they're the star—poof! You're out."

Messianic Leadership at GE

General Electric's iconic former CEO, Jack Welch, personified this kind of autocratic style in which the organization becomes the alter ego of its messianic leader. Welch was famous for dominating meetings, overwhelming those who expressed resistance to his ideas and striking fear into the hearts of employees who expressed anything less than total faith and complete allegiance. At the end of his tenure, GE treated Welch like a deity, giving him a retirement package so extremely lavish that when it was disclosed to the public during his divorce proceedings, Welch decided to walk away from it out of public embarrassment.

His package included free use of a company-owned luxury apartment at the Trump International Hotel and Towers on Central Park West in New York City, along with free amenities such as fresh flowers, wine, laundry and dry cleaning services, a cook and wait staff, a housekeeper, and every other detail down to toiletries, newspaper and magazine subscriptions, even postage. The deal included a free grand-tier box at the Metropolitan Opera, memberships at four country clubs, including Georgia's prestigious Augusta National, courtside tickets to New York Knicks basketball games, box seats behind the dugout at Yankee Stadium and a skybox for the Boston Red Sox, prime tickets to the French Open, Wimbledon and U.S. Open tennis tournaments, VIP tickets to all Olympic events, and unlimited use of a corporate Boeing 737 jet (a perk estimated to be worth $291,869 a month). GE also paid for Welch's limousine and driver in New York, bodyguards when he traveled abroad, satellite TV installations in his New York apartment and his three other homes in Massachusetts, Connecticut and Florida. These fringe benefits were to supplement a retirement agreement that included a pension of over $9 million a year, and a health and life insurance package that Welch negotiated with the GE board of directors in 1996 when he agreed to extend his tenure as chief executive until age 65. On top of that, Welch was to receive a consulting fee of $86,535 for his first month of work each year, plus $17,307 for each additional day. All this to reward a man who already had acquired a fortune through his work at GE estimated at approaching $900 million. The deal that GE struck with Jack Welch to reward him in *retirement* illustrates that the company viewed him as a sort of combined god and king entitled to this largess merely on the basis of his identity.

A genership culture does not seek a messianic figure; rather one who can help those around her achieve their full potential. Indeed, those charged with stewardship of the organization—likely to manifest as a team of individuals rather than a single god-like individual—will seek to create dynamic, evolving teams of people imbued with the qualities of genership. No single person will exercise control over all organizational resources and employees. Compensation and tools for development will be distributed in relation to the requirements of the organization's creative vision rather hierarchically. Diverse perspectives on reality will be embraced and considered in order to strengthen the organization's work. While some hierarchy may be evident, the power to influence specific situations will be dispersed. When the organization confronts a crisis, the entire system will respond with innovation generated at many levels. The organization's creative vision will act as its guide. Dialogue about vision and the immediate reality will be robust and decentralized, providing the energy for impactful innovation.

Abraham Lincoln provides a worthy example of genership in action, particularly in his willingness to appoint strong rivals to his administration while showing the self-confidence to listen to and heed their advice (in much the same way that Obama appointed Hilary Clinton his secretary of state). In her masterwork on Lincoln as a political leader, *Team of Rivals,* historian Doris Kearns-Goodwin describes his skill at taking in diverse perspectives, his ability to learn, to admit error, and to share both credit and blame with fellow team members. Lincoln's famous words from his second inaugural address describe the essence of the creative ethos developed within a genership culture: "The dogmas of the quiet past are inadequate to the stormy present. As our case is new, so we must think anew, and act anew. We must disenthrall ourselves, and then we shall save our country."

Google's culture similarly exemplifies many core characteristics of genership. A powerful example is the company's commitment to employee creative freedom. Google encourages its staff to spend 20% of their time working on a creative project that may have nothing to do with their immediate role or efforts. Major new projects—such as AdSense, Gmail and Google News—resulted from the work of self-motivated employees. In discussing the practice, Google employee Joe Beda writes:

> There is a big difference between pet projects being permitted and being encouraged. At Google it is actively encouraged for engineers to do a 20% project. This isn't a matter of doing something in your spare time, but more of actively making time for it. Heck, I don't have a good 20% project yet and I need one. If I don't come up with something I'm sure it could negatively impact my review.

> The intrapersonal environment at Google is very energizing. When someone comes up with a new idea, the most common response is excitement and a brainstorming session. Politics and who owns what area rarely enter into it. I don't think that I've seen anyone really raise their voice and get into a huge knockdown drag out fight since coming to Google.[xv]

Google's previous Vice President of Search Products and User Experience, Marissa Mayers (subsequently named CEO of Yahoo), speaks eloquently about what makes Google unique:

> Share everything you can… [at Google] we have an incredibly open culture…. It's amazing… when you take a lot of smart, motivated people and give them access to a huge amount of information, how well-informed their choices are about what they want to work on and what needs to be done…. It's helped us manage the organization in a way that's really flat. You may have heard that GE has a 1-to-12 rule, which means for every 12 employees there's one manager. We have a very flat organization, so we've had situations where we have 40 or 60 employees with one manager. And the idea there is that if we can have people who prioritize their own

time and manage themselves... because they have access to a... broad array of information, that works well, and it gives them the empowerment and the feeling of independence that they need to be really successful.

Mayers goes on to describe Google's practice of giving ideas credit rather than giving credit for ideas. While in other companies, employees work hard to make sure that they compete for attention and recognition, gaining credit for every element of their contribution to the organization, the teams at Google work to focus not on territory or personal credit, but on innovation and improving the end-user experience. Mayers describes Google's 20% time as "license" that every staff member has "to pursue dreams."

The leadership vs. genership cultural divide can also operate within families. Bill and Patty are parents working from a leadership construct with their child, seven-year-old Steven. What kind of family dynamic have they created? Steven's parents let him know that they are in charge and will actively plan his future. His parents establish clear rules and Steven needs to seek permission for any deviation. Bill and Patty attempt to serve as role models, hoping that their son will observe and imitate their behavior. They demand respect and behave as overall authority figures in his life, and do not discuss their weaknesses and imperfections with Steven because they want him to feel safe and secure in their custody. Steven is bright and notices when his parents are under stress. But they do not share their burdens, telling their son, "Don't worry, everything is fine."

Don and Christine operate from a genership construct, creating a entirely different family dynamic for their nine-year-old daughter Sarah. They do not actively direct her development according to their own designs, but rather act as counselors assisting her to develop a future that has the potential to be unique from theirs. They help Sarah understand her individualized strengths and weaknesses and to consider personal visions that may depart from their own. When Sarah engages in behavior that Don and Christine don't like, they talk and help her understand the purpose behind their ideas about good behavior rather than resorting to rules. When Sarah wants to ride her bicycle without her helmet, Christine helps her develop an awareness of risk and an appreciation for her health and well-being, allowing Sarah to develop independent judgment about such risks. Don and Christine do not hold themselves out as having great expertise or brilliance, but rather allow their flaws and shortcomings to be visible so that Sarah's view of them remains grounded in reality. By practicing genership, they work in community with their child to co-create her future, and not in a leadership role in which Sarah must either follow her parents' advice or rebel.

Joe is the coach of a high school basketball team operating through a strong leadership paradigm. He believes that a great team should be built around a small group of superior players. He actively works to identify three players whom he believes have the potential to excel, and designs special practices and playing opportunities for them. He feels that the measure of his success as a coach will be based largely on whether these players go on to play for major university teams. Joe's high school practices revolve around his stars, who are expected to carry the team's main performance. The other members understand that there are two classes of players: stars and second-stringers, whose primary role is to support the stars. If for any reason the first class players are underachieving, members expect a loss. The team's success and failure is seen as congruent with that of the stars. The other players on Joe's team see themselves as expendable units. As against the team's elite leaders, this verse from Tennyson's "The Charge of the Light Brigade" captures the followers' sensibility:

> Theirs not to make reply,
> Theirs not to reason why,
> Theirs but to do and die.

The team's stars hold the organization's emotional energy, barking at their teammates to influence their feelings, making them angry when the team's performance is poor and celebrating when their performance succeeds. This emotional evaluation of performance always centers on the roles of the stars, who bathe in glory when the team wins and sulk when it does not. When the team confronts a crisis, members look to the stars to provide heroic performances. Joe will spend the majority of his time working with his best players, leaving the talents of average players on the sidelines. His key players will play most of the minutes in any game, giving them many more chances for success. Over time, this experience will increase the talent differential between his stars and the others, whose abilities will remain largely undeveloped unless they take responsibility to find playing opportunities outside the team to support their growth.

In contrast, Drew coaches a high school team striving to create a genership culture. Unlike Joe, Drew measures his success not in terms of developing star basketball players, but by helping his players learn to practice shared creativity through teamwork. He looks at the complete game rather than individual players, developing roles that allow all players to collaborate through unique and complementary strengths. The shared narrative about the team's success engages the contributions of every player rather than focusing on two or three stars. Observing Drew's team in action, it is difficult to see who is the most important player. At different moments, each will make a significant contribution. All participate in regulating the team's emotional response to its performance, taking turns expressing feelings about immediate reality and progress. Members share actively and equally in the development of strategy in response to challenges rather than standing by passively and awaiting instructions from one or two team leaders. In a crisis moment, the team does not rely only on the contributions of a few; every member fully engages. The team that learns collectively and over time can overcome those who have stronger players but less brilliant teamwork. The team measures success in terms of its ability to magnify strengths and overcome weaknesses.

Practical Steps to Develop Genership Group Dynamics

An individual seeking to practice genership may nevertheless be forced into a leadership role by group dynamics. Dan serves as principal of a new charter school. Every week he brings together its teachers for a meeting to consider the challenges they are facing in the classroom. Dan attempts to draw on the teachers to participate in innovative program design efforts that will improve the school's overall services. Its instructors, however, come from a strong leadership culture that imposed many rules and guidelines on their performance. In the weekly meetings, staff members sit quietly trying to guess what Dan wants.

Several members of the group warm up to him, and begin to think of him as a messianic figure. When he gives any advice or indication of his ideas, teachers tell him he is "brilliant" and they don't know how the school would function without him. Eventually, the group dynamics turn genership into leadership, and Dan falls into the seductive rhythm of thinking for the group, making all the decisions and taking credit and blame for all that happens within the organization.

Similarly, an individual with a propensity to lead could well be converted into a genership practitioner when surrounded by people acting with that mindset. Susan is a strong leader who has recently become the head of an existing charter school with a firm genership culture. As she begins to meet with her instructional leaders, she attempts to assert control over decisions and programs that had been run in a more decentralized, collaborative fashion. She unilaterally sets classroom schedules based on her prior expertise. She fine-tunes budget decisions without engaging those affected and makes key appointments without consulting team members for advice. But instead of rolling over and anointing Susan as their leader, the instructors and administrators band together and surface the conflicts, educating Susan about the power of engaging the creative faculties of every team member. They push back on her academic, financial and personnel decisions, persistently drawing her into substantive dialogues and asking tough but fair questions. Susan sees that a new way is possible and modifies her approach, moving to a style that blends leadership and genership.

Organizational culture can have a deep impact on the balance of leadership vs. genership; creating genership group dynamics is vital to success in its practice.

Focus on Open Dialogue, Not Chain of Command

There is strong temptation within a leadership culture to create hierarchies. Their function is to disseminate messages from the leader to the followers and to ensure command and control of subordinates. Hierarchies work to promote the dominance of the leader and leadership group over other members. The result of this structure is to suppress dialogue among subordinates and to limit it between the leader and other organization members. This has the effect of suppressing learning while promoting paranoia: Followers fear that leaders who have amassed organizational power will use it to punish critics; leaders fear that followers will attempt to unseat them from authority. The antidote to these maladies is to promote transparency—open and direct communication at all organizational levels.

Embrace Conflict

Leaders see conflict as a problem to be solved along the path to building consensus. But genership embraces conflict for its value in innovation and learning. When confronted with conflicting visions and perceptions of reality, those skilled at genership explore these differences and use them to enhance organizational learning—strengthening the organization's creative vision, refining its assessment of reality and sharpening its strategy. Genership not only values conflict to promote learning and growth, it invites new visions and voices into the organization to maintain robust and honest dialogue, while ensuring that members continue to engage creatively, not only with one another but with external resources needed for success.

Tell a Different Story

In leadership, the narrative is about the life and success of the leader or leadership group. Genership focuses upon a new story about the organization's creative work, which describes whether the community succeeds in achieving and fulfilling its shared creative objectives. The protagonist is not any one person or small team, but the creative community as a whole. As the narrative shifts focus from the exploits of one personality (or limited group) to the creative actions of the whole community, the genership culture is reinforced.

Focus on What People Do, Not on Who They Are

In leadership organizations, group processes circle around individual personalities. Their pictures appear on the walls and in organizational literature describing their exploits and tastes, even focusing on aspects of their personal lives. The organization becomes a cult of personality and celebrity. With respect to its creative work, group dynamics focus on the development of stars and heroes who possess purported extraordinary gifts and abilities. What people do can quickly become secondary; their identities matter most. The organization's members take actions not for their intrinsic value but because they trust the leader's decisions.

Fully transcending these dynamics requires every member to take individual responsibility for developing and achieving the organization's vision, celebrating creative work rather than personality. Work is celebrated, not details of the creators' lives. That men and women do something well may justify their work, but does not justify them as individuals. The group and its members understand their identities as separate from what they create. Genership cultures recognize that individuals have dignity and moral worth distinct from their creative efforts. They also comprehend that a good person can fail at a task and a bad one can succeed. In genership, the focus is upon assessment of performance excellence, rather than authorship. Teams of people working together—each with required capability—can produce creations that contribute value to the whole community, irrespective of their moral worth (positive or negative) as individuals judged separately. Studying the lives of creators underscores this point repeatedly. This is true in music, writing, athletics, politics and business—indeed, in every arena of achievement: to produce masterworks does not necessarily turn artists into moral role models.

Everyone Counts, Everyone Cares

Leadership tends to create an organizational culture in which some people are viewed as being more important or integral to organizational life than others. Over time, members low in the hierarchy, despite their value to the organization, become viewed as expendable or unimportant. Because a leadership culture prioritizes the goals and perspectives of the leader, it sees the engagement of followers as a step in the process of implementation; the followers' independent wills must be transformed or dominated. Members who experience the organizational need to transform their will or render it irrelevant soon begin to feel like fungible parts of a machine, stripped of their individual identities in the service of a master being or his cause. They soon cease to care as individuals, leaving concern for the organization's welfare to their superiors.

The contrasting genership culture promotes a view of organizational life in which every person's aspirations and observations matter. Because all members correctly perceive that they are vital to the organization's future, that they have a stake in the enterprise and that their gut feelings, beliefs and actions will determine the future course, they care about both their work and the group's progress: a self-reinforcing process. As members care they become more engaged, and the overarching goals, in turn, increase their level of concern and involvement.

See Purported Heroes and Demigods for Who They Really Are

Within the leadership culture, leaders are often set apart from followers, appearing to be greater and more important than those with whom they work. A key element in building the genership culture is to work purposefully to defeat such ideas, calling upon members to recognize that leaders are human and as capable of making errors as any team member. While all may acknowledge that the leader has positional or functional bureaucratic power, the group understands that this is a function of organizational development and structure, rather than something that results from the leader's mysterious or unusual qualities. Creating a culture in which all members are seen as human and fallible motivates all team members to take responsibility and participate, recognizing that there will be no one to provide rescue if the team fails. For those with strong faith, this recognizes the commandment not to worship false idols and that there "is no god but God."

Look at the System of Play, Not Just at Individual Players

Leaders employ the systems they establish to command personal attention. Group members begin to believe that all of their progress stems from the leader's work rather than other team members and the structure of interdependent roles that they create together. Think of a quarterback who gets the credit for every play even though a group of linemen protect him, allowing him time to make effective passes. Without the linemen, the quarterback's play would be destroyed, yet disproportionate credit goes to the quarterback. In the NFL, fans can rattle off the names of star quarterbacks—Brady, Manning,

Roethlisberger. But the linemen who enable their play remain almost anonymous. It is this way in many organizations. There are numerous players who perform what are often brilliant and difficult roles, yet they are unknown and their work is often attributed to a leader more visible to the audience or constituents who receive the team's work. This dynamic can be mitigated by paying full attention to the system of play, allowing team members to understand and appreciate how they interact with one another, and how their roles combine to form a unified, interdependent whole.

Focus Energy on the Assistants

When leaders are engaged in the messiah narratives or fighting the hero wars, someone must attend to the group's business. Usually this is a person highly skilled in genership, able to draw forth the creative abilities of others. This person often presents as the leader's assistant. Indeed, most organizational charts show all members ultimately reporting through a chain of command to the leader. In focusing on the leader's assistants, one often comes into contact with those in the organization actually engaged in the bulk of its creative work. Genership celebrates the assistants' efforts as the primary creative work that is the group's most important. By focusing on an organization's assistants in a highly creative team, vital work is distributed over many talented individuals who work hard to cultivate creative strength in those around them. A genership culture demonstrates a commitment to training, learning and building teams that never become hostage to one leader or leadership subgroup.

Take Turns

Unlike leadership systems, genership promotes a culture in which role assignments are fluid. Members are free to experiment over time, taking on different group tasks. Even the leadership role is not fixed, but rather moves in a particular challenge to the person with the greatest capacity to meet it. Flexibility in roles allows people to bring new visions and perspectives to tasks. These situations function as experiments; group members provide feedback informing the group whether new approaches should be retained, modified or discarded in view of their contribution to progress. By applying genership, roles are not coveted, owned or defended, but shared and transferred among members as the needs of progress toward the vision require. Learning, training and development allow the group to increase flexibility and dynamics in role preparation and transfer.

360-Degree Feedback: Bottom-Up

In a leadership culture, feedback tends to move in one direction: top-down. Those at the top are assumed to have greater skills, knowledge and vision than their subordinates, so the only feedback that matters is from leader to follower. Even when the leader demonstrates fallibility, there is a tendency in the group to blame this on subordinates who failed to provide the assistance and feedback that the leader needed at a critical moment. At such times, the leader complains of being let down by incompetent or disloyal followers.

Genership differs, strongly committing to 360-degree feedback; members are open to receiving critical advice and guidance from everyone around them, irrespective of the organizational hierarchy. The ideas of those closest to the creative task are accorded equal if not greater weight in the dialogue compared with more global, overarching perspectives associated with the traditional leadership role. In a restaurant, for example, it is not just the cook whose opinion matters, but the waiters who have direct observation of customers' reactions and tastes.

Reward Teaching and Learning

In a leadership culture, the emphasis often falls upon the acquisition of talent, as if there were a perfect person for each role; the goal should be to employ that person. The unstated concept is often that such talent is born rather than made, that in every organization there is a set of idealized roles along with people born to fill them, if only they can be found. The leader is seen to be a kind of talent scout, building a team of stars.

A genership culture understands that to adapt and thrive within a changing environment requires needed capacities to evolve along with its vision. It recognizes that many new roles will be invented in the course of creative work, and that those innovators who produce critical contributions to the organization's vision may develop through a series of roles in which they discover and hone skills through trial and error. Within a genership organization, mentor-mentee relationships are less tactical and more open-ended, focusing on creative development of skills and abilities without necessarily an immediate application. The organization will allow its members to experiment, to explore new interests and skills without a clear sense of how those might contribute to its overall vision. The genership organization understands that one person's failure may be another's eureka moment, and that the wherewithal to respond and adapt in the future is usually not a neat, linear progression; genership promotes and rewards continuous learning as well as ongoing evolution in the conception of tasks and roles. Knowledge and skills are understood to be flexible and transferable rather than inexorably linked to personality and identity.

The Buck Stops Everywhere

A leadership culture promotes a certain kind of bravado in which a single person steps up, owns a task and then delivers a spectacular success because of his singular performance. These messianic and heroic narratives are reinforced throughout typical organizational cultures. The message trumpeted is that individuals make all the difference. The organization needs heroes and a leader to emerge from among them. Organizational failures are perceived to result from their shortcomings, like a batter who strikes out with a man on base in the ninth inning when a homerun could have won the game.

Genership embraces a different narrative in which every person owns the organization's creative work and each has a chance to move it toward success or failure. This moment does not present itself only at a crisis point; rather, it is available every minute of the day. Success grows out of the ongoing embrace of these moments by the organization's team members working together. Members do not feel like there is any one person with sole responsibility for achieving the group's creative vision. They are not engaged in a search for the one great leader who will walk them through the desert; instead, they believe the promised land is something to create together. When the team falters, each member will ask, "What can I do to strengthen our progress?" They do not work to fix blame on others or to find individuals responsible for the organization's work. They take up the part that they can do, collaborate with others to strengthen their work, and press onward with hope and positive feelings about the work's future.

Build Networks, Not Towers

A leadership culture often focuses on the power and glory of the leader and heroes who give rise to him. They sometimes orchestrate this to maintain and strengthen their control or influence over the group. Members themselves often actively participate in creating a celebrity culture that emphasizes imagined superhuman qualities of the leader or leadership subgroup. This manifests as signs and symbols of royalty or deity surrounding the leader in which their visage, personality and history are memorialized with an overlay of reverence and awe as if the places they inhabited and their belongings are somehow imbued with their spirit, giving rise to monuments, museums or even trinkets that celebrate the leader's personality. When these physical testaments are erected to perpetuate the Fallacies, they usually have little or nothing to do with the group's ongoing creative efforts.

In contrast, genership celebrates the creative community and the contributions of many. Rather than dedicate its resources to the deification of one, the group creates community resources that support its overall creative teamwork. Not a statue, but a park bench. Not a plaque, but a playground. Not a cornerstone, but a scholarship. Not a biography, but the history of people and their shared success.

CHAPTER TEN

GENERSHIP: ARRIVING WHERE WE STARTED...
AND CREATING SOMETHING NEW

In the struggle for human progress, communities across the world have searched for effective leaders. Yet leadership as a method for moving communities forward has encountered severe limits. While history has offered many examples of positive leadership, we must admit that leaders have often impeded human progress. Think of the countless despots throughout history who have used leadership skills to seize power and dominate others to the detriment of communities: Hitler, Stalin, Pol Pot, Saddam Hussein. Organizations across the world—from the 10-person limited partnership to the global corporation—suffer daily at the hands of garden-variety tyrants. How does this transpire and what is lost in the process? The fault lies in the Leadership Fallacies that imprison human creativity.

The Messiah Fallacy expresses the belief that someone else has unique creative power—that it is out there in the world inside another person or demigod. We are subject to creativity as an external force rather than wielding this power ourselves. The Hero Fallacy similarly places creativity beyond our grasp, making us dependent on the emergence of the messiah through a process of combat among contenders. Most become spectators to human creativity rather than its authors. The Fallacy of Leadership Nostalgia suggests that creativity occurred in the

343

past through the actions of former heroes and messiahs, and that we now live in a fallen time within which we can only access creativity through emulating the great leaders who have preceded us.

The Fallacies imprison the powerful and fundamental individual capacities waiting to be unleashed through genership; they represent states of being that precede human awareness of the potential within every person. How do we break free, liberating the creative impulses and powers that await productive expression? The keys can be found in the rigorous development of genership practices.

Genership calls for the full engagement of people within organizations—families, friendships, teams, companies—any relationship in which two or more individuals have the potential to work together toward constructive change. The Leadership Fallacies undermine it. Belief in a messiah promising rescue breeds disengagement. Spectators' observing a battle among heroes, waiting and hoping (perhaps forever) for the messiah to emerge, encourages disengagement. The same holds true with Leadership Nostalgia; focus on the past, upon ancient leadership wisdom, increases disengagement from the present, from the flesh-and-blood opportunities and possibilities that breathe here and now. Even the greatest wisdom must be applied in the moment, in a fresh and immediate way.

Genership as a System of Skills

Genership practices form an interdependent reinforcing system that also promotes a cultural transformation focused on building creative relationships that demonstrate transparency, equality and effective dialogue. These practices embrace conflict as a tool central to learning and development in relationships that do not fall prey to the Fallacies.

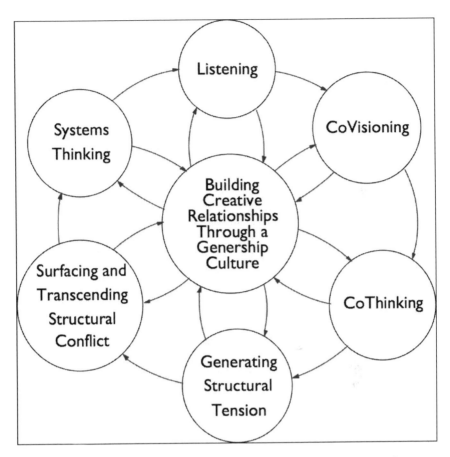

Genership offers a grounded and practical method as much as a philosophical strategy for achieving full engagement. To find real traction in the world, ideas require connection to concrete practices. Listening, CoThinking, CoVisioning and Systems Thinking are as much actions as they are themes, understood through implementation as well as by study. Because genership involves practice, we can begin to do before we fully know, and we can know through *doing* as well as through reflecting and talking. Such knowledge and insight that springs from practice profoundly differs from that gained through passive observation. To act within a drama offers understanding at a more visceral level than that available to the audience. So too with every art. There is tremendous power in the ability to translate ideas into action as a way of mastering meaning and content. The practical nature of genership, its focus on *what to do* as much as what to know or how to think, makes it accessible and offers a universal doorway through which to experience the group's creative life. Genership becomes the focus of experiment, offering the promise of knowledge experienced not from authority but through immediate personal revelation. We begin to trust and credit the profound experience of doing and then discovering something entirely new.

Listening forms the foundation of genership. When we practice listening—and make no mistake, we must *practice*—we become fully engaged. Our ever-strengthening consciousness allows us to observe present reality and—equally important—ourselves. When listening, we become open to ways of observing reality (and our own identity) through the eyes of others, all while expanding and deepening our understanding of what is actually happening. Not only can we discover previously invisible trends, we also become aware of possibilities and potentialities subject to our influence. Listening also expands and informs our personal vision and desire, enriching our sense of what we want to happen; masters of genership continue to strengthen their listening, using this capacity as a powerful tool by applying it to themselves to develop creative power. Genership listening transcends the Fallacies because it eliminates the leader/follower dynamic, locating us in the center of the creative process along with our co-creators.

From a base camp of deep listening, *CoVisioning* and *CoThinking* naturally ascend. As we increase our listening power in interactions with others, they begin to share what they want and how they understand the present moment. Our openness to their aspirations and observations in turn inspires their openness to our own dreams and insights. Working together, we soon begin to generate a dynamic field of vision, placing shared creative claims on the world and collaborating to grapple with the difference between what we want to create and what presently exists. The field of vision evolves over time not only in response to changes in the external environment, including the community beyond the immediate group of co-creators, but also in reaction to developments in the team's aspirations, as new members engage and existing participants continue to learn. The team's collaborations involve an increase in effectiveness as a result of members' remaining fully engaged as individuals in the group's creative struggle. No member sits on the sidelines awaiting instructions from a leader or small leadership group.

CoVisioning and CoThinking propel our full engagement forward. They bring about *structural tension* and ultimately *creative release*. Vision arising from genership always entails departing from what is currently there, creating a tension with present reality, in just the way an acorn destined for growth creates a field of tension with the wind, sun, rain and soil, orchestrating these forces over time into an oak tree. The seed contains an inchoate blueprint that longs for expression in the world, a process that involves work and struggle against forces that resist and compete for creative energy. The practitioners of genership learn to harvest this tension between what is desired and what is manifest. They hold it until reality moves toward the vision like a seed mushrooming into the ground, laying a foundation of roots but also driving upward to the light and heat. A team practicing genership tends to the gap between vision and present reality, generating energy from it like a primal fire; its development plentifully exists in the tension within that gap.

CoThinking and CoVisioning form the nucleus of creative effort—the organizational dialogue between the real and the aspirational ideal. A creative community can be as small as a friendship and as grand as a nation or even a civilization. A genership community learns to embrace creative tension, to experience it as joyful, finding its roots in life itself. Such tension is animating and inspiring, not draining or debilitating. Genership offers the promise of experiencing creative work as thrillingly meaningful, expressing our deepest humanity. Failures and setbacks are recast, reimagined as steps along the pathway to eventual success and fulfillment. A genership culture can energize enduring creative aspirations such as the Civil Rights movement, efforts that exceed the lifespan of particular individuals, bending history's arc toward justice and inclusion not achievable through the works of any one person, single effort or occasion.

In the genership paradigm, creative tension represents the team's *emotional effort* that will be expended in its creative work, all of which requires intense motivation. Reality often presents us with tremendous inertia; motivation grows from emotion within creative relationships, which serve as the greenhouse for Listening, CoThinking, CoVisioning and Systems Thinking. An organization without a healthy creative process that understands conflict as a wellspring of new learning will lack emotion; motivation will also wither. When we step back and see all of the genership themes in context, we can understand them as a kind of energy ecosystem for creativity, which grows stronger because it is fed by the engagement of team members as individuals, not merely as a vicarious echo of a given leader's emotion.

Reality often includes *structural conflict*. We see this clearly when learning to be powerful listeners and deepening our capacity for CoVisioning and CoThinking. As organizations scale, the possibility for creative conflict grows exponentially. We do not necessarily share the same perspectives on reality; we do not always want the same outcomes, nor share the same reasons. Structural conflict may remain hidden until we work in collaboration with others, exploring and embracing desires and perceptions that diverge from our own. These can be conscious or not, siphoning energy away from the creative process and threatening to make it stagnant or even incoherent. This problem cannot be fixed; conflicts in the creative process can only be transcended when they are subsumed within a robust creative system. Michael Jordan had distracting dreams of being a baseball player, but these were overwhelmed by his larger creative passion for basketball, leading him to six NBA championships and the Hall of Fame. He was distracted for one unsuccessful season with his vision of being a baseball player (his father's wish) before returning to secure his place in basketball history. Jordon bookended his flirtation with baseball between two "three-peat" titles, 1991 through 1993, followed by 1996 through 1998, after his baseball distraction. He did not fix his baseball problems through basketball; he simply returned to focus upon his fundamental creative project.

Conflict can be a source of profound learning but can also weaken creativity depending upon how members experience it. This is why a genership approach to conflict is so essential to the strongest possible creative process; conflict is otherwise understood through the Fallacies as part of a quest for power and control, which threatens full engagement. Voices are lost when defeated and dominated. Genership embraces conflict as an opportunity for learning. Discordant voices are harmonized rather than suppressed; diversity remains available for future improvisation as the world evolves. An organization's ability to embrace conflict as an asset depends on having a deeply embedded genership culture.

Leadership often struggles with structural conflict precisely because it lacks the powerful tools that allow creators to build more ambitious and vibrant initiatives filled with positive tension. These skills also allow conflict to be made conscious within the individual and team. Conflicts that remain suppressed continue to cause stagnation or oscillation, producing the familiar one-step-forward, two-steps-back process that we experience when creativity falters.

Systems Thinking allows the other practices within genership to harness the enormous energy of change that surrounds us. It emphasizes the ways in which we are part of our creations, underscoring the insight that to change the world is always to change ourselves. We are not always "of the world." We have a God-given capacity to be outside the world we inhabit through our imagination, reflection and prayer. Nevertheless, we are also deeply connected to reality, embedded in it, at one with it. While humans are spiritual beings who may transcend reality, the possibility for change resides in the utter immediacy of the present moment. Systems Thinking creates the bridge between these two: imagination's unlimited potential and the energy of possibility always present within reality. Thankfully, genership does not call us to master the philosophy, science and art that informs Systems Thinking; most importantly, it is a powerful practice that allows us to harness change within our own creative undertakings, plugging into the natural energy of transformation always abundant around us.

Practitioners of genership use Systems Thinking to close the gaps generated through structural tension. Present reality is made changeable when a team understands all elements of reality through the prism of their shared desires. The field of vision generated by the team allows it to perceive critical variables—those meaningful elements capable of changing. If a team wants to put a man on the moon, he becomes the critical variable. The man's motion can be influenced, the moon's cannot. All creative work is like this. The team comes to grips with what can be changed and goes to work, harnessing existing patterns wherever possible to accelerate progress. A group wanting to travel to another city can understand all the means of getting there. They cannot move the city, they cannot move the roads, they cannot change the laws of physics... but they can move cars, buses, airplanes and their contents. When creators work in teams that experiment with actions, testing strategies to achieve their vision, they begin to master the systems relevant to their creative work. Because individuals acting within a leadership culture tend to celebrate their personality, they cannot perform systems analysis with the speed and accuracy of a team infused with genership capacities. Through systems thinking, creative teams accelerate progress, finding leverage points and designing new structures. When the gaps generated by structural tension are closed, vision becomes reality.

Humans are inherently social and political. Promoting the core practices of genership requires us to attend to *group dynamics* to ensure that the Fallacies do not give rise to patterns of behavior that suppress creativity. Groups marinated in leadership cultures tend toward authoritarian dynamics, giving rise to hierarchies and command structures that limit dialogue and communication—and that promote power paranoia. A genership culture exhibits a radically different character of openness and transparency, empowered by constructive dialogue. It generates maximum power for creative effort through the full engagement of group members, who feel liberated rather than oppressed, who express their individual identities in the team's life and creative aspirations. Those practicing genership do not feel threatened by internal power struggles because members are validated not through their control over each other or proprietary resources, but through their engagement in realizing the group's creative vision. For this reason, conflict is not avoided but rather embraced as a powerful learning tool that develops vision, assessment of reality and strategies for progress.

Genership does not entail a laundry list of skills that can be practiced in isolation from one another; it comprises an integrated set of capacities deeply related to one another. It is an interconnected matrix of skills— an art—not a simple collection of abilities organized for the sake of convenience. It is an organism, not a toolbox; as such, genership's practices exhibit synergy and mutually reinforcing support. The whole is not only *more* than the sum of the parts, it is *profoundly* more, creating potentials entirely beyond the range of their simple extension. Listening, CoThinking, CoVisioning and Systems Thinking are powerful even when independent of one another. But when combined in reinforcing patterns, they manifest a rocket-like escape velocity, allowing us to transcend current experience, reaching above and beyond toward the undiscovered.

Creating What Never Before Existed

T.S. Eliot famously commented that at the end of exploring we often arrive at the beginning strangely feeling as if we have come to know the place only for the first time. His observation profoundly applies to learning. We recognize certain truths as having been there all along, available to us but somehow unseen. The process of exploring ultimately makes truth visible. But genership promises something more: to make visible *new* truths, ones that definitely *did not* exist before. Such birth is a wonder—to have brought something entirely new into being. Through this ability we experience divinity within all life.

If the history of life on Earth was measured over the course of a single day, humans would have emerged during the last minute, and recorded time would all have occurred within the last second. Nevertheless, we can say with confidence that something extraordinary has occurred in the web of life during its last few moments, even though humans represent a small fraction of animal life and an even smaller fraction of all biomass.

With the power of creativity expressed through genership, humans are not merely capable of replicating themselves (a power that resides in all living beings); they can manifest what they invent in their mind's eye. They are capable of introducing new forms of existence. The human brain, that master of patterns, is able to observe sequences of activity and predict how they will evolve in the future. But this ability has transcended its status as an essential survival skill. The human mind has made an evolutionary quantum leap. It can go far beyond predicting the behavior of extant patterns; it now possesses the ability to invent patterns that never before existed. The created world developed by humans has the potential to be as vast as the natural world, as vast as the universe itself.

This power of creativity is deeply encoded in the central Western creation narrative told in Genesis. It is something that we have known all the while, perhaps beneath our conscious awareness, but now can appreciate for the first time. The essence of being human is to express conscious choice. Man has the power to deviate from God's plan; he can also be redeemed. Both the fall and the possibility of resurrection arise from our creative free will, the centerpiece of human existence and experience.

Inherent within the Judeo-Christian tradition and the golden rule—to love others as we would have them love us—we see creativity animated by the power of love. We have nothing but the expression of our lives with which to show love for God. To love others as we would have them love us, we have nothing but our creative choices. Creativity is really our only means to express the love that remains central to the faith that animates most religions of the world. That love should energize creativity makes intuitive sense. Through creativity we have the power to bring new patterns of energy into existence, new structures, new practices and even new souls. Of course, we choose to bring into the world that which we love. To consciously use the power of genership to manifest anything other than what is beloved is either error or dysfunction.

Leadership continues to evolve. It is becoming something better, more expressive of God's precepts, something that calls forth human nature and destiny. Leadership is becoming genership, and we can choose to accelerate this trend. In the words of John Schaar, political theorist and professor emeritus at the University of California, "The future is not a result of choices among alternative paths offered by the present, but a place that is created—created first in the mind and will, created next in activity. The future is not some place we are going to, but one we are creating. The paths to it are not found but made, and the activity of making them changes both the maker and destination."

It is time to change the destination and, in the process, ourselves.

END NOTES

[i] See, e.g., C. E. Shannon, "Programming a computer for playing chess." *Philosophical Magazine*, 41(314):256-275 (1950). The number of possible chess games include "Shannon's number," named after the information theorist Claude Shannon. Shannon arrived at the number 10^{120}. The number of atoms in the observable universe is estimated to be 10^{80}. Shannon's Number is 10^{40} times larger than the number of atoms in the observable universe. Moreover, many mathematicians estimate that Shannon's number significantly *underestimates* the number of possible chess games.

[ii] Anderson, P.W., "More Is Different: Broken Symmetry and the Nature of the Hierarchical Structure of Science," *Science*, New Series, Vol. 177, No. 4047 (4 August 1972), pp. 393-396.

[iii] The reason is straightforward if challenging to imagine: Momentum involves the product of mass and velocity. To observe an object's velocity requires tracking it through time and space, necessarily releasing the concept of exact position, since it will have travelled through a range of space over a span of time. On the other hand, location entails taking a snapshot at a specific point in time, thus foreclosing a measure through time.

[iv] http://johnrapp.qondio.com

[v] "The Four Pillars Upon Which the Failure of Math Education Rests (and what to do about them)," Matt Brenner (2011). (http://www.k12math.org/doclib/4pillars.pdf)

[vi] See, e.g., "The Chess Master and the Computer," Gary Kasparov, *The New York Review of Books* (11 February 2010). (http://www.nybooks.com/articles/archives/2010/feb/11/the-chess-master-and-the-computer/?pagination=false)

[vii] Corning, Peter A., "The Re-Emergence of 'Emergence': A Venerable Concept in Search of a Theory," *Complexity* 7(6):18-30 (2002).

[viii] Albert Einstein, quoted in Morris Kline, *Mathematics and the Search for Knowledge* (Oxford University Press, 1985), p. 219.

[ix] Watt, W. Montgomery. "Hidjra." In P.J. Bearman, Th. Bianquis, C.E. Bosworth, E. van Donzel and W.P. Heinrichs. *Encyclopaedia of Islam Online*. Brill Academic Publishers, ISSN 1573-3912.

[x] *Beethoven's Letters (1790-1826),* translated by Lady Wallace, pp. 45-49.

[xi] Exerpt From Daniel Goleman's Blog, "Are Women More Emotionally Intelligent Than Men?" May 6, 2011. (http://danielgoleman.info/2011/are-women-more-emotionally-intelligent-than-men/)

[xii] See generally the work of Jim Thompson, founder of the Positive Coaching Alliance (PCA) (http://www.positivecoach.org). In the words of Steve Young (PCA Advisor and NFL Hall of Fame Member), "Over the years we have all heard and read the stories of youth athletes' hearts being broken by their experience with sports."

[xiii] Frum, David (2009-03-06) "Why Rush Is Wrong," *Newsweek*.

[xiv] Jay Wright Forrester (born July 14, 1918) is generally credited with being the founder of the discipline of System Dynamics, which deals with the simulation of interactions between objects in dynamic systems. Forrester is a pioneer American computer engineer, systems scientist and was a professor at the MIT Sloan School of Management. For a discussion of how Forrester and others created the Systems Dynamics movement beginning in the 1960s, see "The Beginning of System Dynamics." System Dynamics Society: Albany. Forrester, J. W. 1992. (http://clexchange.org/ftp/documents/system-dynamics/SD1989-07BeginningofSD.pdf)

[xv] Joe Beda, EightyPercent.net
(http://www.eightypercent.net/Archive/2005/03/24.html)

David Castro is a graduate of Haverford College (1983) and the University of Pennsylvania Law School (1986). In 1993, following a successful career both in private practice and as a Philadelphia prosecutor, he was awarded a Kellogg Foundation National Leadership Program Fellowship. He studied community leadership and its relation to improving quality of life. Based upon this work, in 1995 David founded I-LEAD, Inc., a school for community leadership development that has served several thousand emerging leaders across Pennsylvania through its affiliation with Pennsylvania Weed and Seed, and its development of an accredited Associate Degree program in Leadership.

In 2002, in recognition of his work on behalf of Pennsylvania communities, David was awarded an Eisenhower Fellowship, which he used to study leadership and its impact on economic and community development in Turkey. In 2009, in recognition of his work in community leadership and education, the Ashoka Global Funds for Social Change named David an Ashoka Fellow. Ashoka is an international community of the world's leading social entrepreneurs. A teacher at heart, David is frequently consulted as a speaker, serving on panel discussions and contributing regularly via blogs and articles posted through the Ashoka network, the Kellogg Leadership Alliance and the Philadelphia Social Innovations Journal.

Made in the USA
Middletown, DE
15 November 2016